Dr Stephen Langford

THE
LEADING
EDGE

Innovation, technology
and people in Australia's
Royal Flying Doctor
Service

D1010029

Dr Stephen Langford

THE LEADING EDGE

Innovation, technology and people in Australia's Royal Flying Doctor Service

First published in 2015 by
UWA Publishing
Crawley, Western Australia 6009
www.uwap.uwa.edu.au

UWAP is an imprint of UWA Publishing
a division of The University of Western Australia

 THE UNIVERSITY OF
WESTERN AUSTRALIA

National Library of Australia
Cataloguing-in-Publication entry

Creator: Langford, Stephen, author.
Title: The leading edge : innovation, technology and people in Australia's Royal
Flying Doctor Service / Dr Stephen Langford.

ISBN: 9781742588148 (paperback)

Notes: Includes bibliographical references and index.
Subjects: Royal Flying Doctor Service of Australia—History.
Transport of sick and wounded—Australia.
Medical care—Transportation.

362.180994

Typeset by J & M Typesetting
Printed by McPhersons

*For our dedicated staff and supporters over the years,
and to my family, for their encouragement and sacrifices.*

Contents

Introduction

The RFDS (Royal Flying Doctor Service) has been an iconic Australian organisation for more than eighty years. It was founded on the novel approach of using aircraft and radio communications to bring medical care to people living in the most remote parts of our nation.

I have been privileged to work as a flying doctor for over thirty years, a period during which considerable changes in technology have enabled us to implement a variety of innovations to improve patient care. The changes evolve relatively slowly over time when you are immersed in them; but when you reflect on how things were done in the past and how they are done today, the stark magnitude of the transformation becomes apparent.

In terms of communication, for the hundreds of remote out-back locations we dealt with, there were no fixed-line phones, no personal computers, internet or email. Children's schooling was done over a radio and supplies were ordered by radio, connected to the telephone system by the local RFDS base. Routine and emergency medical care also depended on the radio, which was powered by a car battery if the station had no 240-volt generator running.

As doctors, we had no pager coverage in country areas and no mobile phones. If you were out and needed to call the RFDS base, you went to a public phone and put money in. It all seems so archaic. Nowadays even the most isolated place can have a satellite phone with broadband data and internet over the satellite connection.

People sent formal messages by telex or telegram, as there was no fax or email. They could make a radio call to the RFDS and our radio operator would type the message into the telex machine and transmit it. When telegrams arrived, they were read out over the radio. A paper copy would be received in a few months when the recipient came into town and picked up the mail.

In aviation, we flew piston-engine aircraft at around 300 kilometres per hour. These have been superseded by faster turboprops at close to 500 km/h and pure jets at nearly 1,000 km/h when at altitude. Unpressurised aircraft have been replaced with fully pressurised aircraft, while navigation using paper maps, a compass, dead reckoning and some basic radio aids has been enhanced with accurate and universal GPS (global positioning system) receivers. In the dark of night, weather radar tells us where the storm cells are located ahead. Instrument approaches and night landings are now augmented with GPS-based RNAV approaches. If that all sounds a bit technical, then in essence we go faster, higher, more safely – and don't get lost.

In our medical care, what was predominantly 'hands-on' clinical monitoring of patients has been improved with comprehensive portable vital signs and physiological monitoring. We use compact intensive-care-style monitors, which run on batteries and tolerate rough handling, extremes of temperature and changes in altitude. Once, an intravenous line ran by gravity feed. Now infusions are administered with syringe drivers and small pumps.

'Best guess' oxygenation and acid base status have been exchanged for pulse oximetry and point-of-care testing. That is, we can take blood samples and do lab tests in flight using a portable handheld device. Simple respiratory support and hand ventilation have been traded for sophisticated ventilators. Physical examination by our doctors has been enhanced with portable ultrasound scans.

A modern flying doctor carries a smartphone or tablet offering diverse communication options, including messaging, voice and video, plus access to unlimited online medical reference material. What a change from the days of the pedal radio...provided you are in an area of mobile coverage. The contemporary doctor has location information (a GPS in their phone and Google Maps™) and numerous clinical calculators, books and applications in their pocket. Yet, they still need the essential clinical skills, experience and judgement to do the job well, often in isolation, with limited resources.

In this book, I have chronicled the recent history of the RFDS in Western Australia, with a focus on the many innovations of which I have been a part, especially in medical care. I like gadgets and hope you will find the explanation of the technologies interesting. I have endeavoured to provide anecdotes of how they have benefited patients and enabled us to stay at the forefront of what we do. Whether it was the adoption of the low-tech Spil-Pruf® urine bottle (an important advance for medical flights), or high-tech portable diagnostic ultrasound, I think you will find these observations and brief stories fascinating.

In addition to our medical initiatives, I describe improvements in communications and aviation, along with a few insights into life as a flying doctor over this time.

Section 1

Retrospective

Starting out
An exciting but rewarding adventure

It is interesting looking back at decisions we make in life and how they influence the path we follow. I sometimes wonder how I would have fared as a procedural general practitioner on the Mornington Peninsula, which is where I was heading...if it had not been for just one phone call.

After completing a range of hospital positions including general medicine, surgery, anaesthetics, obstetrics and paediatrics, I was embarking on another year of emergency medicine. I had been keen to volunteer as a doctor during the Ash Wednesday bushfires in February 1983 but was locked into roster commitments at my hospital. However, it got me thinking about other things. I was a bit restless, so I wrote to the Royal Flying Doctor Service, as a private pilot, asking what opportunities there were to work as a doctor and do some flying as well. I also applied to the Australian Antarctic Division, with a view to a position at one of the Australian Antarctic bases the following year. Not surprisingly, I received a polite reply from Mr Ken Knight, at the Federal Council offices in Sydney, indicating that it was no longer normal practice for RFDS doctors to fly; but he had forwarded my letter to each of the sections across the country.

About mid-year I had reached a shortlist for Antarctica, then out of the blue I received a phone call from Dr David McDowell, the senior RFDS doctor at Jandakot Airport. He had received a copy of my letter and wondered if I would be interested in a position at our Port Hedland Base in the Pilbara, as the locum doctor was leaving. We had a useful discussion about the role as he had worked there for a year or two and knew it well. Eventually we agreed that I would come over and have a look. I would pay half the airfares, to be reimbursed by the RFDS if I took the job.

An opportunity arose to take a couple of days off in early July to visit. I remember it very well. It was 0 degrees when I woke early that morning in Melbourne, rising to 5 degrees as I drove to Tullamarine Airport. Arriving in Perth that afternoon, it was 25 degrees. David put me up in his home with his wife and young son, then the next morning we flew up to Port Hedland, where the temperature was over 30 degrees.

Almost as soon as we arrived at the base a call came in from Anna Plains Station, about 350 kilometres northeast of Port Hedland and halfway to Broome. It was a classic story but one that we don't actually see very often. A stockman had fallen from his horse in the morning and broken his leg. He had only been found mid-afternoon, after lying in the scrub in the heat for hours as others searched for him.

David suggested we hop on the aircraft, a Piper Navajo, which was just about to leave. So both of us set off with a flight nurse to evacuate the patient. I sat up the front with the pilot, as doctors and nurses often did in those days, seeing a bird's-eye view of the terrain and talking aviation stuff en route: 'What sort of engines does the Navajo have? What's its cruise speed? What's this instrument?'

Soon we found the airstrip – a short, roughly graded piece of cleared dirt adjacent to the homestead – and came in to land. We were met by a ute and a couple of blokes in jeans, dirty shirts and Akubra bush hats, who would take us to the mustering camp where the patient was. This was about a twenty-minute drive away.

As was the custom, we piled into the back tray of the ute with a stretcher and some medical equipment, then headed off.

It is neither legal nor wise to ride in the tray of a utility, but the two compliant doctors and a couple of stockmen did so, while the nurse was offered the courtesy of sitting in the front passenger seat. It was private property and this was how things were done. Roaring along the rough dirt track across vast rusty red dirt plains, spotted with spinifex grass, was a real hoot. Dust trailed behind us. As we hung on grimly to the frame behind the cabin, I chatted with one of my fellow passengers.

'How big is the station?'

'Ah, about a million acres', he said.

Even for me, a city boy, I could work out that this was very big! Not wanting to appear overly surprised, I just nodded. Then I thought I'd continue the dialogue and try to be cool by asking some more farm-like questions.

'How heavily do you graze it?' I asked.

'Ah, about fifty to one', was the response.

'Oh', I piped up, 'fifty head to the acre?'

'Nah, fifty acres per head.' I had blown it! He looked at me like a typical drongo from the city who had no idea whatsoever. This sort of land couldn't sustain intense grazing. There was no rain for most of the year, if at all, and just the occasional cyclone or rain-bearing depression during the summer period every couple of years. I recall he said they had almost 20,000 head of cattle but weren't exactly sure. Livestock roamed freely over the million acres, breeding naturally, and the graziers gained some idea of the numbers only when they did a muster. At up to $1,000 a head for large beef cattle, they had a significant investment here.

We reached the place where the stockman was resting and set to work, giving him pain relief, splinting his leg and inserting an intravenous line because he was hot and dehydrated. He seemed to be more concerned that we did not cut his jeans or lose his boots than with his broken leg. With the help of all the strong volunteers, we transferred him on a stretcher into the back of the ute then drove back to the airstrip, this time at a much more leisurely pace. After loading him into the aircraft, we farewelled everyone and took off before we lost daylight.

Again, it was an exciting experience, watching the sun set in front of us as we headed predominantly westward. We made a smooth night landing on the large airstrip at Port Hedland, taxied back to the base then handed our patient over to an ambulance crew to be taken to the hospital. I hung around with David and the pilot as the aircraft was put away, thinking 'I can definitely do this for a job!' David couldn't have planned it better if he had tried. It was a real *Boy's Own* adventure and although I realised it was not always going to be like this, it certainly seemed to beat the idea of spending a year in the Antarctic with an essentially healthy expedition team.

We visited the hospital and other medical services the next day, looking around the town of Port Hedland and meeting people. It was not a pretty place by any means. Most of the buildings had a rusty hue from the fine red dust which drifted from the huge stockpiles of iron ore at the port, waiting to be loaded onto massive iron ore carriers.

The pubs looked pretty rough, too, particularly down near the port. It was the first time I had seen segregated bars with two entrances. I don't recall any signs but it was clear which bar you went into from the occupants. The two rooms were separated by a double-sided bar in the middle. Both groups of customers seemed quite happy to keep to themselves and there was a mixed patronage of men and women in each. Neither bar was particularly flash; indeed, my recollection was they were downright grotty in appearance and decor. I was told that the entertainment on Friday nights were informal boxing matches at the Pier Hotel. A hospital doctor was given cheap drinks to be there for medical care and to decide if those who came off the worst needed to be taken to the hospital. This all added to the peculiar appeal of the town.

I returned to Melbourne, very excited by the opportunity. I would be able to practise a mix of emergency medicine and remote general practice and spend lots of time flying, which I enjoyed. I would be the only doctor for the region, working with five pilots and five nurses providing a round-the-clock on-call service, but I figured I could handle that. It seemed to be a great experience for a year.

After extricating myself from my Antarctic application and my hospital job, I arranged a tenant for my house then explained to my parents that I was heading off to a diametrically opposed part of the continent. I was back in Port Hedland within a month for a modest one-year appointment with the RFDS. So far, it has lasted thirty-two years.

Across the airwaves
How it was, then and now

To set the scene, let me explain what it was like in the early 1980s as a flying doctor in the Pilbara. I was the sole RFDS doctor and was expected to be available twenty-four hours a day, seven days a week in case of emergencies. This seems excessive by contemporary standards, but at the time that was how most rural doctors and many city specialists worked. I was young and fit and had come from working a busy obstetric and paediatric rotation where we regularly clocked up 100 hours a week. In hindsight, I regret having enjoyed only half a dozen weekends off each year while in the Pilbara and missing the opportunities to explore the region more fully.

There were no mobile phones at the time and in Port Hedland there was not even a paging service, such as the ubiquitous Motorola 'bleepers' which most city doctors carried. We had a radio base in town which housed all the radio equipment and was separate to the hangars out at the airport, 18 kilometres away. A full-time radio operator, Alan Dean, worked the radios every day and was the only administration person at the base. Alan also had a Telecom tie line to his residence. He was able to divert the telephone after hours so that when an emergency phone call came in, he could take it at home.

High-frequency radio

Many remote locations still did not have telephones and relied on high-frequency (HF) radio for communication. Stations, nursing posts, mine sites and remote communities had Codan HF radio transceivers with a special emergency button located on the front. If they needed to call for help outside of the standard daily radio schedules, they depressed the button for up to a minute. This transmitted a special tone that was picked up by a standby receiver at the RFDS radio base. It triggered an alarm and started the main radio transceivers.

The HF radio was also the means by which children received their early education. School of the Air (SOTA) is a remarkable service, which commenced in Western Australia in the 1960s from RFDS facilities at Derby, Port Hedland, Carnarvon, Meekatharra and Kalgoorlie. It provided an innovative distance education program using the HF radio network until 2004 when all teaching became satellite based.

If you were at the base, Alan could turn up the volume for you to hear the teacher talking to each of the students over the radio and asking about their work on the topic of the lesson. The SOTA teachers had radio consoles and office facilities separate to ours, but used the same radio frequencies. Regular medical schedules and other non-urgent calls would have to fit in around the class sessions. The students were of course helped by their parents or a governess in between these sessions. They would also come into town a couple of times a year to meet their teacher. It is amazing to reflect on how many children in rural Western Australia, over a couple of generations, received their early education over the radio. The SOTA service still operates in remote regions.

HF radio waves bounce off the different layers of the atmosphere in the ionosphere and can skip across thousands of kilometres. The frequencies used in each region were selected to provide the right amount of 'skip' to reach the nearest RFDS base, but sometimes different atmospheric conditions caused the signal to skip to another base in the state, or even interstate. We would then receive a telephone call to say that a station in our region was calling. Our radio operator would manually start up the main radios and adjust the tuning until he contacted the caller.

Each remote transceiver had a number of different crystals which corresponded to the different HF frequencies. Once contact was established, different channels could be tried to find the frequency offering the best signal. The frequencies were cleverly allocated so that all RFDS bases had one or two common frequencies but the rest were different. This helped ensure that radio transmissions within one region did not interfere with communications in adjacent regions.

In the event of an emergency outside the regular scheduled contact hours (skeds), callers would push their emergency button, an alarm would be activated and the radio operator would commence setting up communications. Some of this could be done from home, but often the radio operator had to drive to the base and work the radios directly. As the doctor on duty, he would call me at home on a landline to advise of the call. I could be patched by telephone into the radio communications or sometimes I had to go to the base where I could use a secondary radio communications panel directly. This was generally clearer and I had the benefit of being with the radio operator tweaking the controls to obtain the best signal.

Just imagine an emergency. You are on a remote outback station and your husband has sawn off part of his foot with a chainsaw. After administering first aid you start your radio, hold down the emergency call button and hope someone will answer the signal. It might be an RFDS base elsewhere in Australia. Then there is a further delay putting the call through to the nearest base and linking in a doctor. Eventually you receive medical advice about managing the wound to stop the haemorrhage and giving an injection for pain relief, then you wait a couple of hours for the aircraft to arrive. This is certainly not like calling an ambulance in the city and being in hospital in thirty minutes. Everyone did the best they could but you had to be stoic.

Our HF radio system offered simplex rather than duplex communications; that is, only one person could speak at a time or else the signals on the same radio frequency would interfere with each other. Although the distances that could be covered were huge, the quality was often poor and usually accompanied by a high level of background static. With experience, you became more accomplished at discerning what people were saying but it was very difficult at first.

The use of correct radiotelephony phrases and the phonetic alphabet was important in conducting a medical consultation by radio. Each person's communication was concluded with the words 'Over' which then allowed the next person to speak. Part of a routine radio medical consultation would have gone like this:

DOCTOR: *Can you give me his name? Over.*
CALLER: *It's John War...[unintelligible]. Over.*
Can you spell that? Over.
It's Juliet-Oscar-Hotel-November [J-O-H-N].
Whiskey-Alpha-Romeo-Delta [W-A-R-D]. Over.
How old is he? Over.
He's my son and he's fifteen...one-fife years. Over.
And what is his temperature? Over.
It's 39.6, three-niner-decimal-six. Over.

Further discussion about signs and symptoms...

DOCTOR: *It sounds like tonsillitis. We need to give him some antibiotics. Can you go to your medical chest and find item number 109, that's one-zero-niner? Over. [Pause]*

CALLER: *Yes, I've got it, item one-zero-niner. Over.*

It should contain some capsules and may also have the word penicillin somewhere on the label. Over.

Yes, that's right. Over.

Fine. I want him to have one capsule three times a day. Repeat. One capsule, three times a day. Over.

Yes, copy that. One capsule three times per day. Over.

And you can also give him some paracetamol, item one-seven-three, one tab up to four times a day, as we discussed earlier. Over.

Yes, copy that. What about asp...[unintelligible]. Over.

Say again. Over.

Ah, I copied that, but what about some aspirin? Over.

No, let's stick to paracetamol and keep up the fluids. Can you call again on the 7 am morning sked and let me know how he is going? Over.

Yes, will do. Over.

Okay. Talk to you then. VKL out. All stations, VKL standing by for other traffic.

The call sign VKL identified our Port Hedland Base. Meekatharra was VKJ, Carnarvon VJT, Derby VJB and Kalgoorlie VJQ. The Jandakot Base used 6PY as its call sign, similar to broadcasters in Perth, such as the ABC on 6WF.

There were regular schedules every day, usually starting at 7 am, including medical calls and people wanting to be patched through to telephone numbers in Port Hedland or down in Perth. This was the innovative new 'radphone' system, which had just been installed across our bases in 1982–83. The radio operator called the telephone number and explained it was the RFDS and that only one person could speak at a time. He then linked up the call, which involved alternating from transmit to receive as each party spoke. Our radio operator could do this almost without thinking. Rather than listening to both parties intently, he managed to switch back and forth almost automatically based on the pauses between phrases and on hearing the word 'Over'. Alan could carry on a conversation with me while still managing to switch a call.

The radphone service had an immediate and dramatic effect. While there were thousands of licensed users of the RFDS, in 1983 in Western Australia about 145 fixed locations were in regular contact and there were 118 portable radios. Instead of making radio calls to the RFDS base to have them converted to telegrams (radiograms), users could now speak directly, albeit a little awkwardly, to whomever they wished. The RFDS charged $1 for the connection and within the first year, telegrams dropped by one-third from 19,232 to 12,395 while the radphone calls hit almost 12,000 in an incomplete first year.

There was little privacy. Not only could the radio operator hear all the details of the call, but also anyone listening on the same frequency would hear everything. This made some of my medical consultations quite challenging. Without going into detail, we might have a discussion where it was a 'problem down there', meaning a condition involving their genitalia. We would have to discreetly discuss whether, for example, it was a rash, a discharge or a lump, and I sometimes had to make an educated guess based on the sorts of cases I saw on clinics and the probabilities as to the most likely diagnosis. All the time we knew that the caller's neighbours and others on the radio were listening with great interest!

Medical chests

To provide treatment to such remote locations, a cache of pharmaceuticals was needed and this was the role of the RFDS medical chest. It was a large green steel box about 400 mm square that contained supplies of pharmaceutical items, including a broad range of medicines and dressings. Each item was identified by a numbered sticker. To prescribe a particular antibiotic, you only needed to give the caller the number and the dose without having to worry about complicated drug names. In situations where an agent had to be given by injection, we talked through the process of how to prepare the needle and syringe in a sterile manner, how to draw up the correct quantity of the medication, and how and where to inject it. Fortunately, on most stations there was often someone with a nursing background, or someone used to giving injections to livestock, so we could bypass the initial reluctance to do it.

Injections were mostly for giving strong pain relief to someone with an injury such as a fracture or burns. It was always going to take a few hours before our aircraft could arrive, so this was the most humane thing we could do in the interim. On some occasions, other injectable drugs were used. I had one or two cases of anaphylactic reaction, a severe allergic reaction to seafood or something else, where treatment with intramuscular adrenaline, prescribed from hundreds of kilometres away, was life-saving.

We mostly treated with oral medications, or used ointments and creams, or dressings. Without this essential supply of prescription medications, people in remote areas, then and now, would have no means of treating common conditions – tonsillitis, ear infections, conjunctivitis, boils, rashes and the like – their nearest medical help being hundreds of kilometres or days away.

Emergency calls

When an emergency call required us to evacuate the patient, a number of things happened. The base radio operator or I telephoned the pilot and nurse on duty and explained where we needed to go. As the doctor I also had to arrange where we were going to take the patient and talk to the hospital doctors about the case. I then drove out to the airport, with the pilot and nurse doing likewise. The pilot towed the aircraft out of the hangar, checked and prepared it, topped up the fuel and submitted a flight plan in person to the Flight Services office at the airport. The flight nurse selected the medical equipment we needed, took the drugs out of the fridge and loaded the aircraft for the flight.

On arriving at our airport facility twenty minutes later, I would call the base radio operator on a landline to give an estimate of when we expected to leave for the patient's location and try to obtain an update on their condition. Each RFDS base operated independently, tasking our own aircraft and managing the emergencies in our region. If the patient was seriously ill and needed to go to Perth, however, we needed the assistance of a second aircraft from another location to complete the transfer, which was about five hours in duration each way. We would contact the RFDS base at Jandakot in Perth and plans would be made for an aircraft and doctor to come up from Perth to meet us halfway at Meekatharra Airport.

Most of this could be done on the phone but to confirm our movements, the radio operator compiled a message which was then transmitted by Telex. When I look back, this seems so antiquated. The operator would type the message into the Telex machine, which contained long rolls of thick paper tape about 2.5 cm wide. The machine punched holes into the paper tape as you typed. When the message was complete, the paper tape was inserted into another part of the machine and transmitted. The machine, effectively called the receiving machine, and then the punched tape ran through as the letters and numbers were transmitted. At the receiving end, the Telex machine contained rolls of paper about 25 cm wide running on a sprocket drive and the message would be typed out, line by line, as it was received.

This was effectively the same as a telegram. Indeed, one of the services the RFDS provided to remote outposts was to take messages by radio, type them up and transmit them by Telex to the recipients who would receive them as a telegram. On the return side, we would receive telegrams and then call the remote station by radio, reading it out to them and then putting the original in the post to be collected in a few weeks.

Communications were not always about medical issues; often people called in to order supplies. I remember listening to a woman on a station ordering hardware supplies to be freighted up. She also wanted some paint for redecorating her lounge room. When asked what colour, she could only say, 'Oh, something in a nice beige shade'.

I thought how much we take for granted in being able to visit a hardware store and pick exactly the colour of paint we want, whereas people living in remote areas then just had to take the best they could get. These days with the internet, people in even the most remote location can generally shop online and have so many more options.

So our emergency evacuation would get underway. We radioed on the aircraft VHF (very high frequency) to the base as soon as we had departed and had an ETA (estimated time of arrival). The base telephoned or used HF (high frequency) radio to call the patient's location and advise of that ETA so that someone could bring the patient to the airstrip or send a vehicle out to pick us up. This would depend on what was wrong with the patient, what sort of transport was available and whether we needed to do any procedures on the patient prior to evacuation.

For very ill or injured patients, it is often better for the carers to stay with the patient and for us to come in to them. In many nursing posts, the nurse was also the driver of the 'troopie' style of ambulance. If she was up the front driving, then she couldn't care for the patient in the back of the vehicle. In certain circumstances it was better to examine the patients and perform procedures in a modestly equipped nursing post than at the airstrip in the aircraft. Our aircraft were well equipped but there was little room inside and no air-conditioning on the ground. If time was not critical, sorting out the patient at the nursing post 10 kilometres away was more comfortable and convenient.

Once I went out to the Telfer Nursing Post for a young man who had dislocated his shoulder. We had given advice over the phone on some simple manoeuvres to assist with reduction but they had not worked. I flew out to the nursing post, gave some intravenous pain relief and sedation, then easily reduced the dislocation. It was now no longer necessary to evacuate the patient. While we were there, the nurse brought her ginger cat in. It had been mauled by a dingo and had a number of deep lacerations. With some telephone advice from a vet on sedation and local anaesthetic, I spent the rest of the visit stitching the cat, much to the gratitude of the owner, all the while keeping an eye on the young chap whose shoulder we had reduced. We left with no patients but overall it had been a very satisfying evening's work.

Telephones

In the mid-1980s more stations became connected to the telephone service. Telecom installed microwave links along the west coast through to the Kimberley and additional links followed with the North West Gas Pipeline. In a remarkable feat of engineering, the DRCS (Digital Radio Concentrator System) was pioneered by Telecom and NEC. It enabled multiple solar-powered repeaters to be located at 40 to 50-kilometre intervals and provide a link to an exchange up to 600 kilometres away. Pastoral stations and communities in sparsely populated areas could be connected as subscribers and enjoy all the benefits of an automated telephone service.

The station people recounted to me how, ironically, this made them even more isolated than before. In the days of the HF radio, most of them kept the radio turned on during the day and would hear news of what was happening across the region. They would discover that a distant neighbour was pregnant, know when they went to hospital and hear that they had delivered a healthy baby boy. They also heard when a neighbour became ill or died. As more people started to use telephones, the radio traffic diminished and they lost this vital source of news and gossip.

We found that people didn't need to call at a scheduled time any more for medical advice, but would call whenever it was convenient for them. This was more difficult for me because I was often being chased between home, the hospital, the radio base and the airport to provide medical advice, rather than on regular schedules where I could arrange to be in a single location. We ultimately brought in regular schedules for telephone medical advice, just as we had for radio. Later, in 1992, I established a single 1800 number for the RFDS in Western Australia, to help channel all our calls through a single point.

Being on call in Port Hedland in the early 1980s was difficult. With no mobile phones and no pager, you had to stay at home or tell someone whenever you went out. So just a simple trip to the supermarket required a call from the fixed phone at home to say I was going to the shops for forty minutes. If a medical call came in, the base staff either waited until I got home or would hunt me down in the shopping centre. On more than one occasion, they called the supermarket and the public address system was used to summon me to a telephone. If I couldn't use the phone at the shop for a long-distance call to Perth, I would have to find a public coin-operated phone box and make a reverse charges call.

Likewise, going to the local hospital meant people tracking you down between the emergency department, the general wards or maternity. In retrospect, it was incredibly inefficient, but there were few alternatives. We tried a handheld two-way radio system linked to a telephone line, but it was never particularly reliable over the distances between Port Hedland, South Hedland and the airport.

My wife, before I met her, worked as a flying doctor at the Kalgoorlie Base of the Eastern Goldfields Section, from 1988 onwards. They had a number of handheld radios and could call each of their doctors from the base reliably. She recounted to me that one year, two new British locums arrived and were each given their mobile radios and a small car. They set off following each other across the unfamiliar streets of Kalgoorlie until the following radio call was heard by all staff on the channel.

'Mobile 6 to Base, I've had a car accident.'

'Mobile 6, are you alright?'

'Yes, I'm OK, but I've run into Mobile 7!'

In 1988, our general manager agreed to buy me the company's first mobile phone. It was an NEC 9A, a small brick which weighed 0.7 kg and cost $6,995. It transformed my life, as I was no longer frustrated in trying to find a public telephone when paged away from home.

Today each of our doctors has a compact smartphone. We can put incoming telephone calls through directly to the doctor's phone and can send emails with embedded attachments. For example, it is quite easy for many mine-site medics to scan in a 12-lead ECG and then email it to our doctor who can view and interpret it on their phone. We can broadcast SMS messages to all staff when there is a major incident and our doctors can take photos of skin lesions, x-rays and injuries and easily transmit them to someone else for quick advice. While sophisticated technology exists to transmit images, people will still use what is simple and easy. So, instead of high-quality digital x-ray transmission, a simple photo of an x-ray on a viewing box is often good enough.

The convergence of personal digital assistants (PDAs, like the Palm Pilot of the early 2000s) together with digital cameras and telephones has revolutionised how we work. You can photograph an accident site, an injured limb, a broken piece of equipment or an error message and send it to someone for advice, provided you are in mobile phone range. Yet, even now there are still many outback areas without basic telephone or mobile-phone access. When airborne, mobile phones have limited reach.

With the advent of satellite telephones, the HF radio system has contracted to a point where only a small number of enthusiasts use it today. Satellite phones are easier to use and provide better quality most of the time. They also connect directly to the telephone system without an intermediary.

We adopted a marine version of a satellite telephone and installed it in our aircraft in the 1990s. The team in the back of the aircraft previously used HF or VHF radio and our base radio operators or Coordination Centre in Perth would patch it through to someone on a telephone. Now it was easier to just telephone directly from the aircraft. This has resulted in the demise of aviation radio for most medical purposes.

While HF radio and telephone were the common methods of communication of the 1980s and 1990s, we now have video calls available. We adopted a system called Vidyo® in 2011, which enabled our staff to do desktop video calls from their computer, tablet or smartphone. The system works quite well, allowing multiple participants, but still requires a little bit of setup time at each end. Sometimes firewalls and computer administrator settings can make this difficult. People are impatient and will move on to other things quickly if they work easily. I find they revert to simple but clear telephone calls, or popular applications such as *Skype*™.

When I first started in the Pilbara, there were a few nursing posts at mine sites with cardio-phones. These were essentially an ECG (electrocardiogram) machine with a set of speaker cups that could be connected to the earphone and microphone ends of a standard old-fashioned telephone handpiece. The ECG was recorded and then transmitted through the telephone using this acoustic coupler to a cardiologist somewhere in Perth with a similar system.

The concept was fine but inexpensive facsimile machines soon became readily available. Instead of this cardio-phone arrangement, you simply pasted the ECG strips onto a piece of A4 paper and faxed them to wherever was appropriate. It made it much easier for RFDS doctors, as well as specialists, to look at an ECG without an elaborate setup.

Faxes became a very useful means of clinical communication in the late 1980s and are still useful today. Any document, printed or handwritten, can be sent by just pushing some buttons. In contrast, while transmission of images and documents by email provides better quality than fax, there is more time and effort required to scan and send them. With faxes, you have a contemporaneous paper record, which can be added to other patient notes taken at the time.

A reliable comprehensive electronic medical record, compatible with all other clinical record systems, is yet to be achieved. Until it is as easy as typing a phone number and pushing 'send', faxes and paper documents – which are compatible with all medical record systems – will have a place.

Honeymoon over – remote rollover at Sandfire

It was 1983 and I had only just started working at the Port Hedland Base. A young couple had been married in Perth on Saturday night and were driving to Broome for their honeymoon. It was about twenty-four hours of solid driving from Perth to Broome and they were on the last leg, the 600 kilometre stretch between Port Hedland and Broome. Sometime after sunset they swerved to avoid a kangaroo and rolled their vehicle about 20 kilometres from the Sandfire Roadhouse, which was at that time the only stop midway along that stretch of road. When the dust settled, the smashed vehicle lay upside down just off the soft edge of the road. The young bride, who had been in the passenger seat, was now there in the dark, humid stillness of a Pilbara night; her husband was unconscious, suspended upside down by his seatbelt and with an obvious serious head injury.

What do you do? There was little traffic along the road and, in these days, no means of communication unless you had an HF radio. So she waited and waited. Eventually someone came past, stopped to give limited assistance, then carried on to the roadhouse ahead. A bit later, vehicles from the roadhouse arrived and tried to render assistance. At the same time, the flying doctor was called.

The call came in to me at home in Port Hedland. There was limited information except that there had been an accident and at least one person was seriously injured. We are always cautious in launching an aircraft at night to a remote airstrip without a better idea of what the likely injuries are. There are significant safety issues to consider and we often find those who were labelled seriously injured are not as bad as predicted once they arrive from the accident site. Nevertheless, the information that one person had serious head injuries and was still at the accident scene suggested we needed to move quickly.

The pilot was notified, as was the flight nurse, and together we mustered at the Port Hedland Airport and departed for the roadhouse. It was a really dodgy strip, of marginal width, which was adjacent to the highway near the Sandfire Roadhouse. As no one actually owned it, the only maintenance was the occasional grading which occurred at the insistence of the roadhouse manager when a shire road crew passed by doing the roads. A few cartons of beer probably exchanged hands at some point to achieve this.

The pilot was 'Johnno' Wheeler, who had been a cow cocky and station manager himself prior to becoming a commercial pilot. If there was a pilot in our group who had experience in landing at rough strips, it was him. We landed safely on gravel amid the rows of kerosene flares and by the time we were driven to the roadhouse, the patient had already been brought back from the accident in a Toyota Land Cruiser four-wheel drive, on a mattress in the back.

He was in a serious condition, stuporose, with a boggy fractured skull and flail chest from multiple rib fractures on both sides. We carried him into the roadhouse diner and set to resuscitating him and then anaesthetising him. After ventilating him by hand for a while, I connected him up to one of our new compact Oxylog ventilators. His wife had a fractured collarbone and lots of bruises and abrasions but was otherwise stable. She sat up the front with the pilot while the flight nurse and I sat in the cabin attending to her husband.

We needed to transfer him to Perth and the only option available at midnight was to fly directly there, a journey of over five hours, plus refuelling stops. So we set off, stopping first at Port Hedland to refuel and collect more drugs and equipment, then again at Meekatharra.

As dawn broke, we arrived at Jandakot Airport. It was much colder in Perth than up north. As we disembarked and arranged to unload the patient I watched the young bride, tired and dishevelled in a dirty torn dress, traipse aimlessly across the tarmac in bare feet. This is all she had with her, the rest of her belongings were still in the wrecked car by the side of the road 1500 kilometres away. While her wedding was to have been one of the happiest days in her life, here she was, three days later, back in Perth − her new husband critically injured and with many challenges to face in the months ahead if he survived.

I still become emotional when I remember this scene. It makes me wonder just what would have happened if the RFDS as we know it wasn't there? Who would have provided emergency medical care to the victims of this accident, hundreds of kilometres from the nearest hospital or ambulance? When and how would the injured have been taken to the only neurosurgical services in the state?

It reinforces my long-held view that what we do in the RFDS really matters. We make a difference to people's lives every day across the state and it is difficult to envisage outback Australia without the RFDS. I hope that we will continue to always be there for those who live, work and travel in these parts of our nation. They deserve the same level of medical expertise as their fellow Australians in more populated regions.

It is this spirit of the service and its daily importance that has kept me motivated to continue working for much longer than I had initially planned. It drives me to stay passionate, committed and focused on ensuring that our work is not eroded by cost-cutting and budgetary constraints, and that we strive to ensure we are here, doing good work, for decades to come.

Divided then united
Consolidation of our service

'United we stand, divided we fall' is a quotation from Aesop's fables from the sixth century BC but is still applicable in the modern era. When I joined the RFDS in 1983, there were three separate operating sections in Western Australia based on the historic origins of the service. These were the Victorian Section in the Kimberley, the Eastern Goldfields Section out of Kalgoorlie and the Western Australian Section covering the remainder of the state. In the rest of the country, the Queensland Section covered all of Queensland, the NSW Section covered the western half of New South Wales and the Central Section operated in the lower half of the Northern Territory from Alice Springs and out of Port Augusta in South Australia. A small Tasmanian Section provided services in Tasmania and to the Bass Strait Islands.

There appeared nothing particularly wrong with this arrangement at first, with each section providing essentially the same services that were modified locally to meet the needs and existing medical infrastructure in their areas of operation. In Queensland, for example, there was a strong focus on child health and immunisation with RFDS nurses undertaking much of this work in outlying communities. In Western Australia, by comparison, a robust Community Health service had resident nurses across rural areas already providing these services.

It did seem strange, though, that we operated different aircraft types with completely different aeromedical configurations and often used different clinical equipment. Despite some natural rivalry between sections, there was a healthy level of cooperation when required. We in the WA Section might ask the Eastern Goldfields Section to assist if we had an urgent case we could not get to. The Central Section might fly across from Alice Springs to central Western Australia if Kalgoorlie could not get there and Broken Hill often assisted in parts of South Australia or southwest Queensland. There was no reconciliation of costs across borders as, after all, the patients were all Australians in need. However, there was probably a slight smugness sometimes that one section had needed to help the other out.

With time in the role, I became more aware behind the scenes that each section in Western Australia had its own administration, its own accounts and payroll, and its own individual funding arrangements with both Commonwealth and State governments. There were three sets of annual financial reports to members, plus different reports to each government funder. Three presidents, three councils, three sets of elections and so forth. Added to this were the operating differences. Apart from the aircraft, we had different equipment, drugs and consumables, different documentation, training and even uniforms. It seemed that a lot could be gained from having one operating section in the state.

Single operating entity

The idea gained impetus during the 1990s and with careful planning and considerable goodwill, the three sections agreed to form a single operating entity in July 1995. This required the different groups of supporters to give up their exclusive involvement in just one section and become part of a bigger merged entity. It also required a sacrifice by the general managers of both the Western Australian and Eastern Goldfields Sections, Terry Jorgenson and

Syd Winchcomb respectively, to retire and allow a new chief executive officer to be appointed to the new entity, RFDS Western Operations. While no doubt there would have been some internal ructions, on the surface the transition occurred relatively smoothly. This was a remarkable testament to those with many decades of commitment to their respective sections being willing to hand over control in the interests of the service and community as a whole.

Each of the original RFDS sections continued but in a fund-raising capacity only, and the operations of the organisation across the state were vested in RFDS Western Operations. With time, the various assets of each previous section were transferred. The Chairman of the new Board was Ray Campbell and the new CEO Bruce Rathbone. The first three years were challenging as tough decisions were required to better position the service for the future. The size of the fleet was reduced as it was clear that we could not afford to replace seventeen aircraft in future years. Much work started to achieve standardisation in aviation. Likewise, in our clinical services I moved to adopt standardised aircraft equipment, drugs, operating procedures, documentation and training.

We had plenty of challenges to overcome, one of which was that for our Kimberley operations, we did not employ any doctors. We needed to be able to use Derby-based aircraft for any mission, including flying down to the Pilbara or even further as part of a service that was truly statewide. The doctors in Derby had hospital commitments, however, and were not exclusively available to us. I needed a nominated doctor immediately available to take calls from anywhere in the state through our 1800 emergency number. We also had difficulty achieving uniformity in training, priority setting, decision-making regarding tasks and accountability. After some challenging years, we were funded to employ our own dedicated RFDS doctors in Derby in 1999. This enabled us to operate each base in WA as a standardised element of a statewide service.

The Derby Hospital doctors continued to provide outreach clinic services in the region.

The merger of the three sections brought staff under similar employment arrangements. In the WA Section, the late Gaye Richardson (Slater) had led groundbreaking work in creating the first Flight Nurses Award around 1981. While we actually called them 'Flight Sisters' at the time, this was an acknowledgement that there were special skills needed for nursing in the aviation environment and it was not good enough to just throw a hospital nurse in the back of an aircraft. An industrial agreement was applied to all Western Operations flight nurses, just as new aviation agreements were negotiated for pilots. Alison Liebenberg was appointed our new Director of Nursing and Primary Health Care. She came from a strong background in community health and was instrumental in helping settle the employment arrangements and develop standards for flight nurses in the new entity. Likewise, Steve Lansell, who was appointed Director of Aviation and Communications and came from a background of both aviation and communications engineering, guided the consolidation of arrangements for pilots as well as bringing our communications staff together.

In 1999, I oversaw the creation of the first AMA–RFDS Medical Practitioner's Agreement. This brought standard conditions of employment to RFDS doctors. At the time, RFDS doctors were paid 25 to 30 per cent less than peers working in the government hospitals where our bases were located. We benchmarked a bit below the government hospital rates, figuring that our work was more appealing and that our funders couldn't baulk at supporting salary structures less than their own.

A merger was attempted between the Central and NSW Sections but this fell apart and in 2001 the Central Section was renamed Central Operations. Around this time NSW Section, which was providing some of the services in Tasmania and had an air ambulance contract in Victoria, was renamed the South Eastern Section.

Many other changes happened in the tumultuous years following the 1995 merger. Carnarvon Base was closed and the resources transferred to Meekatharra, though the HF radio service remained for a while. All our clinic flights were put onto charter aircraft, so that we could reduce the number of more expensive medical aircraft needed in the fleet and future replacement costs. Our radio services from each base were transferred to remote operation from Perth using a computerised control system called Teknis, which was eventually shut down due to lack of traffic. There was considerable conflict with the Department of Health in WA as we strived to obtain funding to provide a professional, reliable, statewide aeromedical service which was adequately resourced.

We implemented a model of having five uniformly resourced and strategically located bases and using the nearest available for each emergency task. This ensured effective utilisation of all assets and provided some internal performance comparisons. I established a more robust patient database, which enabled us to monitor our clinical workload and its distribution, separate to aircraft operations.

Following the vigorous amalgamation period, Peter Howe took over as CEO in 1998. He came from an extensive background of health administration ranging from managing regional hospitals to ultimately being the CEO of Princess Margaret Hospital, King Edward Memorial Hospital and Fremantle Hospital. He knew health management inside out and had the charm and networking ability to ease the new Western Operations into a more stable relationship with the state Department of Health, which was our major funder.

Bases in Western Australia

Here is a brief outline of the RFDS bases that have existed in Western Australia. When I started my career in 1983 there were eight: Wyndham, Derby, Port Hedland, Carnarvon, Meekatharra, Geraldton, Kalgoorlie and Jandakot Airport in Perth.

Wyndham

The Kimberley bases were managed by the RFDS Victorian Section in Melbourne with a local manager. The Victorian Section was the first division of the AAMS (Australian Aerial Medical Service) to be registered in 1934. It supported the establishment of the very first base in Western Australia, in Wyndham, in August 1935. It undertook its first flight to Halls Creek on 19 August 1935 in the Fox Moth 'Dunbar Hooper' with pilot W. J. B. Reeve bringing the patient back to Dr R. J. Coto in Wyndham.

I had little to do with Wyndham when I was in Port Hedland, as we did not venture that far north in the early 1980s. They had a Piper Navajo and were actively involved in clinics in the eastern Kimberley, to locations such as Kalumburu, Drysdale River, Oombulgurri, Warmun (Turkey Creek) and Mulan (Lake Gregory), as well as conducting emergency flights. The base was being wound down as the Derby Base grew. When the Wyndham abattoir ceased operating and the Wyndham Hospital was down-graded in favour of the expanding town of Kununurra, the base was closed in 1990.

Derby

The Derby Base was opened in 1955 and initially used MacRobertson Miller Airlines to provide the aviation services. Derby was the site of the Regional Hospital, which was a hub for outreach general medical and specialist services, as well as for emergency evacuations. It provided obstetric, paediatric and general surgical hospital services for the entire region and was the focal point for administration of public health. The clinic activities were spread widely across the Kimberley to locations such as Balgo in the southeast, to communities along the Gibb River Road and to other communities in the west, such as Lombadina and One Arm Point on the Dampier Peninsula. Some operations of the Victorian Section bases used subcontracted pilots from local aviation operator TransWest, seconded nurses from the health department's Community Health division as flight nurses, and seconded doctors from the hospital in Derby. Sometimes a case would be flown down to us in Port Hedland and we would transfer the patient the rest of the way to Perth. We flew up to Broome on a couple of occasions, but mostly the Kimberley operation was autonomous.

About 1988, the Victorian Section purchased larger pressurised B200 King Airs, which enabled them to fly directly to Perth, or Darwin if necessary. In the 1990s, the Base Manager was Barb Stott, who ultimately joined the Western Operations team in 1995. At that time, there were two B200s and one C90 King Air in Derby.

In 1999, while retaining the old base building to house our radio equipment, we moved to a renovated house adjacent to the fledgling Derby Aboriginal Health Service to which we were loaning our doctors part time. This remained as the administrative building while we kept nursing and aviation facilities out at the hangar. In 2015, the hangar was renovated to bring all staff to the one airport location.

Port Hedland

Our Port Hedland Base was officially opened on 30 October 1935. Records show they took radio calls and undertook an emergency evacuation at Warrawagine Station and then Marble Bar on the opening day. Perhaps indicative of a Western Australian entre-preneurial spirit, the service was running before the AAMS WA Section had even had its first council meeting and well before it was incorporated in 1936!

The first radio base and doctor's residence were on Richardson Street, facing out to the ocean and the entrance to the port. Three additional base buildings were established subsequent to that, with the fourth opening in February 1981. This was a simple modern brick building with two radio studios and a spare office. Out the back were the remnants of previous bases. What I understood to be one of the original radio shacks was a very small affair, no more than 4 metres square. My recollection is that it was wood framed and covered with asbestos cement sheeting, positioned next to a tall radio aerial with dozens of wire supporting guys. Like everything in Port Hedland, it was covered in decades of iron ore dust from the port facilities. Adjacent to this was the site of the third base. Apparently in the late 1960s, the hipsters had decided to build a novel geodesic dome with a radio base building underneath, such was the fashion at that time. It was supposed to be cyclone proof. Alan Dean, the radio operator, told me that despite its tourist appeal, it was not particularly practical as a working building. We used to laugh about architects and fashion – at a time when we were discarding our body shirts and flares from the 1970s. The building had been dismantled in 1981 and only the circular concrete pad remained, together with a painting of it at the new base.

The radios and aerials at the building in Port Hedland transmitted by UHF (ultra high frequency) to a larger and more powerful HF radio and aerial complex out past the Port Hedland Airport at Pippingarra. I think we had 1,000-watt transmitters, which was about the same power as the ABC. The base building also had the capacity to operate independently with a standby 100-watt HF transceiver and had additional aviation VHF radios to communicate with our aircraft.

We had a modest brick appendage to our hangars at the airport, with only limited room in which to keep medical equipment and a drug fridge. A tiny kitchen area enabled us to make tea and coffee before flight. Half of the brick lean-to was a waiting room with old vinyl couches where patients and passengers could wait before or after flights. In 1999, we closed the radio base in the town of Port Hedland and moved everyone to the airport. This was a practical move which overcame the separation of the town and airport facilities and at a time when we no longer required a resident radio operator. Yet it was still disappointing to see some of our history being left behind. We also lost our post office box number. As far as I was aware, we had used PO Box 3 since the inception of the service in the 1930s and now ended up with an airport address.

The new airport building was jointly occupied by the School of the Air staff from the Education Department as a new facility for their distance education services. Like many architect-designed edifices, it had a large central atrium which wasted space and was rarely used while the rest of the design was a rabbit warren and not very functional. In 2011, we opened a new expanded hangar and office complex with a much larger patient transfer facility. This was to meet the needs of our increased staff and aircraft numbers, which were necessary to support the workload resulting from the considerable growth in the resources industry across the state.

Port Hedland remains the longest continuously operating RFDS base in Australia. There was a single doctor, five flight nurses and five pilots when I worked there. Over the years we expanded to six doctors, seven nurses and seven pilots to provide clinics and telehealth plus multiple crews most days for our medical retrieval service.

Carnarvon

Carnarvon opened in 1955 and in the 1980s had a single RFDS pilot and a part-time charter pilot from another operator, Tropic Air. Between them, they provided regular clinic flights to Shark Bay (Denham and Useless Loop) and to Exmouth and Onslow. They also alternated with Meekatharra to offer some weekend cover using volunteer doctors from the hospital. They could not provide a full emergency service around the clock, however. The presence of an aircraft at the airport may have provided a sense of security to the local population but it was a mirage.

There was a radio base in town and the radio operator for many years was Keith Crooks. Apart from general HF communications and medical calls, a School of the Air service used the radio network.

Meekatharra

Meekatharra had a single aircraft with one or two pilots and nurses. The base was formally established in 1949 but a local committee had organised flights earlier following World War II. The current hospital was built in 1955. From early 1985, we employed our own doctors in the town, providing RFDS services as well as working in the hospital. Initially, they did not fly much at night or on weekends as there wasn't a full spread of pilot and nursing cover. A School of the Air also operated in Meekatharra.

We had two reasonably expensive aircraft spread across two bases at Carnarvon and Meekatharra but could not utilise them fully. In 1995, when the three sections of the RFDS merged, the role of Carnarvon and Meekatharra was reviewed. I spent considerable time looking at the numbers of patients and types of cases managed by each base with a view to consolidating our resources in just one of the locations. For the same cost we could achieve much closer to 24-hour coverage for the people of the Gascoyne and Murchison regions if we pooled our aircraft and staff numbers in one place. While it would have been easier at the time to recruit and retain RFDS staff in Carnarvon on the coast, it meant that those remote locations well inland in the eastern Murchison would have waited much longer for an emergency response.

Meekatharra offered a 360-degree radius of operations. It was also well placed strategically in the centre of the state for meeting

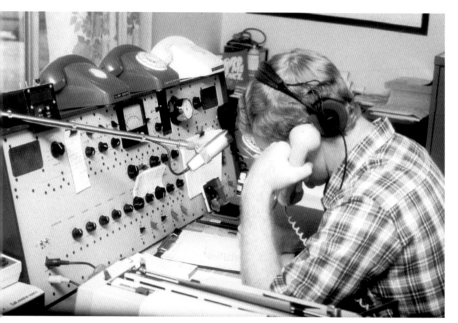

1. A radio console in the 1980s. Medical calls could be taken here using HF radio, as well as communication with aircraft on HF or VHF. The telephone handsets were for calling Flight Service, the Hospital, or for connecting Radphone calls.

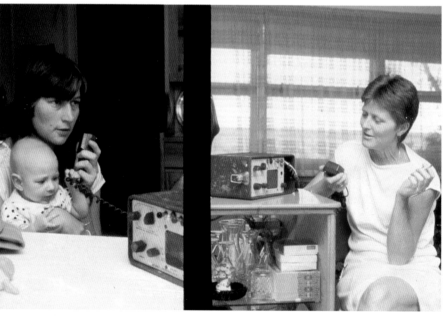

2. Using the HF radio in the 1980s – the only means of communication in remote areas until the telephone service expanded using microwave links and DRCS. A red emergency call button transmitted a special signal outside of normal schedule hours.

3. Typical clinic flight in a Piper Navajo at Nullagine, with Captain Greg Schouten, November 1983.

4. The waiting room, at the Nullagine Community Health clinic.

5. Piper Navajo VH-DEP at Port Hedland in 1984 with the Dental team preparing for a clinic run. The Navajo was used for both clinics and emergency evacuations.

6. Clinics – A tyre blown when landing at Marble Bar in 1984. A new tyre sent out by truck whilst the clinic was underway and replaced during the night.

7. The Marble Bar Nursing Post, attended by the RFDS weekly for 80 years.

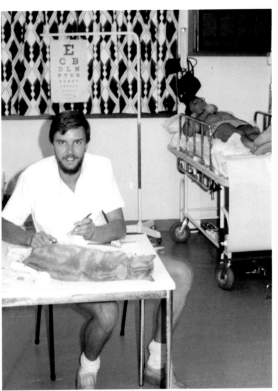

8. A good night's work at Telfer! After flying out and reducing a dislocated shoulder, there was time to suture up the nurse's cat, which had been mauled by a dog, whilst the patient was recovering from his sedation.

9. Evacuation from remote Punmu in 1983. The community was determined to preserve their traditional culture and were living in lean-to shelters.

10. The ute serving as an ambulance for a stretcher patient.

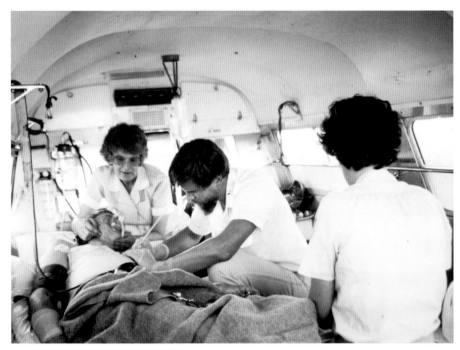

11. Inserting a chest drain in a trauma patient in an ambulance 1984.

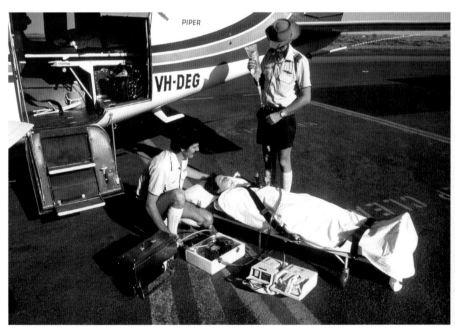

12. Preparing to load a patient into a Piper Navajo, VH-DEG in 1983. A flipper door, aft of the main hatch improved access. The rear stretcher platform can be seen with storage below. Patient is connected to a Bird Mark 7 ventilator in a wooden case, attached to an Oxy Viva, with a LIFEPAK 5 for monitoring. Nurse Reg Andrews and Captain John Wheeler.

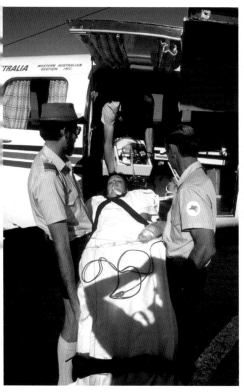

13. The 'mandraulic' loading system. A ventilated patient, being loaded into an unpressurized Piper Navajo at Port Hedland. There was usually an additional person at the foot end of the stretcher.

14. Demonstrating an RFDS medical chest in 1993. The chest contains dressings and medicines suitable for people living in remote areas.

15. Coronary care in the bush. A patient with a heart attack on a station in the Murchison in the late 1980s. Onset of pain was only a few hours earlier. Piper Navajo VH-AYT meets up with the patient who is brought out on a mattress in a station wagon.

16. Flight Nurse Linda Stretch and an onlooker. Patient on our aircraft stretcher with a LIFEPAK 5 monitor defibrillator. A full 12-lead ECG is undertaken using a Nihon Kohden portable electrocardiograph.

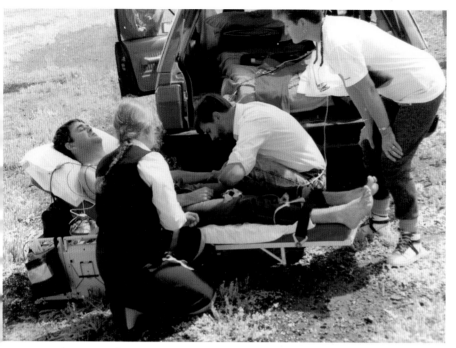

17. With ECG confirmation of a large heart attack, thrombolysis with streptokinase is commenced on site to clear the clot, and quickly achieves a successful outcome.

18. The RFDS bringing care to remote Australians where it is needed.

19. Vickers 77 neonatal transport cot in a Piper Navajo with senior nurse Gaye Richardson. In conjunction with Dr Fred Grauaug at King Edward Memorial Hospital, this established one of the first airborne neonatal transport services in Australia.

20. The dedicated 'Sister Philomena' at Nullagine in the 1980s. Like most remote area nurses she was available to the community seven days and nights a week.

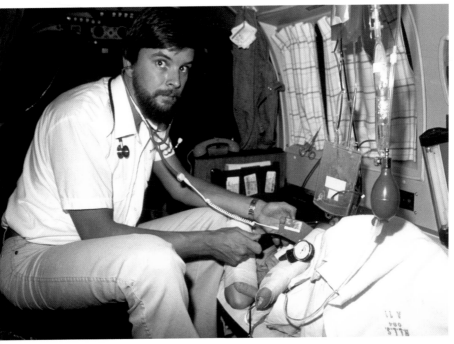

21. Using a Doppler stethoscope to obtain a blood pressure in a small child, prior to the introduction of effective portable non-invasive blood pressure devices. A normal stethoscope is ineffective in a noisy aircraft.

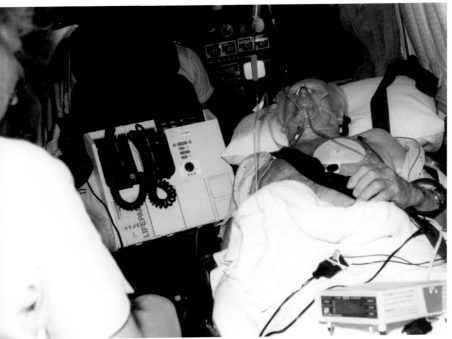

22. A patient with complete heart block undergoing transcutaneous pacing with the LIFEPAK 10 during air transport.

23. The new 'medical' computer in 1986. The latest IBM PC-AT with dot matrix printer. The medical records program written by the author provided information on our aeromedical services.

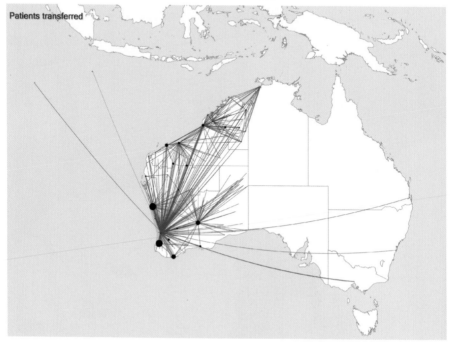

24. Map showing the scope of RFDS aeromedical services in 2014/15, which includes evacuations from the Australian Indian Ocean Territories and interstate transfers to Darwin, Brisbane, Sydney and Melbourne. (Analysis by Helen Bartholomew).

25. The launch of six new WANTS sleds in February 1999 with the C90 King Air VH-FDT in the background. These air and road transportable neonatal transport units, were developed by biomedical engineers at Princess Margaret Hospital for Children in Perth.

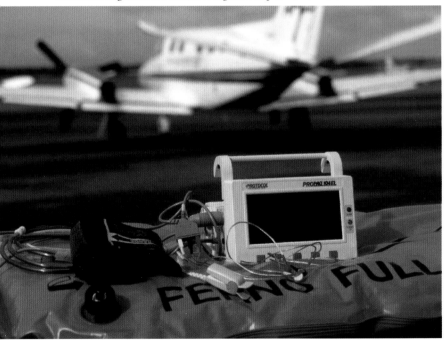

26. The original Propaq monitor and a Ferno vacuum mattress about 1991. The first reliable, robust, portable, battery-powered clinical monitor, suitable for use in flight.

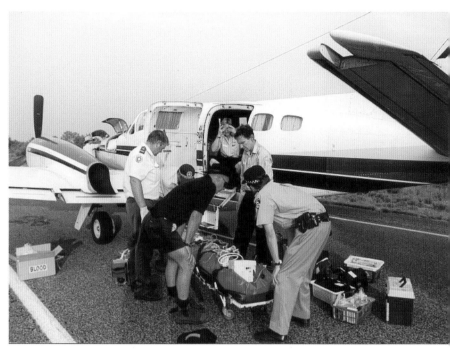

27. A Cessna C441 Conquest II landed on the main road near Pardoo. Preparing to evacuate a young child with critical injuries directly to Perth. (Photo Dr Jim Flynn)

28. The 'Best for the Bush' national health strategy working group in Alice Springs 1993,.
Rear: Dr Geoff King (Qld), Mick Reid (Consultant), Yvette Stern, Barb Stott (Vic),
Middle: Geri Malone (Central), Suzanne Hood (Qld), Dr Stephen Langford (WA),
Dr Ashleigh Thomas (Central), Dr David Greening (NSW), Belinda Shepley (NSW).
Front: Dr Neil Thomson (National) Chris Roff (Vic)

29. A road landing area. Signage on each side of the road has been removed and 'piano keys' painted on the road to identify the runway threshold.

30. Coming in to land on the Eyre Highway, Captain Dick Tippett, February 2003.

31. A road landing near Nanutarra 11 December 2010 by Captain Ross Andrews in VH-OWA from the Port Hedland Base. (Photos Captain Ross Andrews)

32. Rollover near Nanutarra. Four occupants seriously injured. The PC-12 is seen in the distance. The road landing enabled prompt direct evacuation of casualties to Perth. An additional aircraft responded from Meekatharra Base.

up with aircraft from other bases. In June 1996 we announced the closure of Carnarvon. Despite a lot of community unhappiness and political fuss, it was the correct decision. We were able to build up Meekatharra to an effective 24/7 service which still served the sparse populations in the middle of Western Australia. Our Meekatharra teams are regularly used to cover locations in the Kimberley to the north, to Esperance on the south coast, in the Central Lands to the east, and to each of the towns along the western coastline. Without our retention of Meekatharra as an operating base, some of the most remote and sparsely populated parts of Western Australia would have had a much reduced emergency coverage.

The original stone base building in the main street of Meekatharra held the radio equipment. In the late 1970s, a transportable was established adjacent to it as the base administration building, with two staff houses on the same block. It was not until 2009 that a new administration facility was built out at the airport.

Geraldton

At Geraldton there was a single pilot, Captain Ray McLoughlin. He cleaned, polished and took pride in his Piper Navajo like no one anywhere else. It was immaculate and, undoubtedly due to his care and attention, was noted to have the least problems when down in Jandakot for maintenance. There was no radio base in Geraldton, with communications across the region handled from mostly Carnarvon or Meekatharra.

The Geraldton Base, opened in 1977, was effective in moving patients from Geraldton to Perth but, with only a single pilot and nurse, could not offer a full 24-hour, 7-day emergency service. Without any doctors, Geraldton mostly undertook air ambulance-style transfers. When a critical patient arose, an aircraft from Jandakot or Port Hedland stepped in, as there we had our own medical staff.

In 1989, it was decided that we could get better use from the aircraft in Geraldton if it were moved to Perth, so Ray and his pristine Navajo came to Perth and the hangar was sold off. There was a bit of a fuss in the community but the decision was wise. All the patients from Geraldton and the surrounding area were still evacuated but using flight nurses and medical teams from Perth.

Kalgoorlie

While a few medical flights were undertaken by Goldfields Airways in the 1930s, the Kalgoorlie Base of the Eastern Goldfields Section was not formally established until 1937. The area it covered was massive; all the way to the South Australian and Northern Territory borders and sometimes crossing over them. In the early 1980s there were three or four aircraft based in Kalgoorlie enabling at least one to be on clinic runs (often overnight), plus one or two for emergency work, with the last being in maintenance locally. This was a very sound operation with a high level of camaraderie and its own medical and nursing staff and pilots. Patients were brought in to Kalgoorlie Regional Hospital from remote locations and many others were transferred through to Perth, overflying locations that were in WA Section 'territory'. With the formation of Western Operations, it was apparent that additional synergies could be achieved if the Kalgoorlie aircraft was tasked to pick up patients from WA Section locations when en route to Perth or returning to base. In return, the Jandakot and Meekatharra bases could provide increased coverage and backup for locations in the Goldfields.

From March 1973, the base building at Kalgoorlie was located in Piccadilly Street, opposite the hospital. The administration was based there and the doctors had consulting rooms in which they could see patients who had come in from outlying areas normally serviced by the RFDS. The doctors also provided an extensive range of inpatient hospital services, particularly in general medicine and paediatrics. The children's ward was often at maximum capacity and the majority of the patients were from outlying Aboriginal communities serviced by the RFDS. When my wife started there as an RFDS doctor in 1988, she asked 'Who's the paediatrician?' The response was 'You are!' (Ten years later, she became one).

The radio base in Kalgoorlie was a separate building in another part of town. As for other RFDS bases, the radio operator was conscientious and always on call for emergency radio activations.

Shortly before the merger of the three sections in 1995, the Eastern Goldfields built a new facility adjacent to the hangars at the airport and sold Piccadilly Street. The new airport facility incorporated administration, medical, aviation, patient transfer and a visitor centre.

Jandakot

The Jandakot Base is said to have opened in 1964. Dr Harold Dicks and Robyn Miller were flying out of Perth to provide clinic and emergency services. In the late 1970s, there was a short period when St John Ambulance set up an air ambulance operation in parallel with the RFDS from Perth. This was a period of intense rivalry which was probably good for the RFDS overall, shaking any tendency to complacency and pushing it to establish formal employment arrangements for flight nurses and doctors and take a more statewide perspective. Ultimately, the RFDS was directed by the Health Department to undertake all aeromedical work in Western Australia and St John withdrew its air ambulance service to focus on its road ambulance operations.

There was only one full-time doctor in Jandakot, supported by a panel of anaesthetists and other doctors who would provide backup support. Dr Rob Liddell had handed over to Dr David McDowell in 1983, whom I followed. I valued the support of the panel doctors but it was a bit of a 'hit and miss' affair, so I was grateful to be supported in establishing a part-time position to assist with cover on alternate weekends. This meant I only had to work twelve days of twenty-four hours in a row and then had a whole two days off. A number of doctors took on this part-time role while studying to become specialists. They included Dr McDowell (neurosurgery), Dr Bob Graydon (emergency medicine), Dr Stephen Wilson (general practice), Dr Glenda Wilson (emergency medicine) and Dr Rob Condon (public health medicine). By the middle of the 1990s, we had increased the level of part-time coverage – although I recall with horror a stint in 1996 when I had to work seven days a week for almost six months until I could refill the position.

Dr Glenda Wilson deserves special mention. She started as a registrar, training in emergency medicine while she prepared for her exams. As a private pilot, she really enjoyed and understood the aviation component of the work. After passing her exams, she stayed on for a few years until I managed to push her back into the hospital system to complete her specialty training. She returned as a fully fledged specialist in emergency medicine – our first in WA – and has stayed as a loyal and committed RFDS doctor for two decades.

In 1985, there was an eclectic mix of aircraft at Jandakot including two Beechcraft Barons, one remaining Duke, one of two Cessna 421s and a number of Piper Navajos. These were all different and interesting to fly in. We then added the Mojave, the Conquest 441 and, from 1999, the Beechcraft B200SE King Air. Kalgoorlie was operating the Navajo and then moved to the Conquest 425, a slightly smaller airframe than the C441 but with Pratt & Whitney PT6A turbine engines instead of the Garrett TPE331 turbines. The Victorian Section had used Navajos and Beechcraft Queen Airs and by the middle of the 1990s was operating a smaller C90 King Air and the larger B200 Super King Airs.

Apart from the different aircraft operating characteristics, the stretchers and medical fit were different. The Victorian Section aircraft had various fit-outs, most of which were completed by Hawker Pacific in Sydney. The stretchers were not compatible with the other two sections but their most recent King Airs had two useful new features the rest of us did not have. The first was 240-volt AC power and the second was the adoption of the AFTS electromechanical loading system, developed in Adelaide. In the WA and Eastern Goldfields sections, the same basic stretchers were used. These were a very simple chrome molybdenum steel frame with backrest, designed by Graham Swannell, the founder of Aeronautical Engineers Australia. We managed to use the same stretchers interchangeably in the Navajos, the C441s and the C425 although the rear stretcher was sometimes a modified design. This was important as for long flights, using two or more aircraft, you did not want to have to move seriously injured patients from one stretcher to another if you could help it.

When I started, the Jandakot Base was located at Hangar 105. I remember talking to the general manager on the phone from Melbourne before taking the job with a mental image that he was in a large steel hangar using a phone on the wall. In fact, there was a modern brick administration building next to the hangar which was only a few years old. The administration had previously been in a house at 187 Roberts Road in Subiaco, but a sensible decision was made to consolidate administration and operational staff on site at the airport. Engineering was in the adjacent Hangar 107 and had its own set of basic administration offices tacked onto the side. A nursing crew facility was also attached to Hangar 105, opening out airside. It was where all the medical equipment and supplies were kept and could be used for patient handover. It had a small resuscitation room which was completed in January 1983 and was used when patients had deteriorated in flight. A couple of babies had been delivered there after long flights from up north and I undertook a number of difficult resuscitations and interventions in the small room.

A new two-storey building was constructed in 1990. It sat between the two hangars and included a large auditorium and an operations room on the first floor. The operations centre was a significant advance and replaced a much smaller office setup with phones, telex and radios, which had been used in the 1980s. Likewise, the provision of a spacious auditorium was an enlightened decision, creating opportunities for training, seminars, staff meetings, special functions and tour groups.

There have been additional changes to our Jandakot Base facilities. The most significant was a two-storey expansion in 2008, which provided an enlarged patient transfer facility, sleeping accommodation for crews, additional office accommodation and a new training room. We have acquired additional adjacent hangars on the airstrip with a view to a significant redevelopment at some time in the future.

Section 2

Aviation

Aviation in the 1980s
Pistons and prayers

In 1985 we flew exclusively piston-engine aircraft. These included the Beechcraft Baron, the Cessna C421B Golden Eagle and a Beechcraft Duke, yet the most common aircraft in our fleet was the Piper Navajo.

Piston-engine aircraft have reciprocating engines similar to a motor vehicle. The pistons move up and down in cylinders and spark plugs ignite the fuel mixture as they do in a car. The main difference is that aircraft piston engines usually have dual spark plugs and magnetos (the component that creates the spark). This provides more uniform combustion in the cylinder and means that if one system fails, there is still another source of ignition for the cylinder. Unlike a car, the engine is running at full throttle for take-off and then at high revs for most of the flight. As the engine is being flogged most of the time, it needs to be well designed and carefully maintained. In aviation, the power plants need to be as light and powerful as possible; hence they cost substantially more than a similar car engine.

Aircraft piston engines also have a carburettor, which is the inlet throat into which air and fuel are introduced to the engine. Unlike a car, there is the capacity to 'lean' the fuel mixture in the carburettor. When an aircraft flies at altitude, there is less oxygen in the air to achieve full combustion, so the pilot reduces the amount of fuel being sprayed into the carburettor by adjusting the mixture control. This is a manual process and is a bit hit and miss. As the mixture is leaned the engine reaches a point where it starts coughing and is about to stop due to lack of fuel! You then quickly turn the mixture knob back a little to keep it running lean and smooth. This can provoke anxiety in the uninitiated.

Aircraft piston engines provide reasonable power but the type of engine is still relatively heavy for a light aircraft. There is a failure rate from the parts moving up and down with violent force, which is why having multiple piston engines on your aircraft is generally considered safer. In the early days of the RFDS we did use single-engine aircraft, such as the De Havilland DH.83 Fox Moth and the Cessna 180 – magnificent restored versions of each of these are still flying today. However an engine failure resulted in a glide approach and a crash landing. It is also doubtful that much clinical care would have been provided to patients in flight in such small airframes.

The aircraft we flew in during the 1980s were all twin-engined, so in the uncommon event of an engine failure, the other engine would keep you airborne. Safety has always been a high priority in the RFDS for our patients, staff and reputation. There was considerable pressure on our engineers to keep the aircraft maintained to the highest levels, particularly as they were being sent out to rural bases and expected to operate flawlessly in hot weather and on rough strips, with no local engineering support until their next scheduled service.

Having two engines may provide an extra level of safety but pilots still need to be well trained to manage an engine failure. When this occurs in a twin, the failed engine and its propeller, instead of providing thrust, now create a huge amount of drag on the affected side. The aircraft has a tendency to roll and the pilot has to be quick to compensate for the dead engine when it occurs. This requires repeated ongoing training so that the correct responses occur automatically. An engine failure on take-off, under maximum power, is the most critical situation, with no altitude in which to recover. In this situation, the outcome is usually fatal.

I spent many years flying in our Piper Navajos, a versatile unpressurised utility aircraft introduced in 1977. We used them for clinic flights and for evacuations. I would regularly sit up the front with the pilot as we flew out to clinics three or four days per week. This offered me a great chance to learn about the aircraft and aviation, which I was interested in as a private pilot. It also afforded me time to talk about medical stuff, as well as life in general, which was of interest to the pilot.

We developed a strong rapport with each of our pilots through this regular contact, so when the chips were down, as they say, we each had a high level of respect for the other's views. It might be a bleak night with lousy weather and an evacuation would come up. The pilot would ask, 'How bloody crook is this patient?' to which I could respond, 'Well how bloody bad is the weather?'

If the weather was foul and the patient relatively stable, we could have an honest discussion and possibly defer the flight until conditions improved. On the other hand, if the patient was critical, the pilot would trust my judgement and give it his best shot, with the proviso that safety was always paramount. This is when I developed one of my Golden Rules: The first life to save in aeromedical evacuation is your own!

Keeping passengers (and the pilot) entertained

Flying for an hour and a half each way going to clinics became so routine that I was more used to it than driving and always felt comfortable and safe. Indeed, it was much safer than travelling by road as there is less to hit in the air than on the ground! It was often just the pilot and me, although occasionally we would have an allied health worker or a medical student on the flight. The medical

49

students would be invited to sit up the front with the pilot, as it was such an adventure for them. This is where our individual pilot personalities would shine. Without giving away names and details there were one or two who really enjoyed the chance to show off a little, particularly for an attractive female medical student.

First, there would be the taxying trick. The pilot would let the student hold the control column in the co-pilot seat and 'steer' the aircraft on the taxiways, without letting on that the control column has nothing to do with direction of the aircraft on the ground and the pilot was actually steering the aircraft with his feet on the rudder pedals.

'Left turn here...good...right turn here...good.' The student would become increasing confident they had this all sorted, until the pilot would start to turn the aircraft off the taxiway and the student would start panicking that their movements of the control column were no longer working.

'Quick straighten up', he'd tell them, as we would almost run off the taxiway, till he corrected it with the rudder pedals. Ha ha ha! We'd all laugh. 'Yep, done that one a dozen times before', I'd be thinking to myself from down the back.

Then there was the request to the Port Hedland tower for clearance for an 'early left turn'. This really meant that on the very long Port Hedland runway the pilot could become airborne just above the runway, build up speed then do a sharp turn on a wing tip, as we went really close around the tower after take-off. Always an impressive Top Gun style of move, waving to the guys in the tower as we went by.

Finally, we had the steep turn above one of the old Pilbara mine sites en route to our clinic. There were a few very deep open cut pits now full of water. Flying over the top of them, the pilot would ask the passenger if they would like to see one of them, then pull a really steep angle of bank turn, just over the top. The passenger could look across the pilot right down into the pit while *at the same time combating their fear as we seemed to be almost at right angles in a very tight and steep turn above this huge water-filled crater.*

'Yeah, been there, done that one too', I'd be thinking from the cabin. Of course this wouldn't happen today, but at the time, fun and professionalism were able to coexist comfortably. It added a little entertainment to the routine of the daily flights and made for an exciting experience for the student.

Clinic flights weren't without an occasional mishap. On one occasion, we landed at Marble Bar and blew a tyre on the sharp quartz gravel, which made up the surface of the airstrip. As the tyre blew, the rim dug into the dirt and dragged along the runway as the pilot did his best to keep the aircraft straight and slow it down.

It meant a night at Marble Bar's famous Ironclad Hotel: not a particularly salubrious establishment for accommodation but well known for the extent of drinking that could occur in the hotel bar. After all, the town of Marble Bar set a world record for the longest number of consecutive days above 100 degrees Fahrenheit (37 degrees Celsius) over 160 days in 1923/4. For more than six months of the year, the average maximum temperature exceeds normal body temperature of 37 degrees, which was a good excuse for the residents to imbibe considerable amounts of fluid at the hotel on a regular basis.

Not for us, of course. I had a whole day's clinic to attend to. That night a spare wheel arrived on a truck from our Port Hedland Base, 300 kilometres away. The pilot and I deftly fitted it with some help and the following morning were on our way.

Our engineers and pilots had the foresight and experience to keep essential spares at each of our remote bases. Had we not done so, we might have been waiting days for a spare tyre and wheel assembly to come from Perth, or even interstate. Maintaining spares added to costs but ensured we could keep our aircraft operational as much as possible.

Despite the occasional mishap, I have always felt very safe flying in RFDS aircraft. Although we were working in very remote settings, on rough airstrips, in extremes of temperature and weather, with limited navigational aids and all the engineering support down in Perth, our aircraft were reliable and well maintained, and our pilots experienced and capable. Over many decades our chief pilots, engineering managers and overall corporate culture have held sound recruitment, regular training, meticulous maintenance and air safety as inalienable principles. I would much rather fly in an aircraft any time than risk my life on country roads.

Pressures of flight
Aircraft pressurisation

Carrying patients in an aircraft at altitude can have a number of consequences. Some of these are related to the reduced barometric pressure in the aircraft and others are the result of the reduced concentration of oxygen in the air at altitude. Most people are familiar with the sensation of blocked ears that can occur when we gain altitude with a simple drive into the hills, or when we go flying. While there are relatively benign consequences for most people, more serious problems can occur with certain patients when we take them to altitude in a medical aircraft.

The English scientist Robert Boyle demonstrated that with reducing barometric pressure at altitude, a gas will expand. Likewise, the volume of a gas will reduce as barometric pressure increases when we descend. The principle is referred to as Boyle's Law.

Problems occur for anyone with a medical condition where gas is trapped in a body cavity. Patients with a variety of conditions, such as a collapsed lung or a bowel obstruction, can have significant side effects from changes in barometric pressure as the gas expands at altitude.

Until the late 1970s, the only aircraft operated by the RFDS across Australia were unpressurised. The maximum permitted flying altitude was not high enough to position us above most bad weather and still exposed patients to cabin altitudes of up to

10,000 feet. In contrast, pressurised domestic airliners were flying at 25,000 to 40,000 feet with an effective altitude in the cabin ranging from around 4,000 to 8,000 feet.

Pressurised aircraft permit flight at much higher altitudes. They enable aircraft to cruise above bad weather and provide greater fuel economy while achieving faster speeds as the air is less dense. They can do this while keeping the cabin altitude at a much lower level.

Beechcraft Duke

The RFDS in Western Australia was aware of these problems and, in 1972, became the first section to acquire and operate pressurised aircraft. A Beechcraft Duke was purchased and fitted out to carry one or two stretcher patients. This aircraft VH-IFD was followed by a second aircraft VH-UFD.

It was a solid aircraft but there was very little room inside. Two patients were only carried if really necessary, as the stretchers were positioned one above the other, just like bunk beds. To load the stretchers, a sort of gantry arrangement was installed. This allowed the top stretcher to be lifted with ropes and pulleys outside the aircraft, then manoeuvred into the aircraft and positioned above the rear stretcher on a set of brackets.

The Duke was ideal for flights with patients such as those with decompression illness (the 'bends') and other cases where flight at altitude would really cause a problem, such as bowel obstructions and chest trauma.

Cessna Golden Eagle

After a while it was clear that further pressurised aircraft would be beneficial, so in 1975 two Cessna 421B Golden Eagles were acquired, VH-ADG and VH-ADK. These were slightly larger inside and while carriage of two patients was tight, there was a little more room overall. One aircraft was located in Port Hedland and the other at Jandakot Airport.

The Cessna 421s were still powered only by piston engines so their cruising speed was around 180 knots (350 km/h). There were bulbous fuel tanks on the tips of the wings and, to those of us who flew in them, the wings appeared to 'flap' as they flexed up and down during turbulent flight.

Depressurisation

When you fly in a pressurised aircraft, you have to accept that at some time you may become depressurised. It can be sudden and unexpected, such as when a door seal gives way, or is sometimes done intentionally to ventilate the cabin. When it occurs, the altitude in the cabin rises to that of the atmosphere outside the aircraft.

Fumes in flight over Wittenoom

One night in 1984, we were really stretching the capacity of the Cessna 421 aircraft with two seriously ill, ventilated patients on board. One was an Aboriginal man from Marble Bar with a subarachnoid haemorrhage (a bleeding blood vessel in the brain), whom we needed to evacuate to Perth for neurosurgery. The other was a young woman who had presented to the Port Hedland Regional Hospital with severe vomiting during a gastroenteritis outbreak. The diagnosis of a bowel obstruction was missed as her symptoms were similar to those of the other patients suffering 'gastro'. When the diagnosis was finally made, she had a gangrenous bowel and had developed septicaemia and early respiratory failure.

One stretcher was in the normal position on the right-hand side of the aisle and the other located on the left-hand side, atop the seats, which had their backrests folded forward. It was really cramped. As we cruised over the Hamersley Ranges, we smelt something burning in the cabin. We all started to do some serious sniffing but if you have ever tried to locate the source of a smell, you will realise it is difficult to do. Our concern was not just that something appeared to be burning but that in a sealed aircraft cabin, there was the risk of carbon monoxide poisoning eventually incapacitating the pilot and passengers.

After a few more minutes, we became aware of a slight haze suggesting smoke in the cabin. Though our pilot Captain Greg Schouten was young and very capable and we had great confidence in him, this was now serious. We were at 18,000 feet, at night and with smoke in the cabin! He immediately donned his oxygen mask to protect himself from inhaling fumes and we tried shutting down one engine to see if it made a difference. We then restarted the first and tried shutting down the other, but the fumes and smell were still there and seemed to be getting worse. He depressurised the cabin to clear the fumes, while the flight nurse and I put on oxygen masks too. The patients were already on high concentrations of oxygen, so hypoxia would not be problem for them. At the same time, we commenced descending the aircraft to an altitude where we would not need to wear oxygen masks.

By trial and error, we deduced that the burning was coming from something in the electrical system. It is possible to shut down most of the electrical system in an aircraft, including all the panel lighting, and still keep flying. Some instruments have redundant features and are powered by air-driven gyros rather than electrics. We noted an improvement in the fumes but I was now in the co-pilot seat having to hold a torch so that Greg could read the instruments.

It was clearly necessary to land as soon as possible but the only airstrip in the immediate area was the old Wittenoom Airport. We tried to arrange over the radio for someone to come out and put the lights on but that was going to take at least half an hour. After making the standard emergency calls we continued depressurised and proceeded to descend to the circuit area with a view to landing.

Fortunately, it was a clear moonlit night. We had no airstrip lighting and only a torch illuminating the essential airspeed and altitude instruments. As we came in to land it was only the aircraft's undercarriage landing lights that would illuminate a portion of the runway. Pilots train to land with no airstrip lights but rarely ever do so.

I remember that very last bit of the approach vividly; holding a torch on the instruments and watching the airspeed and altitude like a hawk. There was the vague outline of the airstrip ahead of us, the 'rush' as the ground suddenly loomed ahead and was caught in the aircraft lights, and the relief as we touched down and came to a stop before the end of the runway was in sight. We had made an excellent landing in the dark and then taxied over to the shed, which served as a terminal building, before shutting down.

First problem solved. We were down and safe; but now, what about the patients? We were at a remote airstrip in the Pilbara, at night, with two seriously ill patients. Fortunately for them they were sedated and on ventilators so oblivious to all the excitement. However, our aircraft electrics were turned off as the most likely cause of the burning and we had to rely on hand torches for cabin lighting. Thank goodness for the old 'Dolphin' torches of the day, powered by large 9-volt batteries, the size of half a brick. We had many hours to fill in. A rescue flight from Perth was at least five hours away and we only had a few hours of medical oxygen available.

What followed was one of those great examples were people rally to your assistance. Staff from two nearby nursing posts, up to 100 kilometres away, drove through the night to bring us all the portable oxygen and anaesthetic drugs they could muster. Our original supplies were based on the anticipated flight time to our Meekatharra Base — about three hours — not for ongoing care for more than six hours.

We calculated our oxygen requirements and consumption rates and tweaked our ventilators to achieve the duration required with the slimmest of margins. Likewise, we managed to keep our patients stable and fully sedated by using a variety of medications from the various supplies brought to us.

It is hard to imagine a time and place with no mobile phone coverage and even the nearest fixed phone at the nursing post a few kilometres away. All communications were by HF radio to a repeater in Port Hedland and then to an operator in Perth. The old town of Wittenoom in the Hamersley Ranges (now Karijini National Park) was isolated and had no nearby doctors or hospital. We continued our 'intensive care in a phone booth' in the back of the aircraft until dawn, when one rescue aircraft arrived from Perth and another was able to launch from our Port Hedland Base. As the only doctor in Port Hedland at the time and the only one who could not be 'out of hours', I had to go with the crew with one of the patients to Perth, while my colleague from Perth, Dr David McDowell, took the other patient.

What of the depressurisation and its effects on the patients? It was essential to depressurise and ventilate the cabin of any potential toxic fumes but the consequences for the woman with the bowel obstruction was that all the trapped air expanded. We had a nasogastric tube in the stomach to drain it and keep it empty, which is standard practice for this condition. After depressurising, the expanding gas forced much of the bowel contents up into the stomach where fortunately most of it flowed into a drainage bag.

Our conscientious nurse continued with suctioning of this tube throughout the ordeal. It confirmed our teaching that a sudden rise to altitude does have a significant effect when trapped gases expand. Some of the intestinal contents clearly came up into the patient's mouth and if it were not for the cuffed endotracheal tube in the patient's trachea, she would have suffered a dreadful aspiration into the lungs.

The Cessna 421B was subsequently attended to by our aircraft engineers. They found a melted wiring loom beneath the co-pilot seat, where it was easy to smell but hard to find in flight.

Our patients did reasonably well. The patient with the intracranial bleed survived while the young woman had a bowel resection but made a satisfactory recovery.

Other pressurised aircraft

Our two Cessna 421B aircraft made a valuable contribution to our fleet, which at the time was mostly unpressurised Navajos. In 1985 the Western Australian Section purchased a new Piper Mojave, a pressurised version of the Navajo, with a view to expanding the number in the fleet. This did not eventuate and a series of faster turboprop Cessna Conquests were acquired in the 1980s and 1990s instead. Other sections around Australia also started to purchase pressurised aircraft. The big change, however, was the introduction of a new type of propulsion – the turboprop.

Transition to turbines
Introduction of turboprop aircraft

In 1988 we acquired our first turbine-powered aircraft, the Cessna C441 Conquest II. These had a Garrett turbine engine with a propeller on the front – a 'turboprop'. These engines are much more expensive but provide considerably more power for their weight. This meant the aircraft, although bigger, could take off in a short distance and climb out considerably faster. It was like moving from a Holden to a Ferrari. Once airborne with the gear up, the aircraft would rocket away, climbing out at a greater rate and flying around 100 knots (180 km/h) faster than the Navajos could. In the event of an engine failure, the turboprop still had a significant rate of climb, whereas the Navajo could barely climb at all. This provided an additional margin of safety.

At about the same time, the Victorian Section of the RFDS, which operated in the Kimberley, acquired its first Beechcraft B200 King Air, as did other sections around Australia. The Kalgoorlie Base, which was the separate Eastern Goldfields Section of the RFDS, purchased the Cessna C425 Conquest I. These were similar to our C441 but a little shorter inside. All were twin-engine turboprops.

A turbine engine is essentially a series of rotating compressor blades forcing air into a combustion chamber behind them. It spins at very high speed (say 40,000 revolutions per minute) but has minimal moving parts and no violent opposing forces, as in a piston engine, so the failure rate of these engines is much lower. This of course comes at a cost, both in purchase price and maintenance, but it saw us enter a new era of aviation.

As we acquired Cessna Conquests, our pilots needed to step up to flying much faster aircraft, at higher altitudes and up with the 'big boys'; the commercial airliners plying the skies across Western Australia. Things happen much quicker at 500 kilometres an hour. When coming into the circuit at Jandakot Airport, there are many small, slow training aircraft and this requires disciplined airmanship and proper preparation to keep 'ahead of the aircraft'.

We were also now operating pressurised at up to 30,000 feet and sometimes higher. The workload in operating a pressurised turbine aircraft fully IFR (instrument flight rules) was about as much as one could reasonably expect from a single pilot. The next step was to move to two-pilot operations, which were not feasible nor affordable.

The advent of turboprops made non-stop flights from the Pilbara to Perth a reality. Previously it would take over five hours' flying time in a Navajo to travel from Port Hedland to Perth, with a refuelling stop at Meekatharra added to this. Upon arrival, the pilot would be 'out of hours' and not permitted to do a return flight without an appropriate rest break. With the Conquests, we could go direct in three hours, turn around and fly home.

Not only was this better for patient care but more practical operationally. Previously almost every patient I flew with from the Pilbara had to be handed over halfway at Meekatharra to another team, which had flown up from Perth. This added to delays in getting patients to their ultimate destination hospital. Handing over very sick and unstable patients on an airstrip also increased the clinical risks of something being missed or the patient deteriorating. With the Conquests, we effectively almost doubled the operational area that each aircraft could cover. The Conquests also gave us more room.

In the Navajo a single stretcher took up most of the right-hand side of the cabin. It rolled in on wheels after it had been lifted up and into the aircraft. There was an elevated platform aft of this that went into a cut-out section of the tail. A small flat stretcher was located here. It was a bugger to load.

The entire loading process was 'mandraulic'. That is, three to five strong people would surround the stretcher at the door of the aircraft and just lift it up and onto the aircraft floor, which was at waist height. The reverse occurred for unloading. At this time the average patient was much lighter than they are today. Loading issues are discussed further in the Medical section (in chapters 'Lightening the load' and 'Weighed down with big issues').

Although the Conquest C441s were also loaded 'mandraulically', the rear stretcher was able to be secured in a tandem configuration, aft of the front stretcher on the right-hand side of the cabin. We did not need the complex back-breaking loading arrangement of the Navajo. Both stretchers were also interchangeable, which made the loading and positioning of different patients more flexible.

As had been the case in the Piper Navajos, the medical oxygen was installed in the nose of the aircraft. However, as a pressurised aircraft, this installation was a little more complex. First, it was important to ensure that the gas lines coming from outside the pressure hull into the cabin were installed in a manner that would not compromise the pressurisation system. Second, as the aircraft was flying much higher, at sub-zero temperatures, we had to be more aware of the risks of the regulators freezing. In years past, medical oxygen supplies contained a small amount of water vapour. As this passes through the regulator on a gas bottle, the gas cools as it expands. If there is moisture present, it can freeze and cause the regulator to seize up. To avoid this we used a special medical Dry Breathing Oxygen which had very low levels of moisture.

The other issue was to ensure the medical oxygen cylinders were turned on whenever a patient was on board. As a precaution, we usually flew around with the oxygen cylinders in the nose turned off when no patients were on board to prevent any risk of leaks. It was a standard practice for the pilot to turn them back on when we loaded a patient. As far as I recall, they never forgot. It would clearly have been a problem to discover this once we were airborne and cruising at 30,000 feet!

Well hung

At the time of acquiring the Cessna Conquests, we reviewed how we could best store our medical equipment. There was no room in the Navajos or the Conquests to have a separate medical cabinet and most of our supplies were stowed in shelving in the tail of the aircraft. When in flight, you needed to be able to reach commonly used items quickly and easily, often without leaving your seat, particularly if you were in turbulence.

I discussed various ideas with our flight nurses and we came up with the concept of 'wall-hung bags'. In essence, the idea was modelled on the design of shoe bags which some people hang in their cupboards. Instead of a broad panel with pockets in which to put pairs of shoes, we developed a system with pouches in which to put our essential medical consumables.

We designed two padded vinyl panels, each about 1 metre square, which were covered with clear vinyl pouches of different sizes. We laid out all our essential equipment on a table and had an upholsterer produce a prototype, which we then refined further. Gaye Richardson and Jan Edwards, our most senior nurses at Jandakot, were integral to completion of the project. The pouches varied from about 100 mm square to 150 mm by 300 mm to match the various items they would contain. Each pouch was sealed with

Velcro® and had a slot to slide in a card listing the contents. The vinyl panels rolled up to form bags with handles which could be easily stowed in the back of the aircraft, or taken to an accident scene or a hospital.

For a normal flight the first bag was hung on the left-hand wall of the cabin between where the doctor and nurse sat. It contained all the things you would use frequently, for example, syringes, needles, swabs, suction catheters, intravenous line connections and basic tapes and dressings. The medical team could remain in their seats and either person could reach most things they needed during flight. When critically ill patients were transported, the second bag was hung next to the first, as it contained more advanced supplementary items, including intubation equipment.

The aircraft equipment was easy to check and restock, as the wall-hung bags could be removed from the aircraft and taken inside our air-conditioned medical facilities, rather than our nurses sweating it out, checking and restocking in the aircraft. We were the only RFDS section to use this innovative system and it worked well until around 1999 when we started to replace our Navajos and Conquests with the larger Beechcraft B200 King Air. We installed the LifePort fit-out with some storage spaces under the stretchers and there was enough room for additional medical stowage cabinets in the aircraft.

Satellite communications in flight

Air–ground communication has always been difficult when operating over such large distances. While we had HF radio on the aircraft, the quality was often poor with high levels of static. There were some VHF repeater stations across WA but these were not always a reliable means of communication for a nurse to speak to a doctor on the ground, or medical team to speak with a hospital.

In the 1990s, our aviation and engineering group undertook an innovative approach to bring satellite communications to our turboprop aircraft before it was widely available in general aviation.

They selected a marine satellite phone installation with a servo-controlled aerial and modified it to work on our Cessna Conquest aircraft. As the aircraft was manoeuvred in flight, a system was needed that could keep the satellite in focus. To achieve this, the aerial assembly was mounted on the top of the aircraft and covered by an aerodynamic fibreglass dome. It required flight-testing to ensure it did not interfere with the aerodynamics or performance of the aircraft.

The system was installed in the C441 then subsequently in the first series of PC-12 aircraft. There was a problem, however, as the aircraft was moving so fast compared to a typical ground station or marine installation. This was solved with circuitry designed by RFDS staff that could provide information from the GPS navigation system to the satellite receiver, to correct for the speed and direction of the aircraft. We achieved satellite telephone communication from our aircraft, whether on the ground or in the air, across Western Australia, well in advance of other systems coming on the market.

The installation can be seen in photos as a teardrop-shaped dome on the top of Conquests and PC-12 aircraft of the late 1990s and early 2000s.

Safety in the skies
An impressive record

I have always felt very safe when flying with the RFDS, even in the roughest of weather. I have confidence in the maintenance of the aircraft and respect for the skills and professionalism of our pilots.

The Royal Flying Doctor Service has an exceptional safety record. When you consider more than eighty years of flying activity across the most remote parts of the country in all weather conditions, day and night, and landing on rough strips, it is remarkable that there have been so few significant aircraft accidents. Hitting a kangaroo, a bird-strike, or becoming bogged on the soft shoulder of a dirt runway is not uncommon, but in Western Australia there have been only two fatal accidents in our entire history.

Kimberley accident 1956

The first was on 4 February 1956 when a MacRobertson Miller Airlines ex-RAAF Avro Anson VH-MMG providing flying doctor services for the Victorian Section was forced down in a severe tropical thunderstorm en route between Tableland Station and Derby. The pilot, Captain Pieter van Emmerik, two nurses, a twelve-year-old patient and her father were killed.

Boulder accident 1981

The second fatal accident occurred on 30 April 1981, with an RFDS Piper Navajo VH-KMS returning to the Kalgoorlie Base of the Eastern Goldfields Section from Jamieson in the Central Lands. The aircraft struck the poppet head of a mine at Boulder while approaching Kalgoorlie in bad weather at night. A wing was torn off and the aircraft crashed, killing the pilot, the flight nurse, an infant and an adult. A sixteen-year-old female patient was badly injured but survived.

Mt Augustus accident 1981

We were very lucky to have no injuries from a serious accident that occurred on 4 July 1981 at Mt Augustus Station in the Gascoyne. A WA Section Piper Navajo VH-DEE, only about three months old, undertook a night flight to the station homestead adjacent to Mt Augustus, which is a large inselberg (an isolated rock or mountain that arises abruptly from a flat plain).

This near-new Piper Navajo had embarked on a medical evacuation flight from Carnarvon to retrieve a sick child. The pilot was careful in flight planning to avoid the imposing Mt Augustus monocline, which he knew was situated close to the airstrip in the dark on a moonless night. He was required to land with a limited flare path, using only six motor vehicles, as the station strip did not have proper airstrip lighting. His final approach was lower than intended and the aircraft struck trees after turning onto the final approach.

I flew with this pilot numerous times in Port Hedland and he explained to me how he had made an error in the elevation of the airstrip, which sat at 1,200 feet above sea level. Normally when approaching an airfield to land, you overfly at a safe height then let down to join the circuit, which is an imaginary rectangular pattern 1,000 feet above the ground. You fly downwind, parallel to the runway but in the opposite direction you will be landing, turn left 90 degrees onto a base leg and start descending, then another 90-degree left turn onto the final approach leg, where you line up the runway and continue your descent. On this occasion, in the blackness of night and probably fixated on avoiding the mountain, his only visual cues were the distant lights of six motor vehicles on the airstrip. He told me how he remembered the lights were appearing and disappearing, which was attributed to scattered low cloud forecast for the area. In hindsight it was because the aircraft was about 500 feet too low and they were being obscured by the unseen trees between the aircraft and strip.

Shortly after turning onto finals and in a slower approach configuration for this type of landing, the aircraft flew directly into white gums and mulga trees at 100 knots (185 km/h). Both outboard wings were torn off the aircraft, then a larger tree was struck between the engine and fuselage, spinning the airframe 180 degrees as it continued to plough along the ground. When it came to a stop, both the wings and the tail of the aircraft were destroyed and all that remained was the intact cockpit containing the pilot and nurse, shaken but uninjured. As I understand it, the pilot thought at first that he had hit Mt Augustus. They subsequently escaped from the wreckage and slowly made their way through the bush to the people waiting at the airstrip some 500 metres away. This was a miraculous escape, which made a lasting impression on the pilot. Despite this, during many years that I knew him, he never baulked at doing any emergency night flights.

Roo strike at Jandakot

One night I was on duty at our Jandakot Base and took a call to evacuate a patient with a serious head injury from the South West. The pilot on night duty was Captain David Munns, a long-serving and very experienced RFDS pilot, and the flight nurse was Joanne Gorey, also a very experienced RFDS nurse.

It was about 9 pm at night when we loaded our equipment onto the Cessna Conquest C441 aircraft, closed the doors and taxied as usual. I was sitting in an aft-facing seat behind the pilot and opposite the flight nurse. We had the usual take-off roll and then felt the engines really kick in, as they did when full throttle was applied. Just as the pilot commenced rotation, the moment when the aircraft lifts off the runway, he suddenly pulled it up hard and there was an almighty thud through the cabin.

'We've hit a roo', he called out, as the aircraft continued its climb out from the airport. This was Jandakot Airport, the general aviation airport for Perth, and yet even here there were regular kangaroo sightings. As David continued to climb out, he explained to us that he was sure the nose wheel had been hit and he was not going to retract the gear, lest there was a problem getting it down later. He climbed out to a safe altitude, then made contact with air traffic control and the RFDS. We had plenty of fuel so there was time to get the chief pilot and engineering staff in. After an hour or so, we had made a couple of low passes and as best as they could tell with spotlights from the ground, the undercarriage was intact. Still, Jandakot Airport wasn't the place to try and land with no fire service, so we proceeded to Perth Airport.

'Munnsie' briefed us on the way. There was a good chance the nose wheel could collapse when we landed. If that happened, the nose would drop and both props would then strike the tarmac doing serious damage to both the propellers and the turbine engines. The flight nurse and I took up positions in the rear seats to try to provide additional weight in the tail of the aircraft. As we approached Perth Airport, I could see all the flashing lights of emergency vehicles, fire trucks and an ambulance waiting for us to land. We came in and Dave greased it onto the runway holding the nose off the tarmac as long as possible. It didn't collapse and we slowly taxied just off at an exit ramp then stopped. Phew! All clear. Well done!

We exited the aircraft and started to unload our gear while the pilot spoke to the assembled aviation personnel and our own engineering representatives. The aircraft would be left where it stopped until the morning when it could be properly inspected then moved. However, we still had a job to do. Our patient with the serious head injury was still waiting and we were the only aeromedical team available for the night. So we needed to get going.

I recall studying some of the principles of managing combat stress reaction or 'shell shock' in military settings when at RAF Farnborough. The concepts derived from wartime experience included immediacy and expectancy, coupled with brevity and simplicity. That is, you got back in the saddle as quickly as possible, without focusing on what had happened. Intentionally or otherwise, this is what we did. We grabbed a taxi at Perth Airport, returned to Jandakot, loaded up another aircraft and set off on our mission, which we accomplished promptly and professionally. In the modern era I don't think many pilots would do so, but we all just took this in our stride. 'Another day, another life saved.' It was not until I came home the next morning and told my wife of the night's excitement that I started to think about the accident. The kangaroo, about the size of a small man, had bounded across in front of the aircraft. With the pilot's quick action and a lot of luck it had fortunately only struck the nose wheel of the Conquest. Had it struck the much larger targets, either of the propellers, just as we were rotating, the result would have been catastrophic. With sudden asymmetric thrust relatively close to the ground, we were likely to have flipped and crashed inverted.

We had a series of roo strikes during the late 1990s and early 2000s, despite our requirement for someone to drive up and down the airstrip to check it before we landed. Some of the accidents caused engine and propeller damage in excess of $500,000. Our aviation insurers met the costs of the claims, but then took legal action against a number of country shires. It was uncomfortable seeing court proceedings against various local governments in the name of the Royal Flying Doctor Service, as the insurers sued them for inadequately fencing their airstrips. Yet, as a result, many councils installed robust perimeter fencing which has enhanced safety for all users.

Derby incident 2010

On the night of 29 January 2010, a Pilatus PC-12 VH-NWO departed Derby and experienced engine problems 56 kilometres out. Captain Rachel Smart, our only female RFDS pilot at the time, turned back to base and suffered a complete engine failure in the single-engine aircraft approximately 11 kilometres from Derby. In a remarkable display of airmanship, she glided the aircraft back to the airstrip through the night sky and made an uneventful landing. None of the four people on board were injured. Subsequent investigations showed that a number of bolts in the propeller reduction gearbox had failed due to fatigue fractures. The engine had been factory-overhauled by the manufacturer. Such an engine failure could have potentially been catastrophic if it had occurred in a more remote location or not been managed as professionally as it was by the pilot. Pratt & Whitney introduced new overhaul procedures and the RFDS decided not to use loan engines but to own all its spare engines.

Safety culture

Many factors contribute to air safety. They include consistent, conscientious aircraft maintenance; capable, well-trained pilots who are not risk-takers; and to a lesser extent, good decision-making regarding whether we should evacuate patients, particularly at night and from poor airstrips.

We have had only a handful of engineering managers over the past three decades. Denis Coles was in charge of engineering when I started and had years of experience in managing a diverse piston-engine fleet across a number of bases. He was supported by Rae Harris and succeeded by Rob Hartree, Eric Hartley, Paul O'Connor and Darren Barlow. Some of our engineers, such as Ross Burrows and Bob Savage, have served for well over thirty years. For each, the challenge they have accepted is to keep a fleet of aircraft maintained to the highest possible standards and able to operate reliably at our remote bases without further local engineering support. Our patients can't afford to have an aircraft break down when an emergency flight is pending, nor can we afford to be sending engineering teams to our bases to fix unexpected unserviceabilities.

We currently have extraordinarily high utilisation rates of aircraft in our fleet – about 1600 hours per annum for each of the fourteen PC-12s. Each aircraft requires a 100-hourly service, sixteen times per year, which requires considerable scheduling to manage efficiently. Our engineering teams do a remarkable job keeping the fleet serviceable throughout the year.

When I started with the RFDS, the Chief Pilot was Captain Jim Smith or 'Smithy'. He was a bit of a character; an energetic 'can do' sort of guy with a good sense of humour. He retired about the time we introduced the Cessna Conquest C441 turboprops in the late 1980s. His replacement was Captain Chris Beattie, a very professional and cautious pilot who had been our Training Captain for the previous few years. Chris always recognised that we were here for a purpose, to provide emergency aeromedical services, but safety came first. He established a strong culture of comprehensive ongoing training. He retired just before Western Operations was formed in 1995. Captain Dick Tippett, previously the Chief Pilot of the Victorian Section in the Kimberley, took over for a couple of years as we merged a fleet of multiple aircraft types. He was superseded by Captain Michael Bleus, who had been the WA Section Chief Pilot and was head of Check and

Training. Bleus continued our strong focus on selection of pilots and rigorous training procedures. New pilots are already very experienced when offered a position but if they don't come up to his standards in their initial training, they don't stay.

I have worked with Michael since I started; flying with him and sorting out problems. If we have an aviation issue, such as challenges with pilot hours, or other operational matters and it doesn't seem quite right to me, I know I can ring him, emphasise the medical importance of the case and he will sort it out decisively and pragmatically. If it can be done, safely, it will be. If it can't, then I know that's how it is and we can look at other options. Michael has reached the remarkable achievement of being an RFDS pilot for more than forty years. It was tremendous to see his service recognised with the Medal of the Order of Australia in 2014.

Finally, an important contributor to safety is ensuring that we make sound decisions about whether to undertake an aeromedical evacuation or not. Medical teams are not tasked by dispatchers based on a telephone call. Every single flight we undertake has an experienced doctor obtain detailed clinical information about the case. They must weigh up the merits of aeromedical transport against other forms of transport and make a judgement as to how urgently the flight needs to occur and what team should be on the aircraft. The safety record of some services, particularly helicopter services, both in Australia and overseas, is quite poor. A significant contributing factor in many accidents is lack of careful clinical assessment by experienced retrieval doctors before deciding whether to launch or not. We put particular emphasis on assessing the risks of flight against the urgency of patients in our medical staff training.

Navigating the skies

Improvements in airborne navigation technology

It is difficult to comprehend how significantly navigation has changed with the introduction of satellite GPS. Today most people carry a GPS in their phone. It can pinpoint their location to within metres. Yet in the 1980s, such a system did not even exist for general aviation. When flying an aircraft, you followed a map and looked at the road and other features on the ground below you. At night or when there was cloud, there were three core electronic navigation aids to assist general aviation.

The first was the ADF or automatic direction finder. By tuning to one of a number of radio beacons at key locations, the needle on the dial of the ADF instrument would point in the direction of the beacon. This was quite helpful but, depending on altitude, was out of range at 50 to 75 nautical miles.

The second radio aid was a DME or distance measuring equipment. This used radio signal pulses between a DME station at key locations, such as airports, and the instrument in the aircraft. The aircraft receiver could determine the precise distance to the DME transponder from measuring the time delay in the radio signals. It was a clever device invented in Australia at the CSIRO and adopted internationally. It helped the pilot to fix our position more accurately.

Third, we had a VOR or visual omni-directional radio, which interrogated signals from installations, located at most large airports. This type of radio beacon sent a signal that gave information about which 'radial' or bearing you were on relative to the station. In contrast to the ADF, which just pointed to the station, the omni would indicate that you were, for example, on the '135 radial', an imaginary line extending out from the station at 135 degrees. Flying to or from a VOR station you could maintain a precise heading. However, like the other aids, it was out of range at about 100 nautical miles.

These were all helpful in navigating near airports and on main flight routes but for flying out to a remote station in the outback, at night or above cloud, you had to use 'dead reckoning'. This was much more challenging.

We would take off and from our maps set up the aircraft to fly a particular heading. Using the ADF, VOR and DME outbound one could establish the aircraft on the appropriate heading, correcting for cross winds. But once you were out of range, you had to just continue blindly using your airspeed and time to estimate distance and hope that the cross winds did not change too much. Only a few degrees of error, over the course of 100 or 200 nautical miles, could mean you were many miles off course when you arrived at what was the intended destination.

Flying in remote areas, particularly at night, required considerable airmanship by our pilots to navigate to the correct destination and to then land on a dirt strip with a flare path. Just think about it. It is pitch dark at night and you are on an emergency flight, flying across some of the most remote and sparsely inhabited parts of the continent. You can't see the ground to follow any features on a map and there are very few settlements where there may be lights. At the end of one or two hours' flying you are expecting to arrive exactly where you want to be and hoping that there will be lights on the runway.

This could be disconcerting. You are airborne, in the dark, with just the throb of the engines and the altimeter to reassure you that you are high enough not to run into anything. You are dependent on lights being set up by the remote community you are heading to. These were generally not places with electrical lighting but often used kerosene flares, which had to be filled and set out along both sides of the runway prior to your arrival. Unless you were on track, you might not see the airstrip or the dim lights from the community as you approached from 80 kilometres away. If they didn't put out the lights properly, you could find yourself in the middle of nowhere, unable to land. Out in the desert, if you couldn't identify the location you were heading to quickly, you would have to turn around and head home while you still had enough fuel to do so.

Sometimes we would locate a few dim lights on the ground belonging to the station or Aboriginal community we were heading for but no airstrip lights. We would have to circle and try to raise their attention. Eventually we would see the headlights of a car heading towards the airstrip to set up the flare path for us to land.

We were very dependent on the people on the ground putting out the lights properly. When approaching an airstrip at night, the lights needed to be laid out in a standard pattern as this provided visual cues for the pilot in establishing the correct glide path and approach. Trees at the approach end of the airstrip were dangerous and not visible from the air at night. The lights had to be in the right place and the airstrip checked for kangaroos and any ruts or obstructions. The latter was done by someone driving up and down in a vehicle before we landed. By the time the strip surface appeared in the aircraft headlights, you were committed to touch down.

When we acquired our Cessna Conquest C441 aircraft it was recognised that these could be used to evacuate from the Indian

Ocean Territories if an adequate navigation system was installed. In 1988, the aircraft were equipped with the Omega global navigation system, which was based on VLF (very low frequency) radio signals from beacons around the world. It was superseded by GPS in the 1990s.

Nowadays, navigation is substantially enhanced by the worldwide GPS system. It also provides new options for landing at locations without published instrument approaches. For many years, instrument-rated pilots have followed special instrument approach procedures that are published for airports and use the radio aids located there. They offered a safe, standardised method of descending and lining up with the runway, even when the aircraft was in cloud. With the widespread use and accuracy of GPS systems, non-precision instrument approaches are now possible at smaller airports.

Navigating is not just about knowing where you are. When flying at night, in bad weather or in instrument conditions, it is helpful to have an idea of what sort of weather is ahead of you. It is not much fun flying into the midst of a storm cloud at night, being tossed around and subject to lightning strikes. In the late 1980s we trialled some new weather-alerting devices called Stormscopes. These worked by detecting electrical activity within clouds and presenting it on a display, which predicted the severity of storm cells and their direction. They were soon replaced with weather radar when we acquired our Cessna Conquests. This transmits a radar signal ahead of the aircraft and can identify locations of intense rain and hail activity within clouds. The information is displayed on a screen as bright red areas ahead. It is very helpful at night to be able to see ahead and navigate to avoid areas of intense storm activity. Our current PC-12 aircraft have their radar on a small pod on the starboard wing tip.

Every decade, more devices appear and are added to aircraft to improve navigation and safety. While a normal altimeter offers only confirmation of the aircraft's true altitude based on atmospheric pressure, a radar altimeter can see through cloud and provides information on the actual height of the aircraft from the ground below. At night, in bad weather, when you cannot see the ground, it helps confirm you are not too low. When linked to a GPWS (ground proximity warning system), a voice will alert the pilot if they are too low on their approach or too close to the ground. 'Pull up. Pull up.' This system has prevented many accidents at night or in bad weather in general aviation. Enhanced GPWS links the system to a digital terrain database, enabling the system to predict an approaching change in terrain, such as a mountain coming up.

When I used to fly, a transponder was used in controlled airspace. It was set with a squawk code that identified the aircraft to air traffic controllers on their radar screens and provided them with altitude information. With time, these systems developed to provide additional information to other aircraft in the vicinity. A TCAS (traffic collision avoidance system) transmits details of the aircraft to other appropriately equipped aircraft and independent of air traffic control. Another system, ADS-B (automatic dependent surveillance – broadcast), sends a signal from the aircraft to advise of its position according to its GPS satellite navigation. This offers alternative and more accurate position information than air traffic radar. Aircraft can now see on their navigation screens information on the location and movement of other aircraft in their vicinity. This further minimises the likelihood of a mid-air collision in high-traffic areas.

A number of instances have occurred when RFDS aircraft have detected the presence of another aircraft nearby, which they were not aware of otherwise, because of this equipment. As each of these innovative technologies has arisen, the RFDS has strived to adopt them to improve our safety and performance. On some occasions, we have had to wait for the CASA (Civil Aviation Safety Authority) to catch up and approve the devices.

As we move to the future, many more systems are becoming available to make flying safer and will likely be adopted by the RFDS. These include 'synthetic vision', where a computer-generated map of the terrain is displayed for the pilot based on data in a mapping database. The pilot can see the mountains and valleys ahead on the instrument, even if he or she sees nothing out the window. Another aid under consideration is the 'enhanced vision' system, where a forward-looking, night-vision, infrared camera is installed in the nose of the aircraft. Night-vision goggles have been used for decades by the military but they are bulky to wear. These newer infrared camera systems integrate infrared vision into a combined display for the pilot. The pilot can be looking at the instrument display and see the features outside the aircraft, depicted as brightly as if it were daytime.

Built like a Swiss watch
Introducing the Pilatus PC-12

In 1995 the Swiss aircraft company Pilatus launched its PC-12 single-engine turboprop. The company was well known for its robust Pilatus PC-6 Porter, used by the Australian Army during the 1970s and 1980s, with outstanding STOL (short take-off and landing) capability. It seems odd that a relatively small country surrounded by soaring Alps would have a successful aviation industry. Larger countries such as Australia, where aviation is a key means of transport, have struggled to attain this. Nevertheless, Switzerland's reputation for engineering and quality manufacturing, perhaps epitomised by its watches, also translated well to aircraft engineering endeavours.

In the mid-1990s most aeromedical services worldwide used twin-engine aircraft, with the Beechcraft B200 King Air one of the most popular turboprops for the role. Our RFDS colleagues in South Australia decided to take the bold step of moving to this new single-engine aircraft and became a lead customer for Pilatus worldwide around 1995.

We watched with interest, as doomsayers in the aviation industry waited for a catastrophe – an engine failure on a medical aircraft – which fortunately never eventuated. At the turn of the century we, too, decided to adopt the PC-12 in Western Australia and acquired our first four aircraft in 2002.

The purchase of the aircraft followed considerable debate about the relative merits of multiple versus single-engine aeroplanes. A couple of diehard pilots wore black armbands for a while, but they still agreed to fly the nice new shiny aircraft when they arrived! With a single engine, if there is a failure in flight, the consequences could be dire. Just because the engine fails, doesn't mean the aircraft cannot fly, however. It just becomes a glider instead. With suitable training and wise flight planning, a pilot can glide an aircraft many kilometres to land on a suitable airstrip. The greater the cruising altitude at the time, the further the aircraft will travel.

Turbine engines are lighter, more powerful, more economical at altitude and have a much lower failure rate than piston engines. The risk of an engine failure in a single turbine-powered aircraft is much less than in a single piston-engine aircraft.

If an engine fails in a twin-engine aircraft, the pilot must deal with the problem of asymmetric thrust. With full power on one engine and wing, and none from the other, the aircraft will yaw and attempt to roll unless rapid action is taken to correct the asymmetric forces. If not handled properly, this can result in loss of control, particularly at critical stages such as take-off. So having two engines does not guarantee safety. In a single, there is no asymmetric thrust and the pilot instead must focus on how far the aircraft can glide and where to put the aircraft down.

Aircraft don't fly twice as fast with two engines. Indeed, the increase in speed for similar-sized aircraft might only be in the order of 10 to 20 per cent. With a new aerodynamic design, the use of composites and other lightweight but strong materials, the PC-12 is only marginally slower than its twin-engine competitor. Other than for the perceived safety benefit, a twin-engine aircraft can be seen to offer little extra advantage.

There are other economic benefits of a single-engine aircraft. They are cheaper to buy because you are buying one less engine. In our case, this is a saving of around $1 million on the aircraft purchase price. Furthermore, instead of having to do expensive maintenance on two engines, your maintenance costs with a single engine are effectively halved.

Then there is the fuel consumption. With only one engine, fuel consumption is considerably less. As less fuel needs to be carried for a particular flight, the payload of the aircraft (the extra weight that can be carried in place of that fuel) is substantially increased.

All these factors converged to offer an aircraft which was less expensive to purchase, cheaper to operate and had a greater range and payload than an equivalent twin. Being a more recently certified design, the PC-12 also met far more stringent crashworthiness standards.

Medical configuration

Our medical perspective was that the PC-12 would also be better suited to our work. It had a large integrated cargo door, which would make loading patients on stretchers a breeze. There was a separate air-stair door at the front. This dropped down and enabled the pilot and others to enter the aircraft while patient loading was occurring. It also had a completely flat floor, with parallel seat tracks, which was ideal for configuring our medical layout of stretchers and seats. Many aircraft have a wing spar across the floor that limits where roll-in stretchers can be placed. Some have a sunken aisle, or tapered floor shapes, which restrict your layout options further. None of these was a problem in the PC-12.

We were fortunate that the initial aeromedical design of the PC-12 was quite flexible and generic. In 2002, I visited the Pilatus factory in Stans, Switzerland, to observe their production facilities and discuss the layout of our medical interior. It was an impressive operation with the final assembly line in a large building with a parquetry wood floor. Immaculately neat, everything was in its place. You got the impression that the aircraft's final assembly was completed just like a Swiss watch!

I resisted the urge to do things differently and adopted pretty much the same generic medical layout as our colleagues in South Australia. This ultimately meant we had the potential to inter-change aircraft with common design elements if the need arose.

One thing I have learned over many years is the importance of standardisation. Standardised aircraft fit-outs and standardised equipment across a fleet ensures that training requirements are streamlined. In emergency medical scenarios, it is important to have emergency equipment located in the same familiar place in every aircraft. At one stage in the late 1990s, just after the three WA sections of the RFDS merged, we were operating six different aircraft types. No pilot was endorsed on all of them, the maintenance and spares were different, the medical fit-out was different and we could not easily swap around aircraft or pilots between bases without the risk of them not being up to date on a particular type.

In the late 2000s, we achieved a single aircraft type and medical fit-out across the state, based on the PC-12. No other RFDS section today has this advantage.

Our medical interior is simple and elegant. There is a range of systems similar to those in a hospital ward; that is, medical oxygen and suction outlets, 240-volt mains power, DC power and good lighting. We also have a communications panel which enables intercom with the pilot and VHF radio or satellite phone for external communications.

There are two stretchers, each of which are certified to 22G forward and upwards. ('G' is equivalent to the force of gravity, so 22G is twenty-two times that.) A relative disadvantage of the higher crashworthiness of the PC-12 is the need to restrain pas-sengers and equipment to a much higher standard than in other aircraft types, such as the B200 King Air, which was designed and certified to lower standards fifty years ago. The current requirements effectively mean that a stretcher or seat with a 100 kg occupant is expected to withstand a 2,200 kg load (100 kg times 22G). Some serious engineering is needed to keep the stretchers light yet strong enough to meet this.

The basic stretchers we adopted were quite reasonable but needed some tweaking. I arranged for design modifications to provide a gas strut assisted backrest, so that nurses and doctors could elevate the backrest in flight, with a patient lying on it, without straining themselves. To accommodate certification requirements we had to make extra modifications so that the backrest was rigid during take-off and landing, and would not collapse if the aircraft had an accident.

We also improved the stretcher mattress with three-layer foam. Our poor patients might be lying on the stretchers for many hours. They needed as much comfort as we could provide and we wanted to reduce the risk of pressure area problems.

Other modifications were made such as designing an equipment 'arch' or 'bridge' on which medical equipment could be mounted. All patients have a vital signs or critical care monitor attached during medical retrieval. This records basic vital signs such as blood pressure, pulse, respiration and oxygen saturation, and often more advanced measures such as electrocardiogram and capnometry (expired carbon dioxide levels). The equipment to which they were connected needed to be secured somewhere.

My philosophy has been to keep complex medical equipment mounted to the stretchers so that it moves with the patient, in and out of the aircraft, when loading. This requires a flexible restraint system, which can be seen in some of the photos of the PC-12 in action. Again, all our equipment has been standardised so it is interchangeable between any stretchers on any aircraft if necessary.

These objectives all required additional engineering and design work, plus certification in the form of engineering orders to meet CASA and FAR (Federal Aviation Regulation) requirements.

The aircraft has two storage areas and these were laid out to contain important emergency resuscitation equipment in a standard format. When the gear needs to be taken from the aircraft, these airway and circulation rolls are packed in an advanced life support bag with other essential resuscitation items.

The other main component to our PC-12 interior is the stretcher-loading device. This simple, clever compact device was designed in the late 1980s by an Adelaide company, AFTS (Australian Flight Test Services). It comprises a fold-down pedestal attached to the aircraft floor at the cargo door. This encloses an electric screw jack, which lifts the stretcher on a platform into the aircraft. The system is discussed further in the chapter 'Lightening the load'. A full suite of aeromedical retrieval equipment needs to be available for each aircraft. It includes many of the items discussed elsewhere, including cardiac monitor-defibrillator-pacers, critical care monitors with multiple physiological parameters, portable ventilators, i-STAT® point of care analysers, Doppler fetal stethoscopes, syringe drivers and infusion pumps. A range of airway management devices and various splints and prehospital care equipment is also carried. Some items are stowed on the aircraft routinely and others only taken for specific missions. The provision of this equipment and medical fit-out of the new PC-12s was supported by our dedicated Flying 1000 fundraising group.

We took delivery of our first PC-12 VH-KWO in May 2001. The aircraft was ferried out to Australia from Switzerland by Chief Pilot Michael Bleus and Captain Pete Smith. Three more followed in rapid succession before the end of that year: VH-MWO, VH-NWO and VH-VWO, the 300th PC-12 manufactured. Since then we have taken delivery of nearly twenty PC-12 airframes, with a variety of pilots enjoying the special opportunity to under-take this long intercontinental flight to Australia.

First PC-12 medical flight VH-KWO

On 3 October 2001, we made our first PC-12 aeromedical flight in the newly outfitted VH-KWO. The aircraft was flown by Captain John Wheeler under the supervision of Captain Michael Bleus, with Flight Nurse Lynda Ward and me on board. We collected two patients, one from Bunbury and one from Bruce Rock. The aircraft handled well. All our new medical and communications systems, which we had double-checked, functioned without any problems, as expected. It was a nice flight but had a different feel, with a large prop up the front compared to being in a twin.

A new livery

Pilatus has subsequently introduced new variants of the aircraft, the latest being the PC-12/47E or NG (Next Generation), with upgraded avionics and better payload compared with the earliest models. In 2013/14, thanks to sponsorship support from BHP Billiton, RFDS Western Operations purchased four new PC-12 NG aircraft and introduced a new corporate livery to Western Australia. Our CEO Grahame Marshall was keen to ensure our aircraft were readily recognisable in the air and on the ground. The striking livery, which is also used in Central Operations, has an all-red underbelly with RFDS emblazoned in large letters underneath.

Standardisation in the sky
Fleet consolidation

When Western Operations was formed we had seventeen aircraft to manage, comprising six different types across the state: a Beechcraft C90 and B200 King Airs in Derby; Piper Navajos, a Piper Mojave and Cessna Conquest C441s in the WA Section; and Cessna C425s in the Goldfields. Some of the airframes were effectively service 'spares' to ensure there were always operational aircraft in the regions while aircraft were cycled through maintenance. They were not interchangeable across bases, however, as pilots could not be trained and maintain 'currency' on more than about three types.

The new CEO at the time, Bruce Rathbone, realised that a consolidation was necessary to simplify the fleet, improve interoperability and reduce the future capital replacement costs. He set about downsizing the fleet by transferring all clinics to charter aircraft and moving to standardise on a couple of types for our emergency work. The fleet was reduced to only eleven aircraft with effectively two at each of the five bases (once Carnarvon was closed), with the spare eleventh aircraft at Jandakot undergoing service.

The changes were not popular. Our doctors missed the rapport they had established with RFDS pilots when they flew with them on clinics and felt that they were now developing better working relationships with the clinic charter pilots. They were uncomfortable with the perceived safety and reliability of the chartered services and as the aircraft did not have an RFDS livery, the community did not always recognise they were still receiving an RFDS clinic service. When an emergency case happened on a clinic flight, the doctor had to call for the emergency retrieval aircraft to attend as the clinic planes did not have stretchers or medical retrieval equipment, though such situations happened infrequently.

On the positive side, there were no longer situations where the clinic had to be cancelled midway so that an evacuation flight could occur. Instead, our medical practitioners could commence a clinic knowing they could spend the right amount of time with every patient and get through as much work as possible in the time they were there, without interruption. Patients would not have to travel long distances to the clinic only to be turned away.

The reduced fleet size of eleven was a very tight arrangement and often more than one aircraft was in maintenance. Our ability to mount an emergency response with limited resources was often only possible through statewide coordination and our ability to task any aircraft from any base to respond to an emergency almost anywhere in the state. When you call for an emergency service such as police, fire or ambulance, you don't necessarily get a response from your local depot but from the nearest available team. We were doing the same – only on a scale where each base was separated by 600 to 800 kilometres!

When we acquired three special edition Beechcraft B200SE King Air aircraft in 1999, there were plans to design and manufacture a new stretcher loading system. Almost a year went by and the design was too heavy, too bulky and just did not work efficiently. As a last resort, we adopted the LifePort® stretcher system, which was prominent in the United States at the time. While it provided a quick configuration, we endured many difficulties with it and the overall aircraft medical layout in the B200SE King Airs, until they were sold.

After that debacle and with the advent of the Pilatus PC-12 in 2002, it was agreed that there needed to be more medical and nursing input into the cabin design, which was after all our working space. We also needed to adopt a stretcher that would meet the 22G crashworthiness load factors of the new aircraft. We decided on only some minor modifications of the Bucher aeromedical fit-out that was installed in the factory in Switzerland and started to standardise the AFTS stretcher across the fleet of both PC-12s and older B200s.

I have learnt over many years that great care and attention to detail is needed when designing and outfitting a medical aircraft interior. This is a critical care workspace and careful consideration needs to be given to where patients and crew are situated, the location and specification of services such as oxygen, suction, power and lighting, as well as the ease of loading and unloading and the stowage requirements. Once outfitted, clinical teams will spend many hours sitting in the airframe and the poor location of a particular item or under-specification of a service will cause frustration for years. When dealing with enthusiastic engineers, never accept their reassurances that a task should not be a problem because it often is. Never assume anything. A given design or manufacturing task will take all the available time...and some more!

When the last of the Beechcraft B200SEs were disposed of in the late 2000s, we reached the Holy Grail of aeromedical operations with a fleet of solely Pilatus PC-12 aircraft with a standard medical fit-out. Any aircraft could be flown by any pilot and they could be readily interchanged between any of our bases. Any doctor or nurse could embark on an aircraft knowing that the medical equipment was standardised and each item was located in exactly the same place. This might seem common sense but because of the high capital cost of purchasing and outfitting aircraft and slow turnover as they become due for replacement, it took patience and about a decade to achieve.

Jet-setters. It's about time
The first RFDS jet aircraft

As we moved into the new century, it was blatantly clear that we needed to consider a faster long-range aircraft. Demand for medical retrieval was increasing, particularly from the northern parts of Western Australia, as the resources industry flourished and expectations of best practice clinical care meant that more patients needed to be evacuated to Perth. It was no longer acceptable to deny patients the latest treatments available in disciplines such as cardiology, trauma, surgery or general medicine, which were only available in Perth.

Despite being a terrific all-round aircraft, our turboprops were at the limits of their capacity if required to fly patients from the Kimberley to Perth and then return. The round trip took in excess of eight hours, which was the maximum flying time for our pilots in a single tour of duty. This meant that transfers had to be staged with at least two separate aircraft teams meeting up somewhere in the middle of the state. Alternatively, the flight came straight through to Perth and the staff and aircraft were stuck overnight or all day, until the pilot had completed a mandatory rest break.

We made approaches to the Department of Health seeking their interest in establishing a medical jet aircraft but our proposals were unsuccessful. I think it was seen as 'toys for the boys' and the logistical benefits were not appreciated. In addition, our attempts to interest them were based on a significant up-front payment. A proposal to buy a $10 to 12 million aircraft outright was not an easy sell. We also felt that, ideally, such an aircraft should be based in the northwest where the patients were if it was to respond quickly to local emergencies. The additional costs of accommodating extra pilots and hangaring such an aircraft in the northwest were exorbitant at the time.

I had an epiphany, lying by a pool over the January holidays in 2008. Why can't we do what many companies do: just lease the equipment we need and outsource the operation? Why stick to an owner–operator model when we could potentially start a service with much lower initial costs? If we could just get something up and running, I was sure it would prove itself. Indeed, I took comfort from a saying attributed to the Reverend John Flynn, 'If you start something good, no one can stop it'.

I wrote a paper in April 2008 entitled 'It's about time! The case for a fast, long-range aircraft to service the medical retrieval needs of north-west Western Australia', in which I touted the volume of work and benefits of one or more jet aircraft to manage long-distance transfers within WA. I doubt we will ever see a metropolitan level of hospital care in most of the critical care specialties outside of Perth, at least not in the North West, so transfers will continue to be required. Optimism that the demand for aeromedical transport would wane as regional hospitals were improved was naively optimistic, as history has shown.

Our Director of Public Affairs at the time was Lesleigh Green and she came to me excited that Rio Tinto might be willing to support a very substantial community investment project, possibly up to $5 million over a few years. The company provided extensive support to numerous community projects, such as sporting facilities and arts programs, which were of great benefit to many small towns and communities. Yet, I understood they had an appetite for something more significant.

'Well, have I got an idea for you!' I told her. In a genuine back-of-the-envelope plan, I figured that we had chartered jet aircraft recently for between $2,500 and $3,000 per hour. If we could go to industry and offer to buy 500 hours of jet time at that rate, say $1.5 million per year, plus have about $500,000 to cover a medical fit-out and start-up costs, we would fit nicely within $5 million over three years. I factored in no extra medical or nursing staff and no extra drugs or equipment. The idea was that this would simply give our existing teams access to a fast jet for critically ill patients long distances away.

Lesleigh sounded out her contacts and it appeared Rio Tinto might be interested, so we developed the idea further. I thought that a name such as *LifeFlight* would add weight to the proposal and also help differentiate it from our standard RFDS aircraft. It was also possible that down the track we would purchase additional jets or helicopters, commercially funded, if the program took off. We were fortunate that our CEO at the time, Tim Shackleton, and our Board were aligned with the vision and willing to support a pitch for sponsorship.

We had the benefit of a couple of recent coronial inquiries by the State Coroner, Alastair Hope. There had been an unfortunate case where a man in Kununurra had died from a haemorrhage in the brain, which might have been successfully treated had we been able to fly him to Perth quickly and directly. There were other factors involved, too, but at the time the coroner had supported my suggestions about increasing access for Kimberley patients to Darwin and the potential for a long-range jet.

Many times our emergency aeromedical teams had flown someone critically ill to Perth in what was often a 10 to 12 hour saga, then were forced to remain overnight until the pilot had sufficient rest to be permitted to fly back to the north. During this time, the North West regions were devoid of an aircraft and medical teams for at least half a day and there were many cases of delayed transfer occurring.

In addition, we were being asked more frequently to evacuate patients from Christmas Island or the Cocos Islands in the Indian Ocean, as the number of personnel swelled to deal with the refugees arriving by boat. Most patients were Australian workers on the islands but there were some refugees who also needed a medical retrieval to the Australian mainland and there had been a couple of high-profile incidents. In each case we had chartered a corporate jet, paid for by the government agency responsible, modified it to take a makeshift stretcher and medical equipment, and sent it off to do the evacuation. Having our own jet aircraft would enable us to respond more quickly and do a better job with a properly outfitted airframe.

There were also ongoing issues with the transfer of newborn babies with cardiac conditions to Melbourne or Brisbane for complex cardiac surgery, not possible in Perth. Dr Steven Resnick from the neonatal intensive care unit at Princess Margaret Hospital for Children in Perth had discussed the difficulties they faced when trying to put a specialised transport cot and medical team on a commercial flight interstate. Airlines such as Qantas were supportive but there were commercial realities, too. The flights only went when scheduled; booking a block of a couple of rows was not guaranteed; the flight couldn't be delayed if there was a problem getting the baby stable; and loading and unloading all the equipment was difficult. There was great potential to have a dedicated jet available in Perth which could be booked for these flights and could leave when it suited the baby, the medical teams and the receiving hospital.

We put together a preliminary proposal and presented it to a board overseeing Rio Tinto's community investments. Some significant high-profile individuals, including Fred Chaney, Janet

Holmes à Court and of course Sam Walsh, were members. I had some provisos.

First, the aircraft was to be available to all Australians living, working or travelling in remote parts of Western Australia. The RFDS would deploy it as medically necessary and there would not be a preferential service for employees in the resources industry. Nevertheless, while the new jet service would be 'giving something back to the community', it would strengthen our capacity to deal with emergencies affecting workers in the resources industry and so provide added peace of mind to these companies and their staff. The service would be at no cost to the patient, except that we would recover costs wherever possible from insurance policies, companies or government agencies. That included the sponsors. The service would also contribute to improving indigenous inequality in health.

I remember explaining that if we had a worker on a mine site with a broken ankle and an Aboriginal child with serious burns from a campfire, the child would be allocated the aircraft and the worker would be evacuated in a timely manner using whatever other RFDS resources were available to us. I was humbled to hear that this was exactly what our sponsors would expect and were keen to support. No management interference or onerous reporting expectations; just get out there, start it running and enable it to do as much good work as it could.

This was fantastic news. It provided a quantum leap forward for the RFDS and the people we service. I was quoted as saying it was the most significant development in our history since we moved from piston engines to turboprops, and still believe that to be so. I wrote a letter which was published in the *Medical Journal of Australia* explaining the benefits of the new service, which was well received.

Of course we then had to make it happen. I set a target for an aircraft which could carry a minimum of two stretchers and three seats (including medical team) non-stop from anywhere in Western Australia to Perth in all common weather conditions. This was quite a challenge. We have the longest evacuation distances of any state in Australia. For example, the distance from Kununurra to Perth is just over 2,000 kilometres – further than the distance from Perth to Adelaide. The tropical weather patterns often affecting the North West can make flight planning difficult, with a need to hold alternate landing destinations such as Darwin. Yet, I figured there was no point in having a fast jet in Perth responding to a critical emergency in the north, and having to stop to refuel either on the way there or on the way back.

We needed something bigger than the smallest corporate jets and we needed a substantial range. We narrowed this down to either a Hawker 800XP or a Lear 45. An independent aviation advisor and the key companies competing in our tender process came to the same conclusion. Eventually we opted for the Hawker as a similar type was operated for the Premier's Department in the Government of Western Australia and there was expertise in flying and maintaining the aircraft type in the West. It also seemed a good idea to have a similar aircraft to that used by politicians to travel around the state. If our funding came to a standstill after the first three years, we could go to the public and highlight that an emergency service for critically ill patients was going to fold, while the politicians continued to travel around the state in the same aircraft type. It fortunately never got to that and we received support from the Royalties for Regions program for each year of the service.

This was now 2008/09 and we were in the midst of the global financial crisis, as it was called. The Australian dollar tanked so the cost of an aircraft based in US dollars increased significantly. Interest rates rose and commercial finance for an expensive jet for just a three-year contract was exorbitant. The tender process came back with much larger figures than we anticipated. However, we were lucky.

President Obama made it clear to major corporations that if they wanted the government to provide financial support then it was time for the boys to lose their toys. Numerous corporate jets came on the market at almost fire-sale prices and we were able to locate a Hawker 800XP in the United States in excellent condition, with very few hours on it. Our chosen operator, Maroomba Airlines at Perth Airport, was very helpful and flexible. Despite our original intention that they would purchase and operate the aircraft, it became more economical for the RFDS to take out a loan and buy the jet than for Maroomba to go through expensive finance arrangements.

After purchasing the aircraft, we had the fortune to pick a very resourceful company, Hill Aero in Nebraska, to install a medical interior locally. They were relatively small but used to doing many corporate refurbishments and medical fit-outs. Our Aviation Manager and I worked with their design team to come up with an interior, which was relatively simple, flexible and would suit our proposed operation. There was also a need to respray the jet with a new livery.

Initially we planned to have two stretchers on the starboard side of the aircraft but between our first proposals and when we started the aircraft refurbishment, the Ashmore Reef disaster occurred. This was an explosion on a refugee boat off the Kimberley coast which resulted in over forty refugees receiving serious burns. We participated in the evacuations together with Australian Defence Force C-17 Globemasters and C-130 Hercules, but I felt embarrassed at the time that our capacity was so limited. I was certain that we should try to add another stretcher to the aircraft, even if this was only for special situations.

It turned out to be a masterstroke. Hill Aero was able to design a divan that could seat three people – either medical teams or patients – and could be converted to a stretcher if the need arose. This made the aircraft the only civilian aeromedical jet at the time that could carry three stretcher patients all at once, or two critically ill patients each attended by a separate medical team.

I was fortunate to travel to Nebraska for a week to oversee aspects of the fit-out and work on positioning of stretchers, medical gas and power outlets and this third stretcher concept. We managed to find some workarounds to circumvent certain Federal Aviation Authority certification limitations and achieved a very functional aircraft for our purposes. It was great to have a week being creative and seeing the aircraft and its livery take shape. We had really achieved something exceptional.

Our first jet flight

We launched the Rio Tinto LifeFlight jet service in October 2009 and took the jet to a number of key locations in the North West to demonstrate it to the public, to hospital staff and our own RFDS base staff. It was also helpful for ambulance crews to see how patients would be loaded and the differences from a Pilatus PC-12 with which they were familiar. Our first leg was Perth Airport to Kununurra, a flight we achieved in just under three hours with myself, the CEO Tim Shackleton and three Board members. I had put some limited medical equipment on the aircraft for display purposes but I did not fully stock it with drugs and other consumables as we were not intending to use it operationally. This was supposed to be purely a publicity and shake-down flight.

No sooner had we landed around 4 pm than I received a phone call from Dr Brian Collings in our Coordination Centre about a patient at a mine site 150 kilometres from Kununurra. A contractor had been using a very high-pressure water gun to clean scale from the inside of a tank but had accidently cut through his leather safety boot and across the top of his foot. It was not clear whether he had damaged any of his tendons but high-pressure jet injuries can be serious and inject contaminants into the wound as well as damaging tissues. The problem was that our only aircraft at Derby Base was busy and it was unlikely our aircraft could get to the patient until nearly midnight. Was there any chance we might pick the patient up?

There was to be a fundraising reception that night for the local population to come out and see the aircraft. It would start at 8 pm and couldn't be cancelled at short notice. We had four hours to flight plan, fly to the mine site, collect the patient, fly him across the border to Darwin about 400 kilometres away, then make it back to Kununurra. We had to give it a shot. This was when I realised the enormous capabilities of the aircraft we had chosen. Despite having flown 2,000 kilometres from Perth, we did not need to refuel and with two pilots and the computerised navigation system it took only 15 minutes to flight plan and depart.

I would be the doctor on the flight, with no nurse to help and limited equipment but I thought I could manage. We had the referring mine site administer narcotic analgesia and antibiotics and dress the wound to stop the bleeding. Our doctor in the Coordination Centre ensured the patient was prepared and things were organised for our arrival.

It seemed like only a ten minute hop to the mine site. We loaded the patient and then had another thirty to forty minute flight to Darwin. We had not made any formal arrangements for where to land the jet in Darwin but bumbled through. Although rusty at this, I dutifully completed an inflight observation chart, doing my best to ensure it was properly completed and up to the standard we expect of our nurses and doctors. I figured it wouldn't look good if I was admonished about poor documentation. After offloading the patient and organising a handover to the ambulance service, we turned around and flew back to Kununurra. Again we did not need to refuel. I recall it was quite a choppy flight coming back. There was lightning, rain and a number of tropical cells in the vicinity of the airport, but in the jet I felt supremely safe.

It had just passed 8 pm; all the guests were assembled in the hangar but there was no aircraft to see. Our pilot, Captain Steve Young, zoomed in and did an impressive 'go around' which enthralled the crowd. We then made a second approach and landed, joining the festivities almost to a hero's welcome.

We had completed our very first patient transfer and launched the jet in style!

The aircraft met all our expectations and became a vital aeromedical asset for the state. Within our first year of operation, we successfully undertook all the scenarios I had anticipated for it. These included multiple patients on a single flight, two ventilated patients at once, interstate neonatal transfers, support to the ADF (Australian Defence Force) and Australia's Indian Ocean Territories, and many urgent long-distance transfers, which we would not have accomplished effectively without it.

Taking two ventilated patients with two medical teams on one flight is not something we can achieve in our normal aircraft. If you are giving multiple patients an anaesthetic (which is effectively what you are doing with ventilated patients), you need to have a doctor dedicated to each individual. You certainly wouldn't have an anaesthetist in a hospital treating two patients at once, and the air transport environment is far more hazardous. We had two such patients whom we moved from Broome to Perth in the first few months of the jet's operation. The time to load both patients and stabilise them for flight was longer than expected. However, once set up in the aircraft, a doctor and nurse combination was able to sit opposite each stretcher and manage the anaesthetised patients safely and comfortably for the 2.5-hour journey. This mission would otherwise have required two separate turboprop aircraft, each undertaking a 4.5-hour flight and not able to immediately return to base due to the pilot flying hours involved.

Another scenario to consider was to utilise the three seat positions on the divan, as well as the two stretchers, to carry multiple patients.

Full with a family of five

A family of five was travelling in the eastern Kimberley when they rolled their four-wheel drive at speed on a main road. The father and mother were in their late thirties and had three children, aged nine, seven and five. Dad, who was driving, had multiple rib fractures and a collapsed lung. His wife had a possible cervical spine injury and needed to be transferred with spinal precautions on a stretcher. The children had isolated limb fractures involving the arms and a leg.

What would we have previously done? We would probably have evacuated the two adults on a single aircraft to Perth, leaving their children behind, with no parents or guardian, in Kununurra Hospital. The flight to Perth would have taken around six hours and required one or more stops for refuelling, or meeting up with a second team for the second leg. If the crew had run out of hours, they would not have been able to return to the Kimberley until the next day. Then an evacuation of the children might not have happened until day three.

With our new Rio Tinto LifeFlight jet, we were able to rescue the entire family and evacuate them to Perth on a single flight. Mum and Dad went on the stretchers and the three children, with fractures splinted, were able to squeeze onto the divan in the three seat positions. A doctor and nurse team cared for the lot during the fast three hour flight to Perth.

We were also successful in implementing our commitment to interstate transfers of neonates. PMH (Princess Margaret Hospital for Children) purchased a new dedicated neonatal transport system, which was compatible with the *LifeFlight* jet loading system. We trained to ensure loading and unloading would be smooth and seamless, and special stretcher interfaces were established in Brisbane and Melbourne to receive the neonate cot.

The first few interstate neonatal aeromedical transfers went well. The aircraft was able to fly the baby in the special neonatal transport system to Melbourne with a team of three, including an RFDS nurse, a PMH neonatal ICU doctor and a PMH nurse. The trip was just under four hours and, after taking the baby in and handing over at the Royal Children's Hospital in Melbourne, there was still time to return to the airport and fly home to Perth. We developed a process of being warned of any impending transfer, so we could make sure the aircraft was not going to have a mini-service or be deployed for anything else. It was such a setting, being forewarned of a flight to Melbourne, that led to the infamous 'dash under the ash' (see chapter in the Medical section, 'Long distance, small packages') when, in 2011, aviation in southern Australia was seriously interrupted by ash spewing from a volcano in Iceland.

Another satisfying case was assisting the RAAF with a person who had been injured during a training exercise.

RAAF rescue

A training exercise was underway, relating to the defence of airport facilities at Learmonth on the northwest shoulder of WA. There were not many aircraft involved as this was predominantly a ground exercise. Certainly, there was no medevac capability in place. An RAAF member was regrettably struck on the head with an iron bar and the squadron doctor rang us to see if we could assist with a rapid medevac to Perth. Otherwise, an RAAF response would have to be mobilised from the eastern states and would take more than a day.

It was a bit of a fluke but we just happened to have the aircraft en route to Perth, with a medical team on board and a spare stretcher. The aircraft was only 20 minutes away and we were able to divert it. Only a short time later, our stunning LifeFlight jet screeched onto the tarmac and taxied up to the waiting Air Force team. They were impressed! It was not just the speed of the response but the bright shiny medical jet, in a colour other than grey, with a fancy medical interior. We received letters of gratitude and a plaque for our assistance and nearly recruited another doctor out of it.

Pilatus PC-24

The Rio Tinto *LifeFlight* jet has continued to demonstrate the benefits of a jet-engine aircraft for long-distance aeromedical transfers across Western Australia. The increased patient transport capacity and faster travel time makes it a more efficient means of moving patients on single flights, in a single duty period, without crews running out of hours. It has freed up our turboprops to be more responsive to emergencies in their local regions and enabled us to deal with a significant increase in workload over the five years it has been operating.

In 2014, our CEO Grahame Marshall and Chairman Neville Bassett signed an agreement for RFDS Western Operations to be a lead customer for the new Pilatus PC-24 jet – another first for Western Australia. This aircraft will have similarities to the PC-12, being capable of single-pilot operation with exceptional performance into shorter and rougher airfields. It will have the same large cargo door, unusual for a jet of this size, and another couple of metres of internal cabin length compared with the PC-12. It is expected to be in service by 2017/18 and, as a lead customer, we will have the advantage of input into the specification of an aeromedical version and a high level of customer support when it is introduced.

Helicopters

Reflections on rotary-wing aircraft

I am often asked why the RFDS doesn't use helicopters. The answer is that we do use them but we don't own or operate them. Helicopters have many benefits for incidents occurring in difficult to access terrain. However, in remote areas, the capabilities of helicopters, particularly speed, range and payload, are generally too restrictive for the sort of distances we need to travel. Our patients are usually hundreds of kilometres away. If they were closer, they would be transported by road. Our patients may need to be taken to regional or metropolitan centres, which might be 1,000 or 2,000 kilometres away. What would be a four-hour flight in one of our turboprops would take eight hours of flying, plus a couple of fuel stops, in a helicopter. Then there is the noise, the cramped cabin, the lack of pressurisation, the rough flight, the poor cabin heating and cooling to contend with, plus the higher purchase price. If there were a fast long-range helicopter, able to hover or land in a confined location, it would be terrific. Presently the only such aircraft with some of these features are tiltrotor aircraft, such as the Bell V-22 'Osprey' or Augusta AW609, which are way outside our budget.

Helicopters are often referred to as rotary-wing aircraft because the rotor blades are not actually working as a propeller but as a set of rotating wings, each providing lift as they pass through the air. Unfortunately, as the aircraft moves forward through the air at increasing speed, the retreating blade is passing through the air at a diminishing relative speed. Eventually it loses lift. This limits the forward airspeed at which a rotary-wing aircraft can travel to around 150 knots (278 km/h). In contrast, there are no such limitations on the speed of fixed-wing aircraft – well, at least until you approach Mach 1, the speed of sound.

A rotary-wing capability, with sufficient range, would be terrific in the Kimberley. It has the most inhospitable and remote terrain in WA and the least useable airstrips. There are plenty of times when we struggle to find a mustering helicopter with which to extract a patient from a confined area to the nearest airstrip. The population numbers, however, just don't support the sort of investment required to buy, outfit and staff a rotary-wing aircraft; at least not for a not-for-profit organisation trying to achieve the best bang for our bucks. So we cope, using an ever-changing range of aircraft available to us, which fluctuates depending on the economy and opportunities for work in each region.

Rocky landing for an R22

The Robinson R22 helicopter is synonymous with helicopter mustering in Australia. This small lightweight two-seater can be found across the country being used to herd cattle to areas where they can be yarded by teams on the ground. It was late at night in Port Hedland when I received a call through the HF radio system that a mustering helicopter had not returned to base camp and had crashed in a gorge on a station a few hundred kilometres southeast of Karratha. The quality of the call was poor as they were using an HF radio powered by a car battery and with an aerial wire draped over a few trees. They had reached the pilot in the crashed aircraft by foot and he was complaining of severe pain in his back. As helicopters auto-hover and usually crash land vertically, I suspected he had a spinal injury.

There was no airstrip anywhere near the accident site, which was in a rocky gorge not easily accessible by road. However, there was a clearing adjacent to a waterhole nearby in which a helicopter could probably land. I tried to give them some advice on keeping the pilot warm and providing pain relief, but it was going to be a long night as we set about organising how to evacuate him.

With a bit of luck we located a Bell 206 Jet Ranger helicopter in Karratha. It had a bench seat across the back on which we could secure a stretcher. As I expected the patient to have spinal injuries, it wasn't going to be safe to try and evacuate him sitting up. However, it was night and we clearly weren't going to try to fly out there, or land, until daylight.

I organised for our night pilot to drop me down to Karratha with a portable stretcher and some medical equipment then return to Port Hedland. There was only just room for the helicopter pilot, the stretcher and me, so we couldn't take a flight nurse. I also didn't know how long we would be on the ground with the patient. I arrived at Karratha at 4 am in the dark, set up the stretcher and equipment on the Jet Ranger, then we departed at sunrise, around 5.30 am.

It was a beautiful flight out to the station at early dawn although the bright sunrise in the east and long shadows made it a little hard to navigate. Both rear doors of the Jet Ranger had been removed, so we were tracking along at a couple of thousand feet with the air blowing through the cabin and the comforting 'bop bop bop bop' of the rotor blades above. Eventually we identified the smoke coming from a small campfire in the gorge and the pilot carefully manoeuvred in to land within 50 metres of the accident site in a dried-up river bed.

The pilot was still in what was left of the Robinson fuselage. He was lying on the broken seat, which provided padding and acted as a mattress overnight. His mates had covered him with blankets and given him cups of tea but he was still shaken and shivering, as the early morning light had not yet entered the gorge and started to heat it up again. After examining him, I was pretty certain he had some crush fractures to his lumbar vertebrae but, fortunately, apart from other bruises and abrasions, nothing life-threatening. I gave him an injection to relieve the pain. Then we carefully transferred him to the basic stretcher we had brought with us and all carried him to the Jet Ranger, where the stretcher was loaded onto the cabin bench seat.

I was able to use the HF radio they had set up to call the RFDS and provide a scratchy message that we were leaving to head back to Karratha. Once airborne we used the helicopter's VHF radio on our company frequency 129.6 to provide a clearer message to VKL. I asked if we could be met by a fixed-wing aircraft at Karratha. We would take the patient from there back to Port Hedland for x-rays and further evaluation.

Flying back over the Pilbara was again an exciting flight. The patient's legs reached well outside the door openings and I was seated on the floor, looking anxiously at the large openings on each side. We had a brief conversation over the background noise about the accident. It seemed that towards the end of the previous day, he had suddenly lost rotor speed. Working as he was at tree-top altitude, he had only a few seconds to respond and was very lucky to have put the aircraft down in a relatively flat spot among the boulders in the gorge where he crashed. Luckily, it did not burst into flames. I subsequently learned that one of the 'rubber bands' had broken. In the early models of the R22, the power was transmitted from the engine to the rotor through four drive belts, similar to car fan belts. A number of accidents have occurred with the R22 when one or more of these have failed.

We transferred the patient to our Piper Navajo at Karratha, took him to Port Hedland then subsequently flew him to Perth *where he made a good recovery with no neurological deficit. Not so the Robinson R22, which was a complete write-off.*

Helicopters in Perth

Up until 2001, we had an ad hoc arrangement with the Police Air Support Unit in Perth to utilise their Kawasaki BK117 with a minimal medical fit-out when required. The range and payload of the aircraft was limited but it had excellent cabin space. There were clamshell doors at the rear, between the twin booms, which enabled easy waist-height lifting of stretchers in and out of the aircraft. We used it only occasionally, as most of our work was further from Perth than could reasonably be undertaken by rotary-wing aircraft. In one case, we had a fixed-wing aircraft arriving at Jandakot with a time-critical head injury patient for Royal Perth Hospital. It was Australia Day, just before the Skyshow fireworks display was due to commence. This meant traffic was gridlocked on the freeway into the city of Perth and across the Narrows Bridge and Causeway. So we had the Police chopper outfitted and on standby to do the secondary transfer from Jandakot to Royal Perth, which went very well.

At this time, there was increasing interest in acquiring another helicopter for the Police or FESA (Fire and Emergency Services Authority). The need for Perth to have a medical helicopter was used as the leverage. I collated information from a number of other states on the operation of their rotary-wing services and the RFDS prepared a proposal for how we could operate such a service out of Perth. I highlighted the benefits of having all aeromedical services and expertise co-located and the need for clear clinical coordination of which asset to use for specific tasks. There was some controversy because although Perth did not have a dedicated medical helicopter at the time, the large metropolitan population was well served by the road ambulance service and an excellent freeway network. A helicopter would be expensive to purchase and operate. There were few patients who could not be transferred by other means and it would not necessarily provide significantly improved clinical outcomes. Nevertheless, the idea was 'sexy' and appealing to politicians.

In 2002 a tender was opened by the Department of Health and by the end of the year we had offered, in conjunction with St John Ambulance, a combined proposal for a rotary-wing retrieval service based at Jandakot Airport and staffed with RFDS retrieval doctors and St John paramedics. St John could call on the chopper to assist with primary incidents where additional support was needed by road crews, and RFDS would task the aircraft as necessary for longer interhospital transfers. The key to a quality service was having the retrieval doctors and paramedics staffing every mission together, building teamwork and expertise in the rotary-wing environment.

We had an excellent proposal, including hangars adjacent to the RFDS facilities, and it would have worked very well, but it was blocked in Cabinet. To set it up properly was going to cost money, which the Health Department did not have. So it was given to FESA and instead of becoming a medical retrieval service integrated into the health system, it became a 'rescue' helicopter without the comprehensive medical input. A Bell 412EP was acquired with a fit-out similar to that we had proposed; however, the integrated clinical model collapsed.

RFDS doctors have been staffing the helicopter for interhospital transfers for a number of years but we are yet to see standardised equipment, standard clinical protocols, effective coordination of missions and a specialised medical team on every emergency flight. We could have avoided all the teething problems that eastern states services suffered in the 1990s and 2000s and which we continue to experience ten years on. Despite this our retrieval doctors, specialists and registrars in Perth use the Bell 412 up to four times per week.

The Bell 412EP is a very capable aircraft with a reasonably long range and respectable payload. As a twin-engine aircraft, it has Category A performance, which means that when landing or departing a helipad, a single-engine failure should not be catastrophic and the aircraft should be able to recover safely with a single engine. This is important for landing on hospital helipads or in other congested areas. The cabin is U-shaped with the clinical team sitting at the bottom of the U. This offers the chance to carry a single patient transversely across the cabin, or two patients, with access mainly to the head end, down each side of the cabin. The aircraft has a robust winching capability though this is not used much in WA for medical missions. As with all helicopters, speed and range are a problem and for longer flights intermittent fuel stops may be needed.

We can land with patients at Sir Charles Gairdner Hospital or Royal Perth Hospital, but there has been no helipad at Princess Margaret for paediatric emergencies or at King Edward for obstetric emergencies since the service started in 2004. Fortunately, suitable helicopter landing areas have been included in the design of the two new hospitals in Perth, the Fiona Stanley and the Perth Children's Hospital.

RAN to the rescue in Kalgoorlie

A morbidly obese patient attended at Kalgoorlie Regional Hospital with a problem requiring abdominal surgery. She was too large to handle in the operating theatre or in the wards and the anaesthetic was high risk. We were asked to evacuate her to Perth. When it became known that her weight was in excess of 250 kilograms the pilot refused to carry her. We had a floor mat and harness system for such morbidly obese patients but he considered that her weight exceeded the floor load capacity and the limits of the restraint belts we had available for use. This left us all in a dilemma and Kalgoorlie Regional in a tizz. She was too big and unwell for a Qantas flight and a bariatric road ambulance from Perth would be a round trip of probably sixteen or more hours. We couldn't arrange a medical evacuation on the Prospector train either.

As we were tearing our hair out, one of my doctors noticed Navy Seahawk helicopters at Kalgoorlie Airport. Kalgoorlie is a long way from the sea but these aircraft were transiting, on their way back to Perth from the eastern states. He went over to ask them, could they help? The Seahawk is derived from the Black Hawk, an awesome military aircraft with the capacity to carry a number of soldiers in full battle dress or to lift underslung loads, such as artillery weapons. It had a large flat floor in the back and the capacity to carry the load we proposed.

Following some high-level negotiations, it was agreed they would assist with the transfer of the patient with our medical team on board. The patient was prepared for transport in Kalgoorlie Hospital by an RFDS medical team, which then moved her from the ward into the hospital lift. The next call I received was that our team and the patient were stuck in the lift halfway! A technician was called and it took about an hour to free them. The patient was then pushed down one of the main streets in the hospital bed to an area where the helicopter could land.

The rest of the mission went successfully. It was a unique opportunity and with a bit of ingenuity we achieved a successful transfer to Perth. It is not often that the Navy comes to the rescue in the Goldfields.

Other airborne options
Charter aircraft and helicopters

While ideally all our flying is done in our own aircraft, situations arise when we have to use charter aircraft or other vehicles of opportunity. In the Kimberley, we sometimes use a smaller aircraft for a couple of locations with very short airstrips. We use makeshift arrangements, securing a stretcher and all the required oxygen, suction and medical gear on the aircraft. It is not ideal but sometimes it is the only option available.

Over the past decade we have seen an increasing number of small cruise boats working their way along the Kimberley coast. Along that vast coastline there are no communities, nor airstrips, at which we can land. If a passenger suffers a heart attack or trips and breaks their leg, the only way we can rescue them is by using a seaplane or aircraft on floats to land in the sea nearby. Most recently, we have been using a Cessna Caravan with floats. We fit it out with a stretcher and equipment then land, in daytime only, on the sea and taxi up to the rear of the cruise boat. Using an inflatable dinghy as an intermediary platform, the patient can be transferred across to the aircraft.

Likewise, we sometimes use a charter helicopter. Depending on what aircraft is available, we can mount a stretcher in the cabin. On occasion we have had to rely on a two-seater mustering chopper to gain access to very remote settings and can only extricate the patient as a sitting passenger. It's a bit tough if, for example, you have a broken leg, but better than nothing.

On occasion our teams have flown on very large helicopters, such as the Super Puma which service offshore oil and gas platforms. These are a large, two-pilot operation and very expensive. Luckily, RFDS is not paying for the aircraft in these cases. In one of the most challenging rescues of recent times, a number of RFDS personnel travelled from Truscott in the northeast Kimberley to an offshore processing platform to rescue victims of the Ashmore Reef refugee boat explosion in April 2009.

Corporate jets

I first conducted aeromedical evacuations from Australia's Indian Ocean Territories in the late 1980s using chartered jet aircraft. It has always been a challenge to take a standard corporate aircraft and make it suitable for medical transport. There are many issues to consider. For example, we need sufficient compressed medical oxygen for every patient, with a safety margin to cover consumption in excess of the planned duration of flight. Patient requirements vary and our ventilators cannot operate without medical oxygen supplied at pressure. This usually means securing multiple oxygen cylinders in the cabin.

Electrical power is also a common problem. Even if standard 24/28-volt DC power is available on the aircraft, there are usually no power outlets compatible with the aeromedical standard we follow. Normal 240-volt AC mains power is rarely available. Without electrical power we need to be sure that every piece of equipment can run on batteries for the duration of the flight, plus a safety margin. We also need medical suction and adequate lighting.

Loading and securing stretchers is also a challenge. Few corporate aircraft have wide doors and it can be very difficult and back-breaking to get a stretcher up stairs and around the corner into the body of the cabin. Once inside, an appropriate restraint system is required to ensure the stretcher and any attached medical equipment are safe for flight.

Finally, the luxurious interior furnishings must be protected from blood and body fluids, and physical damage caused by loading stretchers and equipment.

You can see that trying to customise any jet aircraft at short notice can be difficult. We have done it in the past but the best option is to have an aircraft that is used regularly for backup and for which a partial medical fit-out is available.

In about 2006 we were fortunate to find an operator, Revesco Aviation, that was willing to make a Bombardier Challenger 601 available for aeromedical work on an ad hoc basis. They offered to modify it to accept a removeable LifePort stretcher installation, which meant that we had a proper stretcher, oxygen and power when configured this way. They subsequently installed a stretcher loading system, which could raise a stretcher and patient up the steep stairs and avoided the occupational risks of physically carrying the stretcher.

The aircraft is very spacious and comfortable, being designed as a medium-sized corporate jet. There are large leather armchairs and even a divan. After a flight in the Challenger, it is a real anticlimax to return to a small turboprop.

An Italian stallion

In August 2010 our Hawker 800XP jet required a major service. It was going to be offline for a number of weeks. We had built up expectations about the availability of the aircraft and had already become heavily dependent on it. Unfortunately, there was no reasonable alternative jet available to us to cover this downtime.

The Italian aircraft manufacturer Piaggio had one of its novel Avanti II twin-turboprop aircraft available for demonstration. It was an awesome, sexy machine and it did not surprise me to learn that the company had a business relationship with Ferrari. As a twin-turboprop aircraft it had unique design features that enabled it to fly considerably faster than similar turboprops such as the King Air.

First, it had pusher props rather than the traditional pulling propellers of most aircraft. It is known that these provide more effective thrust. The airflow from the props does not have to travel over the wings as is the case in conventional aircraft, but can move aft without impediment. With rear-mounted engines, the cabin is also much quieter.

The second feature was the small forward wing: not a true canard elevator but a fixed-wing which assisted with lift and manoeuvring. Third, the body of the aircraft was supremely aerodynamically crafted. There was not a rivet to be seen and the smooth, curved upper surface of the fuselage acted like an aerofoil in its own right. This meant that even the cabin provided lift.

The main wings were swept, offering some aerodynamic advantages at speed, and did not need to be as wide as other aircraft due to the other aerodynamic enhancements and better thrust from the prop configuration.

I went for a flight. It was pressurised and it was fast, climbing out like a rocket compared to some other turboprops. Despite the cruising speed of over 350 knots (648 km/h) it was also very economical.

We managed to install a temporary LifePort medical fit in the aircraft and used it for seventeen patient evacuations, including four ventilated cases and one from Christmas Island. Despite us falling in love with the aircraft, it just wasn't practical. It was a little too short inside to manage two stretcher patients comfortably and the cabin door was very narrow – too narrow to load many of our larger patients. It was also a tight fit in the cockpit. As the sleek nose tapered back sharply to the raked windscreen, it meant that many of our larger pilots were almost wearing the cockpit like a tight-fitting glove.

We said farewell to the aircraft and the Italian demonstration pilots at the end of the month, but it will be worth observing further developments of this aircraft type in the future.

Section 3
Medical

The biomedical revolution
Keeping at the forefront of medical care

We use a broad range of sophisticated biomedical equipment for transporting the diverse range of patients we encounter. There are different requirements for different sorts of patient: for example, severe trauma and acute cardiac cases need different equipment compared with obstetric emergencies, or paediatric and neonatal transport. Each of our aircraft has standard equipment and at each of our bases we have additional supplementary devices, which can be selected for specific missions.

I have prided myself on being an early adopter of new, innovative technology. While there are many types of biomedical equipment found in hospitals, only that which is compact, lightweight, robust and has an independent internal power supply is generally suited to our needs in the aeromedical environment. We are continually evaluating and trialling new gear. When suitable new technology becomes available, which will substantially improve our patient care, we implement it promptly.

In Western Australia, we have been one of the first aeromedical transport organisations to adopt a variety of new technologies over the past few decades. Some of these milestones are:

1970s

- *Vickers neonatal transport cot with ventilator (1978)*

- *Doppler stethoscopes*
- *Portable volumetric infusion pumps*
- *LIFEPAK® 5 portable defibrillator*

1980s

- *Dräger Oxylog® (1983)*
- *Aloka portable ultrasound (1983)*
- *Nellcor N-10 portable pulse oximetry (1985)*
- *Transcutaneous neonatal monitoring (TCM) (1988)*
- *Vacuum mattresses (1989)*
- *LIFEPAK® 10P with transcutaneous pacing*

1990s

- *Satellite telephones*
- *Intraosseous needles*
- *Propaq vital signs monitors with invasive pressure (1991)*
- *Propaq critical care monitors with mainstream end-tidal CO_2 (1994)*
- *i-STAT® point of care testing (1998)*
- *Interpretive and 12-lead ECGs*

2000s

- *Blood-in-motion transport system (Baxter; 2004)*
- *Non-invasive ventilation (CPAP, BiPAP)*
- *Portable ultrasound in flight (2008)*
- *Intraosseous BIG gun and EZ-IO® drill*
- *Mobile medical reference systems (UpToDate®)*

2010s

- *Videolaryngoscopy (2012)*
- *Advanced ventilators (AutoFlow®, inbuilt capnometry, paediatric)*
- *Chemical rewarming blankets (2014)*

I am grateful to the many supporters and benefactors of the RFDS over the past decades who have enabled us to keep at the forefront of aeromedical care. Virtually all our medical equipment and aircraft aeromedical fit-outs have been provided through donations, with government support applied predominantly to operating costs and some aircraft replacement.

Breaking the sound barrier in clinical diagnosis
Using ultrasound

In the early 1980s, the use of ultrasound was becoming a niche in obstetric practice. As a safe, non-invasive investigation, which did not use x-rays, more and more obstetricians were adopting it to help them assess their pregnant patients. I had been fortunate to have exposure to the technology in my year of obstetrics before joining the RFDS. At that time, the training philosophy in clinical practice was 'see one, do one, teach one'. Provided one had an adequate grasp of anatomy and reasonable spatial awareness, it was not particularly hard to use an ultrasound to measure some basic parameters in a pregnant woman.

Unfortunately, most of the machines used in hospital practice were quite large as they contained a CRT (cathode ray tube) display, just like old television sets. They usually sat on a trolley and definitely needed 240-volt AC mains electrical power to operate.

One of the challenges we faced on our flying clinic visits to remote communities was the medical assessment of pregnant women. For some Aboriginal women living in remote settings, it was hard to obtain an estimate of the date of the last normal menstrual period. This was important for a number of reasons. First, many assessments of growth during pregnancy were based on the estimated gestational age. Second, it was particularly important to predict the date at which the patient would deliver in the normal course of events, so that arrangements could be made for transport into the regional centre a few weeks before. The last thing we wanted was to be making emergency flights out for women in normal labour, or for them to deliver a baby in a remote setting with little care available.

Aloka ultrasound of the 1980s.

We were lucky that when I commenced work, the Aloka Company from Japan had just released a new 'portable' diagnostic ultrasound. It was not very portable. The unit was about 30 cm wide, 30 cm deep and 20 cm high and weighed about 10 kilograms, but it was a significant improvement on hospital-based equipment. As I had recently completed obstetrics, our medical director and general manager agreed to purchase one for the substantial sum of about $25,000 using funds raised by our Women's Auxiliary. A large padded case was custom-made from saddle leather, which made the unit even bigger – around half a metre on all sides. However, it protected the device so that we could lug it to and from each of our clinics in the nose of the aircraft.

It worked a treat! Despite having dreadful quality on the 5-inch black-and-white screen compared with equipment today, it gave us the capacity to make accurate measurements of the gestational sac in early pregnancy, or the biparietal diameter (diameter of the skull) and femur length in more established pregnancies. These could be checked against standard tables of normal values and used to predict more accurately the expected date of confinement.

Aboriginal women were usually very shy when attending a doctor and often relied on a friend or family member to provide clinical details during the consultation. I had come to realise that a shy woman, not saying much, was potentially pregnant until proven otherwise. Our new ultrasound gave us the ability to detect and confirm these pregnancies much earlier than would normally have been the case. We could determine whether there was a single or twin pregnancy and what the lie of the baby was, and calculate the dates more accurately.

I was interested in the cultural aspects of demonstrating a pregnancy at such an early age. I had been told that Aboriginal women had some issues in recognising the presence of the unborn baby but found that they showed great interest in seeing their baby and its movements prior to birth.

The ability to undertake diagnostic ultrasound screening in the field in 1984 was a real first for the RFDS and remote medical practice. We grasped an innovation in technology and put it to work in a remote area where there was little infrastructure to help us with diagnosis. It made a significant difference and we have continued to use ultrasound in this way on clinics ever since.

The story doesn't stop there. With new developments in displays and battery technology, it is now possible to buy an ultrasound in a format similar to a notebook computer. With large 12-inch, colour LCD screens and the capacity to use the devices away from mains power, these units are suitable for use anywhere, even in flight. Transducers (the handpieces that transmit and receive the sound waves) have also improved and additional features have been added, such as colour Doppler, to demonstrate the direction of flow in blood vessels.

One of the leaders in this portable technology has been Sonosite. Multiple probes with different sound frequencies (which penetrate to different depths) can be fitted to a single device to broaden its capabilities.

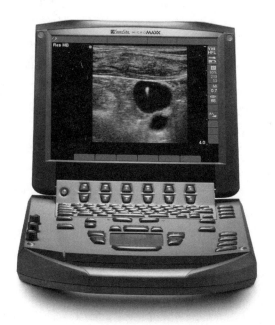

A modern Sonosite portable ultrasound used on clinics and emergency flights.

Since the mid-2000s, we have been taking these portable ultrasounds on our medical retrieval flights. It enables our doctors to detect important features, such as blood in the abdominal cavity, or air or blood in the chest in trauma, and plays a significant role in placement of special intravenous lines into major vessels. Vascular access techniques were previously based on knowing anatomical landmarks and were somewhat hit or miss. Now our emergency doctors can use the same technology available to anaesthetists and intensivists in a hospital to follow on the screen the position of needles, when essential vascular lines are inserted into critically ill patients.

Have scanner, will scan

Having great technology doesn't always mean there will be a happy outcome. I was so excited with my new Aloka ultrasound in 1984. I bought myself a VHS video player with a removeable recording module. It would run on batteries to enable recording from a camera. I then found a video cable that was compatible with the connections on the ultrasound and on my recorder, so that I could make antenatal movies for my patients. This was the latest trend for city obstetricians, so why not offer it to patients on bush clinics? We also bought an old-style Polaroid camera, which could take self-developing pictures of the Aloka screen. When I had a suitable image, I could take a photo and give it to the patient as well as adding one to the medical records.

I really wanted someone to practise on with my new toy and soon discovered that one of our flight nurses was pregnant. It was very early – maybe six to eight weeks' gestation – but she agreed to come around with her husband to my house to have an abdominal scan. I could try out the equipment and they could both have a look.

There we all were on my lounge room floor. The subject was lying on those ubiquitous chocolate brown carpet tiles, which were used to decorate most properties in the 1970s and just never wore out. I put the probe on her tummy and, hey, presto! There it was – a small gestational sac and the flickering of the early fetal heart.

I connected the VHS recorder and made a tape. The quality was mediocre and would be unacceptable today; but here was new life, beating away, to the excitement of us all. We had it on tape for posterity and looked forward to doing more scans as the pregnancy progressed.

Unfortunately it didn't. It was a salutary lesson for me and a reminder that many early pregnancies don't proceed and are lost. I felt awful when I heard that she had suffered a spontaneous miscarriage a week or two later. She and her husband subsequently had two lovely kids, but I learned a valuable lesson: to be less excited until at least twelve weeks had passed and more cautious in what I was looking at and recording.

Breathing a sigh of relief
Mechanical ventilators

In the late 1970s, the practice of transporting a patient on a portable ventilator was not as easy as it is today. Ventilators were not designed for the purpose and even the concept of transferring critically ill patients being artificially ventilated was considered risky.

A small ventilator called the Bird® Mark 7 was used in many hospital intensive care units. While reasonably small, it was not designed for the transport environment. It was not entirely intuitive to use either.

When I joined the RFDS we had one in a large wooden box. You set it up then strapped it to the stretcher, or sat it on the floor of the aircraft. Alternatively, you manually 'bagged' the patient, using an anaesthetic bag and circuit connected to the endotracheal tube. This was long and tiresome over a flight lasting a couple of hours and did not provide consistent and accurate ventilation.

In the late 1970s, the German company Dräger developed the original Oxylog® ventilator. Compact, robust and easy to use, this revolutionised the transport of critically ill patients. The breathing circuit connected to the patient was simple, as were the controls for respiratory rate and volume. There was a choice of 100 per cent oxygen or a mix of air and oxygen available for patients. No electrical power was required: the ventilator would function forever provided a source of compressed medical oxygen was available.

Bird Mark 7 ventilator of the 1970s.

This sturdy yet simple device was just what we needed and we purchased three of them in 1983. They were made so well that, eighteen years later, some of the readily identifiable bright orange Oxylogs were still in use. I remember one of these particularly as it had a plaque on it, 'Donated by the Old Bastards of Wickham 1983'. We could now transfer patients having an anaesthetic and being artificially ventilated on 'life support' over long distances more safely and with better control of ventilation.

Wrenched from the jaws of death

If you ask flying doctors about their most gruesome case, most will have many contenders for the title. In my experience, perhaps the most frightful I can recall is a young woman with a head injury.

I was sitting in the office at Jandakot Airport one day in the late 1980s when Frank Tuson, Supervisor of the Operations Centre, called me and said he had Dr Les Green on the phone with an emergency. Dr Green's call was put through and he calmly told me he had a woman with a spanner in her head. As one might expect, I paused for a moment to consider that statement carefully. Perhaps I had misheard him, so I asked, 'What do you mean?'

'Well, she has a large adjustable spanner in her head. It has entered the right temple and partly exited on the left.'

'Oh', was about all I could reply.

'Yes, someone threw a shifter at the car she was in and it penetrated the windscreen and is stuck in her head. It's still in place.'

I took a breath and we proceeded to quickly obtain some further details about the patient. The woman had been promptly brought to the hospital, where Dr Green, the solo country doctor, had sedated and intubated her to protect her airway and keep her breathing, and inserted an intravenous line to give her resuscitation fluids. This was the A-B-C of resuscitation in action but in a rather unusual case.

'By the way, she's also pregnant, about 30 weeks', Les added nonchalantly.

This was obviously an urgent flight, one that in those days we called a 'flash' flight. Not surprisingly, while we rushed to get ready, I found myself explaining to the flight nurse and then to the pilot what the patient's injuries were, all the time with a sneaking sense that what I had been told was inaccurate.

We departed quickly and flew to this Wheatbelt town about 300 kilometres away. On landing, the doctor was at the airport with the patient, ventilating her by hand. What he had described was exactly what we found – a young woman in her late twenties, with an adjustable wrench, lying transversely through her head. It appeared that by a one-in-a-trillion fluke, after it was thrown at the oncoming vehicle, it had tumbled in flight and struck the windscreen precisely handle first. Perhaps the patient had seen it coming and turned away. The combined velocity of the heavy spanner and the moving vehicle had enabled it to penetrate the glass and then strike the right side of her skull, which it had entered and then become lodged with the handle just coming out the other side behind her left eye.

Otherwise, she was in fair condition. There was little bleeding, her blood pressure and pulse were satisfactory and she was being well oxygenated. We could hear a strong fetal heartbeat also. We connected her to an Oxylog transport ventilator, transferred her to our aircraft stretcher and took off. On arrival at Jandakot, I escorted her to Sir Charles Gairdner Hospital in Perth, which provided the neurosurgical services at the time. As anticipated, there was an assembled throng in the emergency department, all come to help. The patient subsequently went to the operating theatre and had the spanner removed. After a period in intensive care and prolonged rehabilitation, she survived with a neurological handicap but able to eventually return to the town. Her baby was delivered safely and had a good outcome.

A year or so afterwards, I was at a medical conference. A specialist from the hospital used this case and some very impressive x-rays to demonstrate how clever they were at his institution. I couldn't help but feel a little miffed by this. The patient was alive because of a competent rural GP who, despite the extraordinary circumstances, did a terrific job in providing the essential resuscitation that was required. A pilot, nurse and doctor in a small cramped aircraft had also successfully managed this ventilated patient over a 300-kilometre journey so that she arrived in the hospital alive and in a stable condition.

With time, what was once cutting-edge technology was superseded. While it was nice to not have to rely on electrical power to operate the Oxylog, there was no screen to display ventilation parameters and the knobs provided only a rough indication of the volume and rate of respiration. There were also no inbuilt alarms so if there was a disconnection, oxygen failure or ventilator failure, no signal would sound to warn users. The circuit (hose) that connected to the patient was reuseable and had to be carefully disinfected after each use.

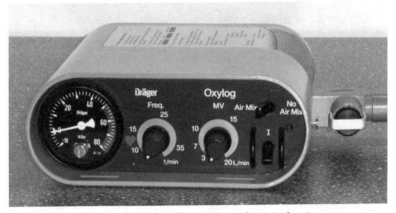

An original Oxylog ventilator of the 1980s revolutionised patient transport.

The ventilators could not easily be used for small children as it was not possible to control the much smaller breaths required using the knobs on the device. However, with the assistance of Dr Alan Duncan, Head of Intensive Care at Princess Margaret Hospital for Children, a special leak attachment was designed for the circuit outlet. In essence, this was simply a small alloy tube with a hole drilled into it which enabled air to leak out. With a 300 ml breath, for example, half of it might leak out the hole and ensured the infant only received a smaller breath of, say, 150 ml. You ignored the settings on the knobs and just adjusted them to achieve adequate chest movement and ventilation of the paediatric patient. This might seem primitive but it was elegantly simple and effective, and it enabled a number of small children to be ventilated on the device during some long flights.

Dräger went on to design other portable transport ventilators with more features, which we have subsequently used. The latest model is the Oxylog® 3000plus. This is a vastly more sophisticated ventilator with complex electronic circuitry and many features, such as altitude compensation, flow measurement, multiple information screens and many different modes of ventilation suitable for difficult adults down to small children.

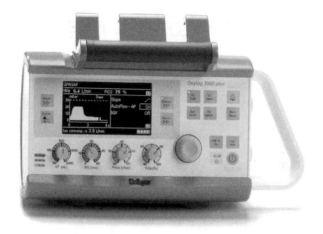

Oxylog 3000plus – a modern transport ventilator.

There are different sizes of disposable circuits (the hoses) for adults and children. This minimises what is called 'dead space' in the tubing and ensures appropriate infection control between patients. Capnometry, the ability to measure carbon dioxide levels in the exhaled air, is built-in, as are advanced ICU parameters which modify the pressure delivered to prevent any damage to the lungs during prolonged ventilation.

The device operates on internal lithium-ion batteries for up to four hours, as well as mains power, and has an illuminated screen and numerous alarm settings.

Shocking times
Defibrillators

A common and life-threatening complication of cardiac disease, particularly heart attacks, is when the heart flicks into an abnormal rhythm called ventricular fibrillation, or VF. In this state, instead of contracting in a regular synchronous manner, the heart muscle fibrillates – a very fast shimmering during which there is no synchronised pumping of blood. Within seconds, the lack of blood flow throughout the body results in loss of consciousness and respiration ceases.

Despite the benefits of CPR (cardiopulmonary resuscitation) in providing some limited circulation and oxygenation for a short period, the only definitive treatment to save life and restart the heart is defibrillation. In the late 1970s defibrillators where quite large, usually mains powered and often only found in hospitals. With the advent of rechargeable nickel–cadmium battery (NiCad) technology, it became possible to produce smaller portable defibrillators. We did not have 240-volt AC power on our aircraft at this time as the weight and size of inverters, which are commonplace today, was prohibitive.

One of the first of these battery-powered units was the LIFEPAK® 5 produced by the company Physio-Control in the USA. We introduced these in the late 1970s and they were available for flights on any of our aircraft. Before this, there was nothing.

They were both a cardiac monitor and a defibrillator. Indeed, the LIFEPAK® was the first electronic monitor which provided information to the medical crew other than a simple pulse rate, respiratory rate, temperature and blood pressure measurement that were taken by the nurse or doctor in flight. We now had a continuous view of what cardiac rhythm the patient was in, whether there were any abnormal beats and if there was any evidence of heart muscle damage to confirm our clinical diagnosis of a heart attack.

LIFEPAK® 5 battery powered cardiac monitor and defibrillator - made a dramatic change to prehospital cardiac care in the 1980s.

During our aeromedical flights, many of which lasted for a couple of hours, the LIFEPAKS® offered the only treatment that could save the patient's life if they went into ventricular fibrillation. At that time, acute cardiac conditions made up 10 to 12 per cent of our emergency calls across Western Australia. We did not have the clot-dissolving treatments we have now, so patients continued to have severe pain and parts of their heart muscle slowly died while we flew them long distances to a regional or tertiary hospital. Data I collated in four months at the end of 1984 showed four cardiac and six respiratory arrests in flight among 1,293 patients carried.

In contrast, in calendar 2014 there were only seven patients who needed defibrillation out of a total of 8,650 retrieved.

Fortunately, we needed to defibrillate patients only a dozen times per year and our success rate was high. This was partly because we were sitting right beside the patient, watching them. If they suffered a cardiac arrest, it would be immediately apparent on the screen and we could shock them very quickly. Studies have shown that the earlier a shock is administered, the more likely it will be successful, which is why 'out of hospital' cardiac arrest usually does not have as good an outcome. The LIFEPAK® had removeable NiCad battery packs which could be very quickly swapped; with a few spares on each flight, we would have sufficient battery life for many hours of monitoring. It also split into two parts, each of which operated independently, so if we were pressed for space we could stow the defibrillator and have just the monitor attached to the stretcher.

In October 1990, Kerry Packer's life was famously saved at a polo match with a defibrillator. He made a large donation to the New South Wales Ambulance Service to ensure defibrillators were widely available in road ambulances across the state; these are sometimes referred to as 'Packer whackers'. St John Ambulance in Perth was already a leader in this. Under the direction of Dr Harry Oxer, basic defibrillators were placed on all metropolitan ambulances in the late 1970s, as he recognised these were the only effective treatment for patients having a VF cardiac arrest. Nowadays small, inexpensive, portable automatic external defibrillators (AEDs) with lithium-ion batteries lasting up to five years in standby mode are commonplace, not just in medical facilities and ambulances but also in airports and other public areas.

Keeping pace with technology
Transcutaneous pacing

A number of different models of portable monitor–defibrillators came onto the market in the 1980s, but the next significant innovation for us was the introduction of transcutaneous pacing in the LIFEPAK® 10 at the beginning of the 1990s.

Most people will have heard of pacemakers, commonly used in the elderly, where gradual deterioration of the conducting pathways in the heart can lead to a slow and erratic heart rate. In these situations, a wire is threaded through the subclavian vein (a large vein in the chest) into the right ventricle of the heart and then attached to a small battery-powered and microprocessor-controlled pacemaker. These are smaller than a matchbox and are usually implanted under the skin, just below the collar bone.

In the acute setting, when someone attends a country hospital with complete heart block, there is no cardiologist available to insert a pacemaker. They are often elderly patients, otherwise in reasonable health, where the natural pacemaker and conduction pathways in the heart start to malfunction due to ageing and degenerative changes. Often the patients have periods where they have a very slow pulse, maybe as slow as twenty to thirty beats per minute, and this often causes them to lose consciousness or have a fall. All they need is to have their heart beating at a reasonable rate and they are back to normal health.

The Royal Flying Doctor Service evacuated many such patients each year to bring them to specialist care where a pacemaker could be inserted. During transport, we needed something to keep the heart ticking along at a reasonable pace. One or two locations, including Carnarvon, had a portable pacing box. One of the general practitioners there, Dr Ron Jewell, had been trained to insert pacing wires, so sometimes we picked up a patient with a wire in place in the heart and attached to a small battery-powered pacemaker on the outside of the body. We flew them down to Perth and the pacing equipment would be posted back to the hospital for the next time a case occurred. Unfortunately, most places did not have the equipment or training to do this and we needed another system to keep the patient's heart beating at an adequate rate.

Along came a technology called transcutaneous pacing, meaning 'through the skin'. Instead of putting a wire into the heart, we would apply large adhesive electrical pads to the front and back of the chest and fire rapid small shocks through the heart to keep it beating. This is not as bad as it sounds; the shocks were not as great as when defibrillating a patient, but nevertheless they caused a small amount of jerking and discomfort over a number of hours.

There were a couple of drugs we could use to pick up the speed and strength of cardiac contractions, but pacing was best in that it enabled us to more precisely control the heart rate by adjusting the rate of the shocks. The technique was to apply the pads and then start delivering small shocks at, say, seventy beats per minute. We could see these as spikes on the monitor screen in addition to the normal natural heartbeats. We then slowly increased the energy level of the shocks until we achieved 'capture'. This was when the electrocardiogram trace suddenly showed a heart contraction occurring following each shock. We would then keep the patient on the device for all of the transfer, which might be a couple of hours of flying plus half an hour in road ambulances at each end.

The equipment was quite clever. If it detected the return of natural heartbeats at an appropriate rate, it would stop shocking and only resume when the rate dropped off again.

Jerked back to reality

When treating and transporting emergency patients in aircraft you become very particular about your equipment and how things are done, and very aware of simple errors that can lead to serious complications. This is why patient transport or aeromedical retrieval has become something of a specialty in its own right. For a patient on a ventilator, for example, if the equipment buttons are accidently knocked to the wrong settings, if the tube becomes disconnected or the oxygen runs out, your patient could become hypoxic and brain-injured within a couple of minutes. Therefore, when handing over patients in hospitals I was always very careful in making sure staff did not touch our equipment and pull things off before they knew what was going on. After all, I had been with the patient for many hours in aircraft and ambulances. They were stable, I knew every little idiosyncrasy of their observations and treatment, and there was no rush to suddenly rip patients from our equipment and replace it with theirs.

Unfortunately, on one such transfer, we arrived with a paced patient in a hospital emergency department, where well-meaning staff suddenly started pulling all the ECG wires off while I was handing over to the doctors. Our LIFEPAK® 10 transcutaneous pacer had stopped pacing and was lying dormant as it had detected an adequate heart rate through the ECG cables. The staff did not realise this. As soon as they pulled off the ECG wires to attach their own monitor, the pacemaker, no longer receiving an ECG signal, started up again. This was quite a shock to them to suddenly have the patient's chest start jerking again at seventy beats a minute. It was also a bit of a shock to the poor elderly lady who was the centre of our attention!

We sorted it out quickly and no harm came of it, but I still use this incident as a reminder when training new doctors: don't trust anyone; keep a close eye on what is happening, especially well-meaning helpers; and maintain a 'command and control' approach to management of your patient.

Challenges with expanding gases
Managing trapped gases at altitude

I noted earlier that problems can be caused when gases trapped in body cavities and equipment expand and contract with changes in altitude and barometric pressure. A well-recognised situation is blocked ears and the need to equalise the pressure on descent. There are many conditions where changes in pressure can have serious consequences. Pressurised aircraft are helpful but we must still be alert to changes of pressure inside the cabin – what we call the 'cabin altitude' – which can influence a number of conditions.

One of the potentially most serious issues is a pneumothorax or collapsed lung. This can occur from an external wound, such as a stab wound or gunshot, which penetrates the chest and makes a hole in the lung. The lung contracts down and the remaining space in the thorax is filled with air and sometimes blood. Another cause can be a lung disease, such as emphysema or even asthma, where a hole occurs spontaneously and the lung also collapses.

When we take such patients to altitude, the air sitting in the thorax expands and starts to press on vital structures in the chest, such as the heart and the opposite lung, causing extreme breathing difficulty. To avoid this we make an incision between the ribs and insert a plastic tube, about the diameter of a small finger, into the chest, stitch it in place, and attach the tube to a one-way valve system. The standard approach in hospitals had been to connect to underwater seal drains. These were large glass bottles containing sterile water that were set up to let the air bubble out through the water but not come back into the chest. These were not practical for air transport so we used a disposable flutter valve called the Heimlich valve. It was a clear plastic cylinder with a one-way rubber valve on the inside. When we ascended to altitude, the expanding air would exit from the valve but could not return. With coughing and deep breathing, the air in the thoracic cavity would also exit but not return. With time, the lung would gradually re-expand as the trapped air was reduced.

A Heimlich valve for relieving the pressure in a pneumothorax.

The problem we encountered was that many patients had blood also leaking from the chest and this valve did nothing to collect it. Various options became available including a bag and valve system developed for the Falklands War. Our preferred solution now is the Pneumostat® valve, which has an inbuilt valve to release air and a small receptacle to collect any blood or secretions.

There are also other body cavities where air can be trapped and can cause problems at altitude. These include, but are not restricted to, the ears, sinuses, stomach and bowel.

Decompression illness

A more complex problem arises with patients with decompression illness, or 'the bends'. This occurs in scuba divers who fail to decompress properly and have bubbles forming in their tissues, such as in the joints, the lungs, blood vessels or even the nervous system. As we ascend to altitude, the bubbles already present will increase in size and more will form as the atmospheric pressure reduces. The bubbles can be very small but have serious effects. It is therefore imperative, for safe air transport, that we keep the aircraft cabin at pressure equivalent to the pressure at sea level as we evacuate these cases to a decompression chamber. Fortunately, our pressurised aircraft enable us to do this.

Equipment

Issues can occur with equipment which contain gases. A commonly used device is the endotracheal tube, a plastic tube inserted into the trachea (windpipe) when we anaesthetise and ventilate a patient. The tube has a thin soft cuff that we inflate with air to create a seal in the trachea. At altitude, this cuff can expand and become quite tight, pressing on the sensitive surrounding membranes and damaging them. To circumvent this problem we can fill the cuff with water, which does not change in volume at altitude, or just add and release air in the cuff, as necessary, to match the altitude and pressure changes.

In the 1980s, medical anti-shock trousers, or 'MAST suits', were in vogue for the treatment of patients with severe blood loss. These nylon trousers contained rubber bladders that could be inflated, rather like large blood pressure cuffs, to apply pressure to both legs and the lower abdomen. When inflated, the pressure squeezed blood from the lower limbs into the circulation and helped increase the blood pressure in the rest of the body and to vital organs. In an aircraft, however, as the suit bladders were full of air, the MAST would expand with increased altitude, increasing the pressure. On descent, the pressure would fall and the patient's blood pressure would drop again.

To deal with this challenge, we sourced a style of MAST suit that had pressure gauges on each compartment, so we could adjust the pressure on climb and on descent. The devices worked well. I recall one patient with a bleeding abdominal aortic aneurysm who deteriorated in flight. We inflated the MAST suit to keep his blood pressure up until we could get him to the operating theatre, where he survived his surgery. The MAST suits eventually fell out of fashion in emergency care over the course of a decade, for various reasons.

There are many other therapeutic devices which have balloons or cuffs, or are inflated in some manner, so it is important in an aeromedical service to always be aware of the effects of altitude and manage them appropriately. You can see that there is more to flying patients around safely in an aircraft than is apparent to the novice.

___

The stoic station hand

Early one Sunday morning in 1984, I received a call through the HF radio system from 8SH Warrawagine Station. Warrawagine is a couple of hundred kilometres from Port Hedland and east of Marble Bar. It is notable for being the first station to call in to the RFDS Port Hedland radio base when it opened in 1935 and to have an evacuation.

The call was from a station hand who was complaining of chest pain and difficulty breathing. As the story goes, he had been working under a four-wheel drive the previous evening when the jack collapsed and the 'diff' came down on his chest. It was a while before he was pulled out and he was pretty sure he had broken some ribs. Having endured severe pain all night each time he breathed, he was now calling because it was increasingly difficult to breathe.

I chastised him about why he hadn't called earlier. His response stunned me. 'I didn't want to call, doc, because I thought you would be busy with emergencies.'

I still marvel at that stoic response. Clearly, he not only had fractured ribs but was also likely to have a pneumothorax.

I telephoned the pilot, Captain John Wheeler, and together we flew out to the station as quickly as we could. On examination the station hand indeed had a collapsed lung so I inserted a chest drain and stitched it in while he was still lying on a couch. I connected it up to a plastic underwater seal drain that we were using at the time and asked the pilot if he could fly back as low as possible as the aircraft was unpressurised.

The return trip to Port Hedland was at altitudes varying between about 1,500 feet and 3,000 feet, which provided a much closer view of the vast spinifex plains than I normally got to see. At the same time, it was fascinating to observe how, with increasing altitude, the underwater drain bubbled furiously as expanding air was vented from the chest.

As expected, the jackaroo made an excellent recovery in hospital, although his fractured ribs still caused him considerable pain for many weeks. Nowadays, I hope that such a call would come in more promptly and our pressurised aircraft would provide a better means of air transport with no pressure changes in flight.

Shining a light on oxygenation
Pulse oximetry in air transport

The human body requires an adequate level of oxygen to function properly. In various illnesses and injuries, delivery of oxygen to the tissues of the body can be impaired. This lowered level of oxygen is called hypoxia.

In lung disease, for example, asthma or pneumonia, the problem is getting oxygen through the lungs into the bloodstream.

In patients with anaemia or blood loss, who have a low level of red cells and haemoglobin, the problems result from the lack of capacity of the blood to bind and transport oxygen to the tissues.

In shock or with impaired cardiac output, a circulatory problem reduces the effective pumping of oxygenated blood around the body to essential organs.

Up until the 1980s, the level of oxygen in the blood and tissues was either roughly estimated by the presence of cyanosis (a blueness of the lips), or more accurately determined by the analysis of a sample of arterial blood using a cumbersome blood gas machine only found in hospital laboratories. Then a marvellous new device, the pulse oximeter, appeared and transformed patient care.

Oxygen is carried in the blood attached to haemoglobin molecules in red cells. Well-oxygenated blood is a bright red colour but when the oxygen content falls, the haemoglobin and blood turns a darker colour. Oximetry uses a probe which can be attached to a fingertip or other skin surface. It shines different frequencies of red and infrared light through the tissue and measures the absorption of the light. While absorption by the skin, fat and muscles is relatively constant, the absorption by haemoglobin depends on how oxygenated and red coloured it is.

Every time our heart beats, fresh oxygenated blood pulses through our fingertip. In essence, the pulse oximeter detects the slight changes in 'pinkness' with each pulse. By measuring the relative absorption of each frequency of red light, it can determine the percentage saturation of haemoglobin with oxygen.

This is very clever yet remarkably simple technology. It gives us an indication of both the pulse rate and oxygen saturation with just a simple probe clipped onto a finger.

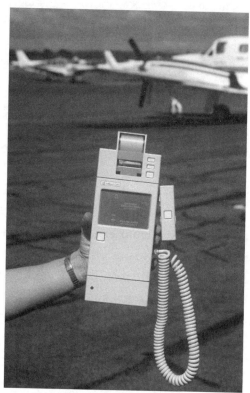

Our first handheld Nellcor pulse oximeter and printer in 1985.

When the devices first appeared in hospital practice they were bulky monitors requiring 240-volt mains power. Then, in the mid-1980s, Nellcor brought out a simple handheld, battery-operated device. This was revolutionary for aeromedical transport. I introduced the Nellcor N-10 portable oximeter to our service around 1985. It enabled us to measure the oxygen saturation of patients in a simple and painless manner, and we could adjust the amount of oxygen we administered accordingly.

Apart from underlying medical problems, carrying patients at altitude in an aircraft exposes them to reduced levels of oxygen in the air they breathe, also causing hypoxia. Our aircraft were nearly all unpressurised at this time and their flying altitude was limited to 10,000 feet. At this level, healthy passengers such as the medical team and pilot were exposed to low-grade hypoxia; for sick patients the effect of the drop in oxygen levels could be quite serious.

When transporting premature babies with lung problems we needed to ensure we provided sufficient oxygen to prevent brain injury but avoid exposure to high concentrations of oxygen, which could lead to blindness and long-term lung damage. With oximeters, we were able to adjust the flow of oxygen to ensure we delivered just the right amount.

Likewise, with anaesthetised adults, we previously guessed how much oxygen to use. Too little was clearly bad for patients but prolonged exposure to high concentrations could lead to lung damage also. With our new oximeters, we could at last be confident we were selecting the right concentrations of oxygen for our patients during flights lasting many hours from start to finish.

It was genuinely enlightening to know the level of oxygenation.

Dealing with clots
Thrombolysis in cardiac care

One of the most important advances in medical care since the beginning of the 1990s has been thrombolysis. 'Thrombo' refers to blood clots and 'lysis' refers to dissolving them. The treatment uses special drugs to dissolve clots in the coronary arteries and reverse the effects of a coronary occlusion or heart attack. In the late 1980s cardiologists started to recognise the benefits of using aspirin, streptokinase and some other drugs to do this but, to be effective, the agents had to be given within hours of the onset of chest pain. When they worked, they effectively cleared the blockage in the coronary artery, with dramatic resolution of symptoms and prevention of permanent heart muscle damage.

Before thrombolysis, we would evacuate patients urgently and try to transport them to a coronary care unit in a city hospital as soon as possible. Yet, because of the vast distances involved, even using aircraft would take many hours. These patients were in severe pain despite treatment with large doses of morphine. They also required other medications to control blood pressure and prevent cardiac arrhythmias.

I would sit there in the aircraft next to them, aware that we were not doing anything to prevent permanent heart damage from occurring. We were just doing our best to relieve their pain, prevent complications and transport them to hospital where they could continue to be monitored as the condition evolved. Sometimes patients would go into ventricular fibrillation in flight. This was a life-threatening arrhythmia and required immediate defibrillation in the aircraft.

Some landmark studies were published in the *Lancet* and the *New England Journal of Medicine* towards the end of the 1980s showing the benefits of both simple aspirin and streptokinase in improving the outcome from heart attacks. It was clear to me that the new treatment would be very beneficial to patients in remote areas so I adopted it promptly, even though it was moderately expensive and usually only given in a hospital setting. It was imperative that it be given early, within about six hours, if it was to work well. Instead of just waiting till the patient reached a coronary care unit many hours after the onset of pain, we made the drug available on RFDS flights so it could be administered as soon as we arrived. It meant we could bring the latest tertiary hospital treatment to patients in the bush and start it sooner, having a quicker and more effective result.

I commenced with streptokinase, which at the time was about $300 for a single dose. There could be some complications following administration but our aircraft were well equipped. It was much better to start the treatment immediately than to miss the chance of a successful outcome clearing the clot. Initially we would inject it at the remote setting and take off once the patient was stable. With experience, I found we could load the patient quickly and start treating them during flight if necessary.

Chest pain at Payne's Find

A man in his late forties was visiting a station in the vicinity of Payne's Find, a tiny gold prospecting settlement on the great northern highway about 500 kilometres north of Perth where there was no hospital or nursing post. The station owner called and gave a clear story of severe central chest pain coming on suddenly. This was consistent with a heart attack. I gave the usual advice regarding drugs from the medical chest and use of morphine and tasked an urgent priority one flight. In a remote setting like this, we knew that if the patient went into ventricular fibrillation they would not survive without immediate access to a defibrillator.

Fortunately, there was an airstrip at the station, although in pretty poor shape. Nevertheless, it was a clear sunny day and CAVOK (cloud and visibility OK), and we managed to land on a pretty overgrown strip of gravel in our Piper Navajo.

Our patient was brought to the aircraft in the back of a station wagon, lying on a camp mattress and still in serious pain. As the treatment was new, we set up and took a 12-lead electrocardiogram which confirmed the changes of an anterior myocardial infarction (a heart attack involving the coronary arteries that supply blood to the front of the left ventricle). We started the patient on oxygen, transferred him to a stretcher on the ground at the back of the car, connected him to a monitor–defibrillator and put in an intravenous line. Then we administered an ampoule of streptokinase slowly over thirty minutes.

Within only a few minutes of finishing there was a flurry of unusual rhythms on our cardiac monitor and we noticed the ECG changes indicative of a heart attack starting to revert to normal. Here we were, in the middle of the bush beside the gravel airstrip, with the patient reclining on the stretcher in the sunshine and starting to look and feel much better. 'This new drug is fantastic!', I thought.

Only a week or so later, I had another case where a woman at Northampton suffered a heart attack on the golf course. We flew in, commenced our treatment and had the same short period of irregular rhythms before the symptoms resolved. This was a remarkable change in clinical practice and, despite the cost, we enthusiastically implemented it across the state.

Over the following years a number of newer agents have been developed that have enabled us to continue to provide the same level of care to patients outside the reach of a tertiary specialist centre. The newer drugs are not cheap – at one stage we were paying $2,300 per dose for tenecteplase (Metalyse®) – but the benefits in effectively reversing a heart attack and potentially saving a life well outweigh the cost.

Packaged up in polystyrene
Vacuum mattresses

When we are evacuating patients with multiple injuries over long distances, their injuries need to be properly splinted, especially if the spine is involved. Unfortunately, there is often a need to transfer these cases between a number of different stretchers, from the site of their initial accident to arrival at a tertiary trauma centre.

In the 1970s and 1980s, we used the Australian-designed Jordon frame to transfer suspected spinal injuries. Plastic slats were carefully slid under the patient from one side to the other and then connected to a frame assembled around the patient. The entire assembly would then be carefully lifted. While good in principle, it was not ideal in practice, with bits of the body flopping where the slats were loose. This was superseded by scoop stretchers, which are still in use today. Two wedge-shaped blades are slid under the patient from each side and then connected at the head and foot end, before scooping the patient up. The scoop is then removed as it is uncomfortable to lie on for more than a short period.

The trouble was the repeated handling of the patient. Someone injured in a motor vehicle crash might be lifted from the roadside on a scoop stretcher, transferred to a road ambulance stretcher, then taken to a nearby country hospital where they would be transferred to a resuscitation trolley in the emergency department. When they required aeromedical evacuation to Perth, they were transferred back onto a road ambulance stretcher to be taken to the airport, then transferred across to the aircraft stretcher prior to loading onto our aircraft. In Perth, this was all repeated in reverse.

These frequent transfers can be risky if the patient has a spinal injury and cause discomfort from any fractures each time. We need to splint patients well to minimise movement during flight, particularly in the case of turbulence. Hard backboards, as are sometimes used during road ambulance transport, are extremely uncomfortable for flights lasting many hours. They can cause significant problems with pressure areas, leading to bedsores.

In the mid-1980s I had the opportunity to visit some of the emergency medical services in Europe and was impressed by the newly developed vacuum mattresses that were coming into use. These were airtight vinyl or nylon and similar to an air mattress, except that they were full of polystyrene balls (just like a beanbag). You sucked the air out rather than inflating them.

Patients are placed on the mattress, which is then connected to a small handheld vacuum pump or a medical suction device. The air inside is withdrawn and the mattress is carefully moulded around the patient. This causes the polystyrene balls to be drawn together tightly and they eventually form a firm splint, which matches the shape of the patient.

It is fascinating to see how a soft and floppy mattress suddenly becomes a lightweight but rigid splint, wrapped around the patient, following their curves and providing even pressure and support. Once the straps are applied across the body, the patient can be lifted and carried, or slid, from one stretcher to another, with minimum movement. They are truly packaged up in a 'total body splint'.

We imported the first of our vacuum mattresses in the 1980s and have used a variety of brands and models since then. They are not absolutely rigid but we find they provide adequate splinting, as well as comfort, and avoid the pressure area problems which can arise in seriously injured patients who endure long periods of immobilisation. The original design has since spawned a variety of improvements in shape and supporting slats, and offshoots such as smaller vacuum splints for limbs.

While not an Aussie innovation, we recognised the value of such simple but effective technology and adopted it as soon as we could, to better our patient care.

Sounding out the situation
Doppler stethoscopes in flight

Over the years, up to 10 per cent of our emergency evacuations have been for complications of pregnancy. These fall into half a dozen simple categories. Most commonly, we evacuate women in preterm labour or with premature rupture of the membranes. These women are going to deliver a premature infant, which will require specialist care once born. Rather than waiting for the baby to be delivered and then trying to retrieve it from a small rural community, I have adopted a proactive in utero maternal transport approach for the past thirty years.

Transport of the unborn baby in utero offers a much better transport medium than even our most sophisticated neonatal transport units. There is plenty of published evidence in the medical literature on this. The baby is kept warm, well oxygenated and protected, and can be moved to a location where they can be delivered with all the required specialist services ready and waiting.

It takes confidence and good clinical judgement to do so. Many clinicians not familiar with this approach would baulk at the thought of putting a woman in labour into a small aircraft for a couple of hours, to fly them 1,000 kilometres to another centre. Yet, it can be done safely, and our data and experience shows no deliveries during transport, in about 5,000 cases, over the past decade.

The other emergencies we transfer include pre-eclampsia and haemorrhage. Pre-eclampsia is a condition in which the pregnant woman develops a very high blood pressure and can ultimately go on to have seizures. The treatment of pre-eclampsia is ultimately early delivery, to protect both the mother and fetus. We still try to eke out a few extra days or weeks, however, to enable the unborn infant to grow and develop further.

At the time I completed my obstetric training, these patients were all kept sedated in a quiet, darkened room to try to minimise any stimuli that could lead to seizures. When I joined the RFDS, it came as a surprise to realise that I would need to put these patients in a loud, noisy aircraft and subject them to hypoxia, turbulence and flashing strobe lights at night, as we evacuated them to major centres for care. It seemed contrary to what I would be doing in the hospital setting. Yet, with careful use of drugs to prevent seizures and control the blood pressure, we were able to achieve very satisfying outcomes.

Antepartum haemorrhage (before delivery) and postpartum haemorrhage (after delivery) are serious and frightening aspects of obstetric care. In antepartum haemorrhage, the loss of blood can lead to the death of the baby and even the mother. In postpartum haemorrhage the mother can die. These are challenging situations in regional centres, let alone in rural and remote settings with no surgical capacity. They form another of the common reasons for aeromedical evacuation.

In such a vast state with limited regional infrastructure, the majority of patients end up in Perth where there are highly specialised obstetric and neonatal facilities. While obstetric problems can often be dealt with by regional obstetricians, it is the lack of neonatal intensive care facilities to deal with the premature newborns that necessitates aerial evacuation over long distances to a capital city.

When caring for such patients, there are different ways of monitoring the wellbeing of the unborn child. In a hospital, a cardiotocograph machine is used. It measures and records uterine contractions as well as the fetal heart rate. Various patterns of how the fetus responds during contractions can help provide information on its wellbeing.

A simpler way of monitoring fetal wellbeing, used for a century or more, is just to record the fetal heart rate. If it is bounding along at a normal and regular rate, it provides reassurance that the baby is alive and coping well despite the underlying obstetric problem. If it slows significantly during contractions or between them, this can suggest the baby is stressed and at risk. The complete absence of a fetal heart rate confirms death of the baby in utero. It is therefore important to be able to measure the fetal heart rate during transport as part of the overall clinical monitoring of the patient.

Unfortunately, aircraft are noisy. Using a normal stethoscope in flight is effectively impossible. The background noise level drowns out the soft sounds we would normally be listening to: a patient's lungs or their heart, or while taking a blood pressure. The fetal heart rate is similar. The sounds can be usually heard with a normal stethoscope, a Pinard stethoscope (the conical device often used by midwives) or even the normal ear resting against the abdomen, but not in a noisy aircraft in flight. Fortunately, we can use a Doppler ultrasound to provide audible information on the heart rate. By positioning and angling a probe over the pregnant abdomen, sound waves can be bounced off the moving heart wall and provide a return signal which equates to the fetal heart rate. As we are using an electronic device, the volume can be amplified and routed into earphones or a headset to improve clarity.

We commenced using handheld battery-powered Doppler fetal stethoscopes in the early 1980s and have continued to use them ever since. They provide reassurance to our flight nurses that the baby is alive prior to and at the end of the transport and confirm that they are stable during the flight.

A fetal Doppler stethoscope as used for monitoring the fetal heart in flight.

Worrying signs in the Wheatbelt

We diverted a flight nurse in flight to retrieve a pregnant woman who had presented after a small antepartum haemorrhage to a hospital in a Wheatbelt town. The locum doctor did not have obstetric experience and, as is increasingly the case, there were no midwives in the hospital. The patient clearly needed to be transferred to a larger centre for ongoing obstetric care but obtaining a clear obstetric history and observations over the phone prior to flight was difficult, due to the inexperience of the referring staff. The patient was stable and, as all RFDS flight nurses are trained midwives, we diverted the flight nurse who was alone on the aircraft.

On arrival, as is standard practice, the woman was examined at the airstrip and a fetal heart rate recorded using the Doppler. Well, our nurse tried to measure it, but it wasn't there. There had been no fetal movements for some time and the heart rate just couldn't be detected by any means.

This is a very sad and challenging clinical situation to be confronted with. A young mother full of hope, expecting transport to a tertiary hospital in Perth to complete her pregnancy but oblivious to the fact that her baby has died. Do you tell her there and then at the airstrip, in the presence of her husband farewelling her for the flight, or do you proceed without comment?

It's a big call for the RFDS nurse. Is she really sure she can't hear the heart rate? Could she be wrong and cause unnecessary grief? If the fetus has died, there is nothing different to be done to manage the problem, either at the airstrip or in flight. She still needs to be transferred to the city. From a medicolegal perspective, however, we need to note that the infant has died prior to transport and to let the receiving hospital know what to expect. Of course it is important to keep patient informed, even if the circumstances are not ideal and it is heartbreaking to do so.

Technology can help us be more certain of our findings than just simple clinical examination, where there is usually some leeway that we might not be correct in our assessment. Unfortunately, we don't always find the answers we want.

Drilling down to the core of the problem
Intraosseous infusion

One of the most challenging aspects of clinical medicine is dealing with seriously ill or injured toddlers. It is essential to gain intravenous access – to insert an IV drip – so that fluids, drugs, pain relief and blood can be given quickly and easily as required. Not only are the veins of infants smaller in diameter than in an adult, but they are often hard to find in the chubby arms and legs of children this age. To complicate matters further, if the child is dehydrated or has lost blood, the vessels are often collapsed and even harder to identify and cannulate.

Over the years, various techniques have been used to try to overcome this problem. They have included minor surgical procedures, such as a 'cut-down' where we make an incision in the skin and try to identify the vein directly. This can be time-consuming in an emergency and is not always easy to do. Other methods have included administering fluids rectally, or intra-peritoneally (that is, through a needle directly into the abdominal cavity). These methods were not very effective as they did not ensure rapid access to the child's circulation; however, they were the fallback position for remote area nurses and our staff in the 1980s.

In the major paediatric hospitals around Australia, under excellent conditions and with a range of specialist staff, gaining intravenous access in children was not a major problem. In remote areas, with severely dehydrated children due to gastroenteritis, or other infections and injuries, it was a much greater challenge not just for flying doctors but also remote area nurses.

A Cook® intraosseous needle. These were screwed in by hand.

In the early 1990s, special needles appeared which were marketed by the Cook company in the USA. They were designed to penetrate bone and enabled clinicians to insert an intravenous style of line into the bone marrow space in certain long bones. The bone marrow is well perfused with blood and it has been shown that drugs and fluids administered into this space are distributed through the rest of the circulation almost as quickly as if they had been given directly into a vein. Infusing fluids into the marrow space was actually an old technique but it saw a resurgence when these specially designed needles became available.

We were quick to adopt this new intraosseous technique and it provided a rapid and technically easier approach to paediatric resuscitation in emergencies. We encouraged remote locations to ensure they had intraosseous needles and it has subsequently revolutionised emergency vascular access in sick children.

Paediatric trauma at Merredin

It was the mid-1990s and I was called to a motor vehicle accident at Merredin, roughly halfway between Perth and Kalgoorlie. A three-year-old Aboriginal child had been struck by a car. On our arrival, the child was shocked and likely to be bleeding into the abdominal cavity from an injury to his liver or spleen. It was extremely hard to find any veins on his skin and while often you can just feel them, in a child with significant blood loss such as this, they were flat.

We pulled out the intraosseous needle from our emergency kit and I began carefully rotating it back and forth into the upper anterior tibia. I had practised this on chicken legs before. You had to be patient and not force the needle too hard, as it could suddenly penetrate the outer surface of the hollow bone then pop right through and out the other side of the bone.

After about thirty seconds, which seemed more like ten minutes to me, I felt the gentle pop as we entered the marrow space. I drew back blood to confirm we were in the right place, then connected a large syringe and flushed through the first 200 millilitres of resuscitation fluid, before connecting to an intravenous fluid line and pump.

The needle wasn't very steady at all (it only goes in about a centimetre) but our flight nurse, using all the ingenuity for which our nurses are so highly regarded, constructed a supporting structure around it, using a cut down paper drinking cup then lots of adhesive tape.

We packaged up the patient then got out of there quickly to fly to Perth. Towards the end of the flight, we had been able to resuscitate the child enough to find a vein and insert a normal intravenous line as well. A simple but effective new technology certainly helped us to save a life on this occasion.

Since then, there have been further developments to refine the ease of insertion and make sure the needle stays in place, and to develop the technique for use in adults. One device was the BIG (Bone Injection Gun®). These were small and disposable and could fire a spring-loaded needle into the bone to achieve rapid access.

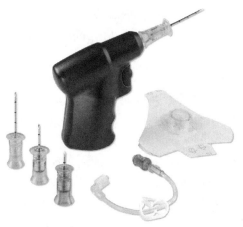

An EZ-IO battery-powered drill for inserting intraosseous needles into bones.

Most recently we have adopted the EZ-IO® drill system. This is a small portable drill, powered by a lithium-ion battery, which drills a needle into the bone. They are quick and easy to use and come with a range of needle lengths. The needles have a broad hub and sit much more securely in place, avoiding the risk of falling out which could occur with previous techniques.

The whole concept of using a power tool to drill into a child's leg may appear barbaric to the uninitiated! However, whether with local anaesthetic or not, the technique is very quick and surprisingly painless. We are able to use this approach in adults but with longer needles.

Every RFDS aircraft now has an EZ-IO® drill and the problem of obtaining rapid vascular access in seriously ill children is now effectively solved with new technology.

Information from exhalation
Capnometry in transport

The stimulus which drives the human body to breathe and prevents us from holding our breath indefinitely is not usually a lack of oxygen but a build-up of CO_2 (carbon dioxide) in the bloodstream. Our respiratory control centre is exquisitely sensitive to small changes in the level of CO_2 and uses this to finely regulate our rate and depth of respiration.

When a patient is anaesthetised, we take over responsibility for ensuring the level of ventilation is appropriate. Too little or too much ventilation will result in significant fluctuations in blood CO_2 levels, which can have adverse effects on patients.

Once the problem of measuring oxygen in flight was solved with pulse oximetry (see earlier chapter in this section, 'Shining a light on oxygenation'), we still needed to do better to manage CO_2 levels in our ventilated patients. It was another decade before something suitable appeared.

In the mid-1990s, hospital anaesthetists started to use devices to measure what is called end-tidal carbon dioxide. These capnometers used a sensor which passed light through the air exhaled by the patient. By measuring the absorption of light in the exhaled air, in comparison with a reference cell, the device could continuously estimate the level of CO_2 in each breath. The very last part of an exhaled breath contains a level of CO_2 which is equivalent to that in the bloodstream. By measuring the CO_2 at the end of exhalation, we could predict the level in the bloodstream, which is what we were aiming to control.

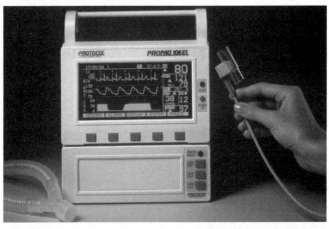

A fully configured Propaq monitor of the mid 1990s with capnography.

As with most biomedical devices, these new capnometers were bulky, expensive and mains powered. In 1994, a United States company developed a new portable monitor, the Propaq, which had capnometry as an optional extra. The monitors were small, battery powered and rugged, and designed for military and prehospital care. With the capnometry option, they cost the equivalent of a family-sized car (around $30,000 at the time) but they provided state-of-the-art monitoring for seriously ill patients.

As rapid adopters of new technology, I could see the immediate benefits of end-tidal CO_2 measurement and we were the first aeromedical retrieval service in Australia to import the devices and place them into service.

Capnometry is usually used with ventilated, anaesthetised patients. The sensor is attached to the endotracheal tube – the plastic tube inserted into the trachea – near where it exits the mouth. It provides an independent measure of respiratory rate and the graphical waveform of CO_2 levels confirms that we are ventilating the lungs adequately. The devices also include inbuilt alarms for CO_2 levels and an apnoea alarm which is activated if no breaths are detected.

The technology is not perfect. It makes an assumption that the air being exhaled at the end of a breath provides a reliable estimate of the level of CO_2 in the bloodstream. This applies if lungs are reasonably healthy and gas exchange is occurring without restriction, but in serious lung disease the transfer of CO_2 between the circulation and the lungs may not be normal. Nevertheless, the devices became a core part of our armamentarium and are now considered mandatory in any critical care patient transport.

The Propaq monitor was our first comprehensive physiological monitor, providing information on multiple parameters. It became almost an international standard for aeromedical transport and we used it, essentially unchanged for twenty years, as our standard portable ICU-style monitor.

Saved by the bell

An elderly woman with an intracranial haemorrhage was being transferred from a regional centre to Perth for urgent neurosurgery. She was sedated, paralysed and ventilated. Shortly after take-off, as the aircraft was climbing out at full power, with the medical team strapped in their seats, there was a ventilator failure that resulted in complete cessation of breathing.

Capnometry was in use and alarmed within seconds, as it was no longer registering any exhaled carbon dioxide. This enabled the medical team to rapidly correct the situation which otherwise could have had tragic consequences.

Managing pressure
Invasive pressure monitoring and
inotropes

Measuring a patient's blood pressure is one of the most basic clinical observations or so-called vital signs. Most people are familiar with a blood pressure cuff being applied to their upper arm and a blood pressure either being manually taken by a doctor or nurse with a stethoscope, or sometimes by a machine.

In an aircraft, the background noise levels preclude the use of a stethoscope and the vibration can make machine estimations unreliable. If patients are critically ill or have a low blood pressure, using various external cuff methods is not sufficiently accurate. The gold standard in this case is what is called invasive blood pressure measurement.

A fine plastic tube or cannula is placed within a blood vessel, in this case an artery, and connected up to a circuit resembling an intravenous drip line which includes a pressure-sensitive transducer. This then measures the true pressure within the blood vessel on a continuous basis and displays it on the monitor screen.

With the adoption of portable critical care Propaq monitors in the early 1990s, we also had the capability to start using invasive pressure monitoring on some of our patients. One measurement was called central venous pressure. It gave an indication of the pressure of venous blood flowing back into the right atrium of the heart. Most commonly, however, we used an arterial cannula in the radial artery at the wrist to give us invasive blood pressure. This is particularly important when treating patients with very potent drugs (called inotropes) which increase cardiac output and blood pressure.

To measure invasive blood pressure the medical team needs to insert an arterial cannula and set up the infusion, pressure transducer and then calibrate or 'zero' the setup, so we are sure we are recording the true pressure. Thereafter we need to check the setup at altitude in flight. We have been able to provide the sort of beat-to-beat invasive pressure monitoring found in intensive care or an operating theatre for almost two decades.

Accompanying this technology is the more regular use of inotropic drugs to raise blood pressure and improve the circulation in patients who are seriously ill. These drugs are extremely potent and related to the well-known adrenaline, which is responsible for supercharging our physiology in a 'fright, fight, flight' response to stress. They need to be given in carefully controlled doses, which is when devices such as syringe drivers and infusion pumps are essential.

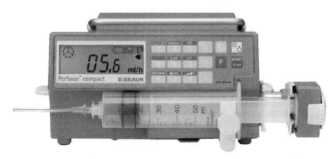

B Braun syringe driver for administering infusions of potent drugs.

A highly concentrated solution of the particular drug is diluted and added to a syringe which is then placed in the syringe driver and connected to an intravenous line. The driver slowly depresses the syringe plunger at rates as low as 1 millilitre per hour. This rate can be titrated to match the invasive blood pressure reading until the optimal level is achieved. This system is smoother and provides a more accurate and even administration of drugs than can be achieved manually or through other methods of intravenous administration.

There are many brands and styles of syringe driver on the market, mostly designed for hospital use. We located the B Braun device, manufactured in Germany, more than a decade ago. It is ideal for our purposes, small and compact, and runs for many hours on replaceable batteries.

Getting to the point of the problem
Point-of-care testing

One of the challenges doctors face in dealing with critically ill patients during a long flight, as well as when providing care in remote settings, is lack of access to normal laboratory services. There are many blood tests that are used to monitor and guide treatment. Without them, we cannot provide the highest level of clinical care that we aspire to.

One of the core groups of tests is electrolytes, such as the sodium, potassium and calcium levels in the blood. Abnormalities of these occur with gastroenteritis and dehydration, and acute and chronic renal disease, and can contribute to cardiac arrhythmias. A blood urea is also often measured in conjunction with these. The abnormalities can be corrected but only if one knows what the levels are.

More difficult to test, yet critical for patients being ventilated, are what are called 'blood gases'. These are a measure of the levels of oxygen and carbon dioxide in the blood, together with other determinants of respiration and acid-base status such as pH and base excess.

In the mid-1990s only large regional hospitals had machines that could measure blood gases. To have any of these tests done required blood being sent to a laboratory and a laboratory scientist called in. About the same time, I saw a new device at an international medical conference which was clearly a breakthrough. It was branded as an i-STAT®. It enabled a suite of about eight tests to be done at the bedside with a high level of accuracy in only two minutes. The technology involved using disposable cartridges, about the size of a Dictaphone tape, which contained biosensor chips able to perform multiple analyses at once.

The concept has been called point-of-care testing as it allows clinicians to do their tests at the bedside and obtain almost immediate results. For the RFDS, it meant we were able to undertake biochemical tests which were not available in many of the hospitals we flew to for emergency cases. It also enabled us to perform laboratory tests in flight. It was clear that this would be a terrific step forward but it took a couple of years before we could import the devices from overseas.

In 1998 we became the first aeromedical service to have access to this technology on our retrieval flights. For approximately $8, we could obtain a set of results including blood gases, electrolytes, haemoglobin, blood glucose and urea within two minutes. The device was handheld and battery powered and could print to a small portable infrared printer.

This was a great step forward for managing seriously ill patients and was really cool, too! We could arrive at a major tertiary hospital emergency department and hand over a printout of blood tests done in the ambulance bay, knowing that it would take the hospital doctors much longer to get the same tests done.

The i-STAT® analysers were around $9,000 each but when we saw what they could do, and the improvements to patient care, we just had to adopt them. Nowadays the devices are widely used in hospitals and other settings, with the point-of-care concept popular and cost-effective.

A big fuss over tiny things
Neonatal transport: cots and monitoring

Newborn babies, particularly those born prematurely, are delicate things. During the twentieth century, the perinatal mortality rate, that is, the rate at which newborn babies died, plummeted due to improvements in antenatal care and neonatal care. Great strides were made worldwide in care of premature infants and Australia was at the forefront of much of this. As many of the problems were related to immaturity of the lungs or other respiratory problems, providing assistance with breathing on a mechanical ventilator was one of the key elements of treatment. From the 1970s onwards, the survival rate of very premature infants continued to improve with advances in neonatal intensive care. Amid the challenging ethical issues of potential long-term disabilities in some premature infants, large centres of excellence continued to improve outcomes in babies it was previously thought could not be saved.

Aligned with this was the development of neonatal transport services, led by figures such as Dr Neil Roy in Melbourne. The concept of the NETS (neonatal emergency transport service) was to have a specialised team with an infant incubator and mobile intensive care equipment being able to travel to outlying hospitals and bring premature or seriously ill newborn babies back to a major centre. When I worked in Melbourne in the early 1980s, before joining the RFDS, I had to call on the neonatal retrieval service to collect premature infants I had been involved in delivering.

On arriving in Western Australia, I was surprised to learn that a similar service was not only available in Perth but that an airborne system had been established across the state and the RFDS was part of it. The late Dr Fred Grauaug from King Edward Memorial Hospital for Women had initiated a road service and the RFDS had been involved in development of two air-transportable neonatal cots to service remote areas. This airborne neonatal retrieval capability was one of the first established in Australia.

Two standard aircraft stretcher frames had been modified with special neonatal cots, the Vickers Model 77, in the late 1970s. This cot helped keep the newborn warm, provided oxygen and had an inbuilt simple mechanical ventilator, which could be used to keep the baby breathing adequately. The Vickers units were relatively lightweight and had an internal rechargeable nickel–cadmium battery which would keep the ventilator running when disconnected from power, such as when loading and unloading from the aircraft. This was critical because if the ventilator stopped, the baby stopped breathing.

The heating system drew too much power to be battery powered but would work on either hospital mains power or on our aircraft 28-volt DC power. The stretcher included two large gas bottles, one containing medical oxygen and the other medical air, which was blended to adjust the concentration of oxygen delivered to the infant. All up, the self-contained system weighed about 80 kilograms, to care for a baby which might weigh only 1 kilogram. (The weight of these units hasn't improved since then, with neonatal transport units today weighing well over 100 kilograms as more equipment has been added.)

One of the Vickers systems was kept at our Jandakot Base where it could be used to respond to locations in the southern half of Western Australia, and the second was located in Port

Hedland where it could be used to respond to newborns in the north. Our flight nurses were familiar with the equipment as they checked it every day and, between a small number of nurses, did all the airborne retrieval flights. We usually took a neonatal paediatrician or registrar on the flights as they had the most experience in this specialised area. The combination has worked quite well for many years. While the doctor from the hospital has the expertise in management of a premature infant and in performing procedures, the RFDS flight nurses are familiar with all the aircraft systems, power, communications and loading, and are more seasoned fliers. When the weather was rough, particularly in our unpressurised Piper Navajos, there were many times when the paediatrician would be incapacitated by air sickness while the RFDS flight nurse continued caring for the baby in the cot.

In Port Hedland, we relied on the paediatrician from the hospital to come out and go on flights. In the 1980s and early 1990s there was only one paediatrician on duty seven days a week for the entire region. Flying on our aircraft meant he or she was gone for most of the day. Having completed busy terms of obstetrics and neonates, I accompanied newborns in the Vickers cot on a few occasions when the paediatrician in town had other seriously ill children to manage. These were only those cases that were relatively stable on the ventilator and not severely premature.

Extubation at altitude

On one such flight we were in a Piper Navajo, an unpressurised twin-engine aircraft. We were flying down the middle of the state at 10,000 feet and across the Hamersley Ranges. It was hot and there was the usual moderate turbulence. The flight nurse and I sat in facing seats on the left-hand side of the aircraft with the Vickers cot on the right-hand side, no more than 30 centimetres away, with the two 'portholes' in the Perspex cover through which we could place our hands to access our patient. It was cosy.

Our baby was about 1.5 kilograms and lying in the cot with an endotracheal tube in its trachea and being ventilated. These tubes are very small in a neonate, only a few millimetres in diameter, similar to a ballpoint pen refill. They are secured in place as best as possible with adhesive tape wound around the tube and then across both sides of the infant's face. There is only a centimetre or so leeway from being pushed down too far into only one of the lungs, or pulled back too far and out of the trachea above the vocal cords. If the tube is kinked, pulled out or disconnected, your means of ventilating the baby is lost.

Compared to the small diameter of this endotracheal tube, the connection pieces and hoses which join it to the ventilator are quite large. So you have the baby's head, a tiny short segment of endotracheal tube coming out of the mouth or nose, and then another relatively large connection valve. It is important to position these well so there is no kinking or traction on the endotracheal tube.

There we were, droning along on what was to be a two-and-a-half hour flight to our refuelling stop at Meekatharra when suddenly, WHAM! The whole aircraft rose dramatically and then fell away as we hit a large pocket of turbulence. The flight nurse and I both rose in our seats and hit our heads on the roof, but fortunately we were partly restrained by the seatbelts which we had learnt to wear at all times. Not so for the small baby.

I have a vivid recollection in slow motion how, as we rose from our seats, the infant likewise became airborne inside the cot. It struck the clear lid and then thudded back down onto the mattress with the tube pulled out, all at the same time. Aaaaargh! Suddenly we had lost the airway and the ventilator would no longer be ventilating the baby properly.

How do you deal with this in a small cramped aircraft in flight? There is no room to easily intubate the neonate in the cot *and we needed to stay restrained in our seats in case of further violent bumps. I grabbed a pillow and put it on my knees while the flight nurse removed the baby from the cot and laid it on the pillow in front of me. We tried with a self-inflating bag to ventilate the child through the tube but it was clearly not working, so we removed it quickly and commenced bagging the baby with a mask. I then proceeded to re-intubate this child as it lay on my knees. It's an interesting technique but you can raise or lower your knees to bring the child into a better position as you try to pass the endotracheal tube down a very small hole around the tongue and through the vocal cords. In these small patients we usually pass it down through the nose as, once it is in place, it is easier to strap across the nose and face than a tube coming out of the mouth.*

We were successful in re-intubating the child, securing the new tube and reconnecting to the ventilator. It all went well and the baby appeared less affected by this sudden emergency than we were. Thereafter, I determined we couldn't let this sort of thing happen again so we invented a neonatal 'seatbelt'. It was simply some velcro straps which we could put across the infant and the ventilator hoses to keep them all secure in the event of future turbulence in flight.

The Vickers 77 cots served us well for nearly twenty years. Further monitoring was added as it became fashionable and then replaced when something new arose. One such technology was TCM (transcutaneous monitoring), a means of estimating the oxygen and carbon dioxide levels. In any serious ill patient, particularly with respiratory disease or being artificially ventilated, knowing the blood levels of oxygen and CO_2 are important in guiding treatment. The best way to measure this is by taking an arterial blood sample and analysing the concentrations of each. A means of obtaining the information that did not require taking repeated blood samples was highly sought after.

The technique of TCM was developed on the basis that if a small area of skin is heated, oxygen and CO_2 are released and these can be analysed with a sensor applied to the skin. While not an exact measurement of arterial gases, it provides a guide to whether oxygen and CO_2 levels are rising or falling in the patient. We first started using the TCM technique in the late 1980s. It was fiddly to apply the electrodes and gel but the results were helpful. It went out of fashion, particularly when pulse oximetry came in, but like many things in medicine, the pendulum has swung back and thirty years later an improved version of the technology is again in use.

In the late 1990s, it became apparent that we needed to update our Vickers neonatal cots. Dr Corrado Minutillo, who was in charge of the WANTS (WA Neonatal Transport Service), and Mr John Stasiw, head of biomedical engineering at Princess Margaret Hospital, embarked on a plan to build six new units from the ground up. We worked together to do everything possible to minimise the weight of the new neonate units, while ensuring that the equipment and controls were easily accessible by clinical staff in flight and there were no obstructions when loading in and out of aircraft or road vehicles.

Whatever was built had to be compatible with a variety of aircraft and road ambulance stretchers. A design was proposed that had a flat base and was universal in terms of what stretcher it would fit on; indeed, the concept was that it should be able to fit on any stretcher and be restrained using the seatbelts normally applied to patients. The concept worked well but it was still heavy. Smaller gas cylinders were used together with smaller, lighter monitors and a minimalist frame. However, the incubator component, including battery power, was still a significant weight. They weighed around 140 kilograms all up and needed six people to lift them. At our bases we eventually installed a hoist in each of our hangars to lift the unit on and off our stretchers.

We launched the units in February 1999, with each one given a name for someone who had contributed significantly to neonatal care in Western Australia. 'Paddy' was for Dr Paddy Pemberton, head of the neonatal NICU (intensive care unit) at PMH for many years, and 'Fred' was for Dr Fred Grauaug from NICU at King Edward Memorial Hospital, who had introduced neonatal retrieval to Western Australia in the 1970s.

They worked well for five to six years until the new director of WANTS decided to purchase a new style of cot developed in Queensland. Groan. We had the system and procedures running smoothly and here we were, about to change again. The attraction was that the proposed units were supposed to be much lighter in weight (around 80 kg) and some of the existing equipment could be swapped across to the new Mansell Neocots, saving costs for PMH. The cots had been designed by engineers at the University of Southern Queensland. The clever way they had saved weight was to redesign the incubator. Instead of using a 40 kg neonatal cot, they decided that a lightweight acrylic 'bread box' with a heating unit inside was all that was needed. Considerable weight was saved but by the time the new units were all configured with additional monitoring equipment and a Stephan® ventilator weighing 12 kg, they weighed over 100 kg again!

An assumption was made that as these were used in Queensland on RFDS aircraft, they would be compatible with WA aircraft. Unfortunately, stretchers are different in most states of Australia. As we were using the Pilatus PC-12 with a much higher crashworthiness rating than the King Airs used in Queensland, we had to use a completely different stretcher type. Considerable effort goes into marrying up the medical needs of patients with the requirements for aircraft certification. There are also occupational health and safety issues to evaluate when it comes to lifting and loading.

Dr Steven Resnick inherited the role of director of WANTS, renamed NETSWA (Neonatal Emergency Transport Service WA).

After a couple more years of modifications and stretcher interfaces, we now have a system that works satisfactorily and is compatible with both road and aircraft stretchers. A shorter version of this same system was acquired by PMH to use on the Rio Tinto *LifeFlight* jet for interstate transfers.

Surfactant

One of the most important problems in premature babies is immaturity of the lungs. Without having had time to develop fully, the lungs are prone to cause breathing difficulties at birth. Lungs are like delicate sponges containing millions of tiny air sacs or alveoli. When these sacs expand there is a natural tendency for them to collapse again due to surface tension from their moisture lining. A substance produced by mature lungs called surfactant reduces the tendency of the lungs to collapse, but in premature infants this is not present in sufficient quantities.

The development of artificial surfactant occurred in the early 1990s and enabled our neonatal colleagues to better manage respiratory distress syndrome in infants prior to transport. It was very expensive and had to be given in a very controlled setting under paediatric supervision, as it involved an aerosolised form of this greasy liquid being squirted into the lungs of a baby already in respiratory distress. Yet, it worked; its cost was less than our flying costs and it could ensure a better outcome for babies, which of course was everyone's goal.

Nitric oxide – not a laughing matter

Many people will have heard of nitrous oxide (chemical symbol N_2O), commonly referred to as 'laughing gas'. It is a gaseous anaesthetic agent with analgesic properties that can cause a sense of euphoria in those who inhale it. It was once commonly used by dentists and in obstetric and anaesthetic practice, and occasionally by medical students for pranks. There was a short period in the

1980s when we tried to use the Entonox® system to deliver a mixture of nitrous oxide and oxygen to patients, particularly maternity patients in labour. Our midwife flight nurses were familiar with it and it provided fast, short-duration pain relief during contractions.

Nitrous oxide has two problems in an aeromedical environment, however. The first is that the analgesic properties are less effective at altitude. This is because the concentration (partial pressure) of the gas in the bloodstream is much less. The second problem is that it can diffuse into areas of the body containing air: for example, the bowel, collapsed lungs, the middle ear or sinuses. It is then slow to diffuse out, causing pain and pressure effects with altitude changes. Overall, it is cumbersome to carry and use, and not very useful in airborne medical care.

Nitric oxide (chemical symbol NO) is different and not as much fun. Exposure of adults to large concentrations of nitric oxide can cause sore eyes, coughing and headache. Nitric oxide stimulates vasodilation of blood vessels, which leads to increased blood flow. This is the mechanism by which common angina medications (sprays or tablets under the tongue) or drugs for erectile dysfunction do their work. With that heritage, it is somewhat surprising that it can be used by inhalation, in very small doses, in neonates and other intensive care patients with pulmonary hypertension or other lung disorders. The opening up of blood flow to the lungs is beneficial in improving oxygenation in these very sick patients.

The neonatal transport units were modified to restrain the gas cylinders safely as well as the control system, which allowed the very small amounts (measured in parts per million) to be delivered into the infant's ventilator circuit at an accurate dose rate. In the event of an accident, nobody wants these flying through the cabin.

Not surprisingly, the idea of carrying this reactive gas in an enclosed aircraft and administering it to a patient was quite concerning for aviation regulatory authorities. Despite very small babies actually breathing the nitric oxide, we had to consider the effects of the exhaled gas and the small but potential risk of the cylinder leaking and the entire cabin being filled with the nitric oxide. This could potentially cause incapacitation of the pilot, with symptoms such as headache and difficulty with vision.

So we needed to obtain a variety of certifications and put emergency procedures in place in case the cylinder accidently emptied its contents into the cabin all at once. This required testing in an aircraft on the ground, emptying a cylinder of nitric oxide into the cabin by remote control then measuring the concentration in the cabin. The work was done by Aeronautical Engineers Australia in Adelaide and we were fortunately able to share the research findings for our own Pilatus PC-12 aircraft in Western Australia.

When we fly with nitric oxide on board, a portable gas monitor is placed near the pilot's instrument panel to provide a warning if a high concentration is detected, due to an unobserved leak. The pilot will don his or her emergency oxygen mask if this occurs. A similar alarm is also carried on the neonatal cot in the cabin. So far, no problems have ever arisen.

With all this technology, we certainly make a big fuss over tiny things.

Long distance, small packages
Transporting cardiac babies across the country

Princess Margaret Hospital for Children in Perth (soon to relocate to a new Perth Children's Hospital) is a highly regarded tertiary paediatric hospital. With our Western Australian population just one-tenth of the entire nation, only a small number of complex heart abnormalities arise in newborn babies each year. It is difficult to maintain specialist surgical expertise with low numbers, so certain babies need to be moved to larger interstate centres for surgery. This has been the case for decades and will likely continue.

When we established the Rio Tinto *LifeFlight* jet, one of the roles I was keen for it to play was to assist with the transport of seriously ill cardiac babies to the eastern states for surgery. The previous system had been suboptimal. A transport could occur only when there was a scheduled commercial flight to the required interstate destination and at least three rows of seats were available. If there were delays on the ground, they could adversely affect the critically ill neonate. Likewise, problems with the baby could potentially delay the flight and all the other passengers. Large commercial aircraft do not have medical oxygen, suction or power available and loading all the required equipment is difficult. Airlines like Qantas tried to accommodate the needs of the neonatal team but it was never as good as a dedicated on-demand service.

When our jet service was established, we were able to offer the teams caring for these small babies the chance to fly on a properly configured medical aircraft. They could depart when it best suited them to go to whatever destination was necessary. There was enough room to carry a paediatrician, two nurses and a family member if required. The transfer could usually be accomplished in a round trip on a single day without an overnight stay.

These cardiac babies are very sick with life-threatening problems receiving very delicate and precise neonatal intensive care. What I liked about the idea was that after loading the baby and specialised equipment onto the aircraft, the team could take their time, making sure everything was in order and the baby stable. When they were ready, the jet could taxi, blast off and be in Melbourne in less than four hours.

We expected to have only about ten such flights per year but they would arise at random intervals. Over the first two years, we accomplished a number of them very successfully.

Dash under the ash

It was 15 June 2011 and the eruptions of a volcano in Iceland had sent a huge cloud of volcanic ash swirling around the planet. I woke in the morning and heard the news that this ash cloud was coming up from the south and was likely to have a significant impact on flying out of Perth and the southwest of Western Australia. Already there was talk of Perth Airport being shut down to regular public transport flights and I started to think about a neonate with a heart condition who we were planning to fly to Melbourne for cardiac surgery the next day.

We had an urgent meeting first up that morning to discuss the impact of the ash cloud on our operations across the state. Fortunately, it was not going to be a big problem in the north but for aircraft coming south, there could be issues landing in Perth.

Our Chief Pilot, Captain Michael Bleus, was monitoring the meteorological situation and confirmed that we could continue to fly our PC-12 aircraft, provided we kept them below about 15,000 feet. Above this, the ash cloud extended to an altitude of over 30,000 feet and there was concern about the potential impact of volcanic ash on aircraft engines.

Most aviators are aware of the legendary tale of a British Airways Boeing 747, which lost all four engines over Indonesia when it flew through volcanic ash. Even if there was no failure of the engines, there was potential for extensive damage to turbines from gritty ash particles. It was not unreasonable for our smaller PC-12 to remain in the clearer air below 15,000 feet, but much larger passenger aircraft could not operate that low and it would result in significant extra fuel consumption.

As we sat around the board table, I asked what could we do about our jet flight the following day? The situation was not going to improve and, indeed, likely to be much worse. Current predictions were that this would last some days and Qantas flights out of Perth were already being cancelled. I knew that our baby was not getting better; if we missed the opportunity to transfer it, the child may not survive.

Flying a commercial jet is normally done at altitudes of 30,000 to 40,000 feet to make the most of speed, range and weather. However, a jet is still just an aircraft and potentially could fly low, at least until it cleared the extent of the ash cloud. This is where having an understanding of both aviation and medicine makes a difference. I phoned my colleague Dr Steven Resnick in the neonatal unit and explained the situation. We both knew this baby needed urgent cardiac surgery and a couple of days' delay might be fatal. Could they stabilise the child and be ready to transport by lunchtime if I could organise the flight? 'Yes, if we have to', was the reply.

Our Rio Tinto LifeFlight jet was operated for us by Maroomba Airlines, established and owned by Captain Steve Young. Always a pragmatic individual, I phoned him and told him we needed to get the baby on its way to Melbourne before it was too late and asked if they could do it straight away. He told me that Perth Airport was now closed to all large commercial airliners so it was too late.

Never one to accept 'No' the first time, I hassled him about why couldn't we fly below 15,000 feet to keep under the ash, at least as far as, say, Kalgoorlie? Then the jet could refuel and fly at normal altitudes to Melbourne? Bugger the extra fuel burn – we really needed to have this baby moved! Sure, it is not normal practice to do so, but the aircraft is capable of flying that way. He agreed to have a look at the meteorology report and see if it might be possible.

The rest, as they say, is history. Almost every media team in Perth was at the airport interviewing disgruntled passengers whose flights had been cancelled. When the news got out that the RFDS jet was actually going to take off on a mercy mission to transfer a small baby to Melbourne, they broke into a frenzy. Hordes of media and cameras flocked to the hangar where we based our jet to film a piece of the action and provide a new angle on the news.

I let drop that we were making a 'dash under the ash' to fly this cardiac baby to surgery and it became an instant headline. We earned some great publicity but, most importantly, baby Bevan reached Melbourne and received the life-saving surgery needed.

The flight went pretty much to plan and our tiny patient was successfully treated despite needing complex cardiac surgery. The family have been fabulous supporters of the RFDS ever since and never flinch at coming to events or giving interviews when we need help with fundraising events.

Premature payloads: labouring under a misconception
Transporting women in labour over long distances by air

Starting in the late 1970s, there were some remarkable advances in neonatal intensive care, which continued to push down the age at which a premature infant was likely to be 'viable'. It meant that for a woman who went into labour very early, the outcome she could expect for her baby was better, but usually only in a specialised centre. While the exact cause of early labour in most patients is unknown, there are many factors associated with the onset of premature labour. There are also some drugs which can help stop labour, or at least suppress it for a while. One of these is the common asthma drug salbutamol, though used in much higher doses.

When I first went to Port Hedland, fresh from an obstetric post, the idea of putting a woman in labour into an aircraft to fly her nearly 1,500 kilometres to Perth seemed preposterous. Even in my previous post where I was only 50 kilometres from Melbourne, we would first deliver the premature infant and then seek a NETS team retrieval if the outcome was satisfactory. Yet, after starting in the North West, I realised I was labouring under a misconception, if you'll excuse the pun. I discovered that some women could be safely flown to Perth without delivering, if we maximised the dose of salbutamol we gave them.

The benefits were very clear. The best way of transporting a baby around is inside the mother's uterus. There was plenty of evidence, even in the early 1980s, that the outcome of infants born in non-specialist or country hospitals and transported later was inferior to those delivered in a specialised tertiary centre in a capital city. Once a premature infant is born, it needs to be very carefully cared for and can become cold, hypoxic and hypo-glycaemic quickly. In particular, premature infants usually have immature lungs. Their breathing and oxygenation can deteriorate significantly without specialised neonatal ventilators and advanced respiratory support techniques.

So if we were to achieve the best outcome for our patients in preterm labour in the most distant parts of the state, we had to try to transfer them to Perth undelivered. It took quite a while to convince doctors and others that this was possible and we have to continue to coach them to this day. It is so easy just to say, 'Oh no, that's too risky', but this then commits the woman to having a suboptimal outcome for her child.

We instituted an aggressive treatment regimen with salbutamol given intravenously and I did dozens of flights initially, pushing the dose up until we stopped the contractions and successfully transferred the patients to Perth intact. They would experience a rapid pulse while they were on the drug and develop the shakes, which were direct pharmacological effects; but we achieved an enviable result in that nearly all low and very low birthweight infants from across the state were delivered in just one hospital, King Edward Memorial Hospital in Perth. The outcomes for these babies are superior to those small numbers of premature neonates who are out-born and suffer long transfers in neonatal cots to Perth over many hours.

People new to this process worry that the pregnant woman will deliver in flight. With great flight nurses, all of whom are midwives, and our salbutamol regimen, this just does not happen. Sure, if a patient arrives at the airstrip about to have her baby, then our staff do not take off. They return the patient to the hospital or, very rarely, deliver them at the airport! However, once on board the aircraft, inflight delivery is rare.

We have evacuated approximately 500 women with complications of pregnancy every year for the past 30 years. Not all these patients are in premature labour and may have other complications including haemorrhage, high blood pressure (pre-eclampsia) or obstructed labour. Over that period, and with a database of around 15,000 patients, we have had about 10 deliveries during flight, and almost every one of these women was at 'term', not in premature labour. Likewise, we have had no significant complications from the treatment regimen.

My view has been that when we 'buy time' by suppressing labour, every hour that we delay delivery equates to getting the patient 400 kilometres closer to Perth in our modern turboprop aircraft. We managed to cope in the days of slower piston-engine Navajos where it was a five to six-hour flight from the Pilbara. So now, when it takes just over three hours, it is relatively easier. Most flights are conducted by a flight nurse alone, usually with a second patient on board.

We have published two research papers in the medical literature, one in 1988 and another in 2012, demonstrating our success with this process. It was born out of necessity. Where else in the world are women in labour put in an aircraft and flown up to 2,000 kilometres to a tertiary hospital? The distances are akin to Rome to London, Washington to Miami, or Brisbane to Melbourne. Our geography and distribution of hospitals necessitates this process and we continue to carry it out successfully.

No one gets it right all the time, so it is fair to outline one of the challenging cases where the outcome was not so rosy.

Problem with prematurity

I was working at our Jandakot Base in Perth in the early 1990s when we received a call to retrieve a young girl in premature labour from Karratha. She was only sixteen and, as the story unfolded, had been sent out from Ireland to live with relatives in Karratha because of the shame of being pregnant out of wedlock. From a contemporary perspective, it is hard to appreciate that this was a significant issue for the family at the time and in Ireland, where termination of pregnancy was not an option. My understanding was that the plan was for her to have the baby in Australia and have it adopted out; but of course, we did not discuss these things with her.

The referring GP noted that she was very premature, perhaps 28 weeks or fewer, but he was not sure as she had not had any antenatal care in Australia yet, nor an ultrasound scan. Her case was complicated by premature rupture of the membranes and a fever, suggesting intrauterine infection. Due to the prematurity and potential complications from intrauterine sepsis, she needed to be in a tertiary hospital in Perth. There was limited obstetric care where she was and no local specialist. The aircraft and crew at the nearest base in Port Hedland were busy, so the only option was for us to fly up from Perth. This would be about three hours each way in a pressurised Cessna Conquest, plus the time to flight plan and the handover time on the ground in Karratha. It was going to be close from the start but we needed to give it our best shot, as there were no other reasonable options.

I was flying with Flight Nurse Joanne Gorey, with whom I had worked many times before. We reached Karratha in the middle of the day and handed over at the airport in the sizzling heat.

With a very premature baby and the membranes already ruptured, we did not do an internal examination of the patient for fear of stirring things up. However, we did confirm she had a fever and made sure she had received antibiotics and was on a salbutamol infusion to slow her contractions down.

We took off and headed to Perth. Despite trying to suppress her labour it was clear she would need to deliver as soon as she reached a tertiary hospital as continuation of the pregnancy at this stage was not an option. As the flight progressed and with about an hour to go, Joanne started to become concerned that the patient was close to delivering. Little indications like curling up her toes and wanting to push were tell-tale signs. We hung in there, with our fingers crossed, as there was really not much else we could do. We had our salbutamol running at full dosage and radioed ahead to see if another flight nurse could be ready to help on our arrival.

As the aircraft descended to make a straight-in approach and landing at Jandakot Airport, Joanne could see a 'head on view'. We touched down and the pilot taxied to a quick stop outside the hangar where we delivered a very premature-looking baby.

Past experience and a bit of adrenaline kicked in. I managed to intubate the baby with our smallest endotracheal tube. We were also able to insert an intravenous line into the stump of the umbilical cord and keep ventilating the infant. Another nurse brought over the specialised neonatal cot. I set up the neonate on the ventilator quickly and we raced the baby to the neonatal unit at Princess Margaret Hospital by road ambulance.

On arrival they weighed the child and, to our surprise, found it to be only 550 grams: extremely premature and at the absolute limits of viability.

Later in the day we heard that the child was not doing well, was septic and would not survive. The young mother had a partly retained placenta but fortunately made a satisfactory physical recovery in King Edward obstetric hospital.

In Perth, at least she received the best medical care and would have had access to staff with expertise in providing emotional support at such a difficult time.

Airways in the airborne
Advanced airway management

If you complete the most basic of first aid courses, you will learn about the A-B-Cs of resuscitation: airway, breathing and circulation. It should not be surprising that managing the airway is top of the list in advanced resuscitation and emergency care also. We encounter generally two types of problem. The first group are patients where there is a risk to patency of the airway, from trauma, blood or just heavy sedation. We need to ensure we keep the anatomical region from lips to larynx open so that the patient can continue breathing unobstructed. The other group of problems are cases where the patient is critically ill or in respiratory failure and we need to provide respiratory support to help them breathe in and out. This is usually managed by intubating them: inserting a tube into the trachea and placing the patient on a mechanical ventilator to keep them breathing.

In all these cases, an inability to 'secure' the airway can lead to obstruction or inability to ventilate the patient. This is life-threatening and needs to be dealt with quickly and reliably. Anaesthetists spend many years training in different techniques to deal with difficult airways and have many devices at their disposal in a hospital. They also have the ability to plan a range of measures for managing patients who are having an elective procedure.

In the emergency care situation, and particularly in our remote practice, our options are more limited. We don't have the range of staff and equipment of a large hospital in our aircraft and we usually don't have a choice whether to intervene, or much time to plan our approach.

For many decades the basics of airway management involved using a bag and mask applied to the face, or intubation with a standard laryngoscope. The laryngoscope is a bit like a torch. It has a metal handle containing batteries and a long curved blade with a light bulb near the tip. The laryngoscope, as the name implies, allows you to see over the tongue and down to the larynx, which is the opening through which an endotracheal must be inserted to enter the lungs. The technique has been in use for a long time but can have problems. When patients have small jaws, limited mouth opening, large tongues, fat short necks, blood or vomit in the pharynx, or numerous other problems, it can be extremely difficult or impossible to intubate them in the conventional manner.

Over the years, doctors have trained in a variety of manoeuvres to pass the endotracheal tube through the vocal cords into the trachea. Once this is achieved, a cuff surrounding the end of the endotracheal tube is inflated and the tube is then secure. In between attempts to do this, one has to resort to ventilating the patient with a bag and mask to keep their oxygen levels up. This can go on for some time.

A serious problem arises if you find that you can no longer adequately ventilate the patient by any means and can't intubate them either. If they don't breathe, they will die. In such an emergency, a 'surgical airway' is needed. This is a diplomatic way of saying you have to cut their throat, just below the larynx, and insert a tube into their lungs through the neck. This is called a cricothyroidotomy or tracheotomy.

The decision to undertake the procedure is probably more challenging than the procedure itself. It takes confidence to bail out and say to yourself, 'I need to do this', rather than keep persevering as the patient deteriorates.

I count myself lucky that I have never had to do a surgical airway other than in training, but a few of my RFDS colleagues have. I have sweated it out but always managed to sneak the tube through the cords the conventional way.

Rescued from a rock fall

One of my colleagues in the Eastern Goldfields RFDS was the legendary Dr Peter Carroll. His reputation extended not just to his work activities. It was on one of the routine flying clinics he attended in the late 1980s that he was called to assist a miner who had been injured in a rock fall in an open cut mine. As he was on a clinic, Peter did not have a flight nurse with him or much emergency equipment. The patient had received a massive blow to his face from a rock. Both his jaw and lower face bones were badly fractured and there was uncontrolled bleeding coming from the mouth in the nearly unconscious patient.

In a tale typical of the flying doctors, Peter gave some sedation, cut the patient's throat, inserted a plastic tube into the trachea and connected it up so that he could ventilate the patient with a resuscitation bag. He found a wad of women's sanitary pads and packed them down into the mouth and throat to stop the bleeding. The patient needed to have a cervical collar on, to splint his neck in case it was fractured, but the cervical collars did not have an opening for the tube coming out of the patient's neck. So Peter got his scalpel and carved a hole in the plastic collar so it would fit.

With an IV line inserted and intravenous fluids pumping, doctor and patient got into the aircraft to fly straight to Perth. You can imagine the reception in the emergency department at Royal Perth Hospital. The patient covered in blood and dirt with a tube sticking out of his neck and pads out of his mouth — but alive and in a relatively stable condition, having flown 500 kilometres direct from the accident site. The doctor was looking just as dirty and scruffy but cool as a cucumber. Another day's work with the RFDS!

A vicious assault

I was on duty one day when I received a call from a solo GP in a Wheatbelt town. A woman had been attacked by her partner. He had swung an axe at her while she was standing, seemingly in an attempt to decapitate her. The axe had gone high and been embedded in the side of her face, causing a massive deep injury from her left ear through her cheek down to her mouth. The side of the face was an open wound with blood, mushy tissue and bone fragments gaping from the hole.

There have been times as a flying doctor when I have questioned man's inhumanity to man. How could someone have intentionally done this sort of thing to another person?

We flew out as quickly as possible, arriving at the airstrip during daylight, and were greeted by the volunteer ambulance, with a senior hospital nurse in the back. They had driven 50 kilometres to the airstrip to meet us. The poor patient was lying on the stretcher, unconscious but breathing and with a huge blood-soaked combine pad over the wound. One quick look confirmed my fears: this was a really serious injury, the likes of which I had never seen before. The side of the face was literally laid wide open.

It was not just the severity of the injury that concerned me, but the knowledge that this woman was likely to obstruct and we had to secure the airway before we could move her. It was too far to travel back to the hospital, so we would have to do it there in the ambulance at the airstrip.

I was pretty stressed. It was hot, the ambulance was cramped and this was by far the most difficult airway I had ever encountered.

I was going to have to manage it in less than ideal circumstances with just the help of the flight nurse. If I failed, I might have to cut a tracheotomy, which was just as daunting an alternative.

The flight nurse raced back to the aircraft and started bringing all the gear we needed over to the ambulance, while I tried to examine the injury, protect the airway and plan my approach. I checked that the IV was running, drew up some drugs to provide sedation and muscle paralysis, and checked that the suction and oxygen were all ready at hand. This is when the teamwork between an RFDS doctor and flight nurse is critical. You have plenty to think about and must trust the nurse to remember things you might have overlooked, to anticipate what you are likely to do and what you are going to need.

I relaxed a bit and proceeded to intubate the patient. Despite the horrendous injury, the face was very loose and it was relatively easy to identify the vocal cords and insert the endotracheal tube. We secured it in place, connected the patient to our ventilator and packed the wound with combine pads to control the bleeding. The patient was successfully transferred and arrived at Royal Perth Hospital in pretty good condition, considering everything. However, there were a few stunned looks from the emergency department staff when they saw what we had dealt with in getting the patient to them alive. Unfortunately, the outcome was not so fine. The injuries to the face and neck structures were extensive and unfortunately the patient succumbed to them in the following days.

New gadgets to manage difficult airways

In the late 1980s a British anaesthetist invented a new device, the LMA (Laryngeal Mask Airway). This was like an endotracheal tube but instead of having to go through the vocal cords into the trachea, there was an inflatable cushion on the end. The cushion sat inside the throat but over the larynx like a small mask. When inflated it achieved a reasonable seal, enough to enable ventilation. We adopted these LMA tubes promptly. In an emergency, even if you could not intubate the patient, you could usually place an LMA. They did not completely protect the patient's lungs from inhaling blood or other secretions but at least the patient could be kept breathing.

Over the years, gadgets have arisen to help perform a surgical airway more quickly and slickly. One of the first we used was the Portex Mini-Trach® set. As the name implies, it was a mini-tracheotomy kit. It contained a small scalpel to cut a hole in the throat and a tube to insert as the airway. The tube was really too narrow to enable effective continuous ventilation in an adult, but the fact that everything came in a pre-packed sterile kit meant that it was quick and easy to use when a surgical airway was needed. We introduced these in the 1990s to all our aircraft.

Because a cricothyroidotomy or tracheotomy tube enters the neck and doesn't have to go all the way from the mouth into the trachea, they can be quite short and about the size of a curved little finger. More gadgets were developed, such as the Rusch Quicktrach® and the Melker Cricothyroidotomy kit. The former was a tracheotomy tube with a very sharp stainless steel needle inside which was inserted into the neck just below the Adam's apple. The Melker system, which we adopted, enabled us to start the process with a needle and then dilate up the hole so that the tube could be slid in. Alternatively, a scalpel could be used to cut down through the cricothyroid membrane and the tube could be inserted directly into the trachea. The benefit of the kits was that everything came pre-packed and ready to go, and thought had been given to making the sets and the procedure as streamlined as possible.

In recent years, particularly with fibre-optics and cheap high-resolution LED screens, better laryngoscopes have been developed. What I used in the 1980s had a small light bulb near the end of the blade. You had to make sure it was properly screwed on so it did not come off down the patient's throat and the level of illumination was as poor as an average household torch. Fibre-optics meant that the light source did not have to be at the tip of the laryngoscope blade anymore but could be further back in the handle and more powerful.

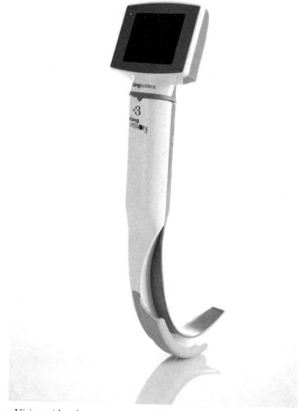

King Vision video-laryngoscope with LED screen and disposable blades.

With advances in electronics, it became economical to produce laryngoscopes with an inbuilt camera in the blade tip. Instead of having to look down the throat and see the vocal cords directly, you now could insert the laryngoscope and watch the image 'indirectly' on a small video screen. Some of these devices started at $10,000 to 20,000 but by 2012, the cost of a small handheld video-laryngoscope was under $1,000. It was fabulous. They had disposable plastic blades with an inbuilt camera and light source, which fitted on a battery-powered handle with a small colour LED screen on top. After use, rather than sterilize them, you just threw the blades away as they were so cheap.

This was clearly a great new piece of technology to introduce to our aircraft. It was compact, lightweight and provided another relatively easy method of securing the difficult airway, rather than moving to a surgical one. A number of our doctors have used the King Vision® video-laryngoscope to great effect, to resolve some very difficult cases and save lives. We are currently looking at disposable flexible fibre-optic scopes. The days of the conventional direct laryngoscope may well be numbered.

An alarming situation
A novel in-house oxygen failure alarm

It is all very well to have the latest ventilators but if the oxygen system on the aircraft fails, is turned off, or the supply runs out, our ability to mechanically ventilate a patient ceases. I have insisted that our aircraft oxygen system is designed so that we cannot have all supplies of medical oxygen connected at once. Enforcing this level of redundancy in our aircraft fit-out ensures that if there is a massive leak, such as a burst hose or defective fitting, we will still have one cylinder of medical oxygen to spare.

Failure of the oxygen supply can be insidious and occur initially without being noticed. Our clinical staff pay special attention to oxygen supplies in flight, particularly with critically ill, ventilated patients, but there is still a risk of failure, particularly in a noisy aircraft, in bad weather, or with a difficult patient distracting their attention. The idea of having an alarm to warn of a fall in oxygen pressure makes sense.

The basic Oxylog ventilator we first operated in the 1980s had no electrical power and no alarms. There was no option to purchase an off-the-shelf device that would warn us of oxygen failure or a ventilator failure. I put this problem as a challenge to Captain Greg Schouten, a clever pilot with an interest in electronics, and encouraged him to see what he could do. With a little experimentation, he came up with an elegantly simple solution. There was a fitting that we connected into the ventilator circuit and a short piece of tubing joining it to a box containing a pressure sensor, the electronic circuitry and a buzzer. The device monitored the fluctuations in pressure with each breath. If there was no change in pressure over about eight seconds it would alarm, as this meant either the oxygen had run out, the ventilator had stopped, or the circuit (patient hose) had disconnected somewhere.

All up it was going to cost about $100 per unit. 'Terrific', I thought, 'let's do it!' Unfortunately, other views prevailed. We would need product liability insurance of some sort in case the device failed and there was an adverse outcome. After all, this was to be used as an alarm on a critical piece of life-support equipment.

'Hold on', I protested. This was to help warn of an equipment failure. At that time, we had nothing and so were at risk. The likelihood of the ventilator or oxygen failing, and then the alarm itself failing, was much lower than the risk of the failure in the first instance. Surely, it would be better to have something rather than nothing? Yet, I lost the argument.

I put the device away in a cupboard and pulled it out occasionally to play with it. Over at least 20 years we did nothing to solve the problem. Newer ventilators came with alarms to warn of an oxygen failure or other errors, but we still didn't have any warning about failure of one of the key systems in a medical installation.

In the mid-2000s, I was enthused again after a minor incident in which the aircraft medical oxygen was turned off by mistake. I contacted the major gas suppliers to hospitals and engaged them to develop a compact version of the gas warning panels they put into hospital medical gas installations. It took ages to do and because it was for an aircraft, there were additional certification requirements for power supplies, restraint of the device, plumbing it into aircraft oxygen lines and the like. We got nowhere.

So I asked Greg again if he could build a small box with a loud audible alarm and flashing light, which would automatically turn on when the oxygen lines were pressurised and then alarm if the pressure fell below a set threshold. He came up with a similar device, but this time, with the help of our engineering team including guys like Rob Howe, we had it certified and installed in all our PC-12 aircraft. This was a small but very important innovation to enhance the safety of our patients in flight. Perseverance eventually pays off.

A bloody good idea
Dealing with haemorrhage and blood loss

There are many medical procedures we do on the ground which we can do in flight if we have to; it's just harder to do them. As an example, we can insert vascular lines and chest drains, or anaesthetise and intubate a patient. However, we don't have the skills or facilities to do any surgery. While we can provide a high level of critical care to most patients, if they have a surgical problem, which involves internal bleeding, we are unable to stop it easily.

Perhaps one of the most distressing elements of our emergency work is having a patient slowly exsanguinating but being unable to control the bleeding. Most people are aware that if a patient has a large wound, direct pressure and dressings will control the bleeding. But what can you do when the bleeding is deep inside the body in an inaccessible location and not amenable to pressure or bandages?

There are options to help deal with this challenge, albeit none of them offers the perfect solution. They include minimising movement which may contribute to ongoing blood loss (for example, by splinting fractures); ensuring coagulation status is as good as possible (for example, by reversing anticoagulant drugs); or managing the blood pressure so it is not too high (which increases blood loss), but not too low (which results in damage to vital organs).

In some circumstances, the bleeding may be confined in a body cavity and will settle with gentle handling if we allow the body's clotting mechanisms to do their job. In other situations, such as severe haemorrhage after childbirth, we can use drugs to stimulate the uterus to clamp down and help control blood loss.

Splints

Some fractured bones can bleed extensively, particularly the bones of the pelvis and the femur (thighbone). For long bones such as the femur, the best means of stabilising them is to apply traction. When I first started in the RFDS, there were a couple of traction splints we used: the Hare splint and the Donway splint.

Hare traction splint.

The Hare splint comprised two long telescopic metal rods with a padded transverse bar at one end, which you situated under the patient's buttock, and a ratchet device at the other end. We would apply an ankle strap, attach it to the ratchet and start cranking, which applied increasing traction to the lower leg. Although this all sounds a bit medieval, it worked quite well, providing strong traction, stabilising the fracture and, in turn, reducing the bleeding into the thigh.

An innovative alternative was the Donway splint, which had a similar structure comprising two long metallic tubes connected to a transverse bar at the buttock end. The foot end was a U-shaped tube that lengthened pneumatically. It looked a bit like a trombone in design and we used a bicycle pump to increase the pressure in the splint, which increased the degree to which it expanded and the amount of traction provided.

These worked well but were large to store and relatively heavy. More recently we adopted a very compact lightweight splint called the CT-6, which weighs under 500 grams and is less than 30 centimetres in length when folded. It is made of a number of carbon-fibre rod segments that join together like a portable fishing rod. A string and pulley system provide the traction at the foot end.

T-pod pelvic splint.

When the bones of the pelvis are fractured, internal blood loss of a couple of litres can occur. The pelvis is a structural ring with the vertebrae attached at the back and each leg below. To provide effective temporary splinting, circumferential traction is the key.

In the past, this was achieved crudely with bed sheets wrapped around the pelvic area and tensioned. In the 2000s we adopted a device called the T-pod. It resembles the corsets and women's garments of the eighteenth and nineteenth centuries in that there is a padded band applied around the pelvis at hip level, then tightened by pulling on a series of strings. Lightweight, disposable and relatively easy to apply, it does an excellent job until the patient arrives in hospital.

Unfortunately, when patients are bleeding into a large cavity such as the abdomen, it is not possible to apply pressure or control the source and patients need urgent surgery. The sorts of problems that severely challenge us are ectopic pregnancies, ruptures of the liver or spleen, bleeding peptic ulcers or oesophageal varices. We can try all the measures above to mitigate the bleeding but need to transfuse blood to compensate for that being lost. This can be a problem in rural and remote areas and in emergency settings. When we fly to an accident site hundreds of kilometres away, where there is no hospital, we don't usually have any blood products available to us. Indeed, many small country hospitals do not stock blood products either. They need to be constantly replaced with fresh supplies every two to three weeks and will not be used regularly if there is no surgery or obstetrics being undertaken.

In the late 1980s, we had two cases at Meekatharra Hospital in close succession where patients bled to death. One was a motorbike rider who came off his bike and struck a road sign at high speed, almost amputating his leg at the thigh. Despite the best efforts of all to control the bleeding, there was no blood available in the hospital at that time, even though it was the only hospital in almost 1,000 kilometres of road between Dalwallinu and Newman. I spoke with Dr Bill Beresford, who was the Deputy Commissioner of Health at the time and whom I had known from when he was the Senior Medical Officer of Derby Hospital and involved with the RFDS. The ARCBTS (Australian Red Cross Blood Transfusion

Service) was more than willing to provide a system for delivering and rotating blood products through the hospital if it had the appropriate blood fridge, procedures and monitoring systems in place. With Dr Beresford's support, a fridge was purchased and a system put in place. This has not only served the local community well over the years but has also enabled the RFDS to borrow blood for emergency flights originating from our Meekatharra Base. There have also been occasions when RFDS aircraft heading to Perth from up north have stopped at Meekatharra and picked up some life-saving units of O negative to use during the remainder of their flight.

In a normal hospital environment, blood is not given without very careful cross-matching to ensure it is completely compatible with the recipient. Most people are aware that there are four main blood types: A, B, AB and O. Each of these can be categorised as positive or negative, depending on the presence of the 'Rh' or Rhesus factor. In addition, there are dozens of minor types which can cause incompatibility. The best way of ensuring there is no reaction is to mix the patient's blood with the donor blood before giving it – a process called cross-matching. Unfortunately, this is not possible in hospitals without laboratories or in the field, so we opt for using O negative blood. This is sometimes called 'universal donor' blood, as it is the least likely to cause a reaction in the majority of recipients. This is what we take to use in flight if we have no cross-matched product.

When heading out to a patient with major trauma, an obstetric emergency or gastrointestinal bleeding, this is the sort of blood we would request from the local hospitals at our RFDS base sites at Derby, Port Hedland, Meekatharra and Kalgoorlie. In Perth, we used to obtain blood products from either the ARCBTS or Royal Perth Hospital, which took some time to arrange. The blood had to be selected and packed, then delivered by taxi, courier or even police car to Jandakot Airport. Often we would wait more than an hour for it to arrive.

In 2002, I started investigating whether we could have our own blood fridge and blood supplies at our Jandakot Base, to enable us to respond more quickly to these types of emergency. There were a few issues to resolve. The first was to get endorsement from the ARCBTS to supply us with blood products. The second issue was to have appropriate storage facilities and procedures to hold it. The third was to ensure we could transport blood products safely in flight at the right temperature.

Our own blood bank

I did a deal with the nearby St John of God Hospital at Murdoch and the ARCBTS that if we received units of fresh O neg and did not use them during a three-week period, we could transfer them to the hospital to ensure utilisation before they expired. We obtained a specialised blood fridge and put in place protocols and twenty-four hour monitoring relatively easily. As we had a Coordination Centre staffed around the clock, we set up an alarm system so that if a problem arose, the director of nursing or I would be called at home to come in and sort it out. Managing the blood taken on flights that was not used and was returned to our blood fridge needed special attention. If it had been heat exposed, it would be unsafe to take on subsequent tasks or to hand over to the St John of God Hospital.

I was lucky to have employed a project officer, Patricia Barrett, who was previously a laboratory scientist. Together we identified a blood transport system, originating in Germany, with very special freezer bricks. These were not your normal blue freezer blocks put in the Esky for a weekend barbeque. They contained a special phase change material, which kept its temperature constant until completely thawed. Blood bags that touched them would not freeze and could be kept at the right temperature range, between 2 and 10 degrees, for many hours. The bricks or 'elements' came in sets, which surrounded the bags of blood. A special insulated carry bag with reflective foil on the outside held the blood and elements.

We undertook a research project over a few months using bags of intravenous fluid as simulated bags of blood. Small data-loggers with inbuilt thermistors were placed with the blood, inside and outside the transport bag. We trialled our system in simulated high-temperature transport environments, elegantly accomplished in the boot of a car in our carpark on days when the temperature was in the high thirties. When we analysed the data of ambient temperature and blood unit temperature, we found that this system could be used to transport blood on long flights of up to twelve hours and it would still be at the correct temperature on return. This was an exciting finding. While we wrote up an internal paper, like much of our internal research and development, we should have published it more widely in the medical literature for others to use.

To ensure that every unit of blood is not heat affected, we apply a small temperature data-logger to each bag when we receive it. If the blood has not been used within three weeks, we download a temperature printout of each bag and provide this to the laboratory at St John of God to prove it is safe.

The great advantage of the arrangement is that blood is readily available for emergency flights. Our medical teams can take it even if they are not sure it is needed, knowing that if it is not used, it will not be wasted and can be safely returned to stock for another case. Rather than waiting for blood to arrive, we can depart more quickly. When we use the helicopter, we can also take blood with us. Over the past decade, we have been able to give blood to many patients during aeromedical retrieval, which has been life-saving.

Gunshot at Narrogin

One of our emergency physicians Dr David Poff was setting off from Perth for a patient at Esperance with haematemesis and melaena, the medical jargon for vomiting blood and bloody diarrhoea. It is hard to control this sort of bleeding and he took emergency blood for the flight, just in case. Shortly after departure, a call came in about a patient with a gunshot wound to the abdomen who was bleeding profusely. There was little surgically they could do for the patient in the local hospital and his only chance was rapid transport to the trauma service at Royal Perth Hospital.

The flight to Esperance was diverted to Narrogin and arrived within thirty minutes. The patient was able to receive uncross-matched O negative blood during flight, helping keep him alive until arrival in Perth. This was an unexpected but bloody good outcome! It would not have happened without our own blood bank at Jandakot Airport in Perth.

Some problems have a silver lining
Burns management and burns dressings

I suffered serious burns to my hand, arm and face in a chemistry experiment in high school in 1972. I won't go into more details about the rocket fuel and explosives we were trying to make. Enough said, I ended up in the burns unit at the Alfred Hospital in Melbourne and required some months of follow-up treatment. This not only kindled my interest in studying medicine but left me acutely sensitive to the plight of individuals who suffer burn injuries.

It was at the time of my own burns that a new treatment became available; SSD (silver sulphadiazine) cream. It was supplied in small tubs and was a cool 'cold cream' preparation, which was applied to burns with a spatula. The problem with full thickness burns is that they breach the wonderful barrier our skin provides. Not only does the burn area allow a large quantity of fluid to escape but the damage also enables infection to enter the body. The development of SSD provided antibacterial qualities associated with both silver salts and sulpha-based antibiotics. It was very soothing but messy to use and could result in dark staining.

We have carried many patients with burns over the years. It is a very challenging task for just a few hours in an aircraft and I respect those who work full time providing burns care. In the confines of the aircraft, the smell of burnt hair and tissue at close quarters is very unpleasant. With large burns, there is an enormous amount of exudate oozing from the burnt areas and, when combined with SSD cream, the patients are very slippery and messy to handle in a small aircraft. By the end of a flight, the sheets and absorbent pads we have used to absorb the fluid are all soaking wet, as are the stretcher seatbelts and anything else touching the patient.

Nevertheless, as it takes many hours for patients to be flown from remote areas to the burns units in Perth, it is essential that we provide early treatment. We need to protect them from developing infection and sepsis, which can cause difficulties with surgical treatment and grafting, or lead to death from widespread septicaemia.

Over recent years new wound dressings have been developed that are impregnated with silver compounds. They are lightweight, less messy to apply and provide an equivalent antibacterial barrier to SSD to minimise infection. They are not cheap, however. The cost of silver-impregnated dressing material required for, say, two patients, each with critical burns covering 40 per cent of their body surface area, is currently about $8,000.

Many country hospitals cannot afford to carry this quantity of silver burns dressings and they would not be used very often. Yet, it is important to have them available when a serious burn injury occurs. We were involved in evacuating patients from the Kimberley Ultramarathon held near Kununurra in 2011. A bush-fire swept down a valley and engulfed a number of elite runners, causing extensive burns. This was covered extensively in the media and was subject to a parliamentary inquiry.

It was clear to me that we needed to be able to respond better to such events across Western Australia and to provide the very best of treatment as soon as possible, including the new Acticoat™ dressings. With some lobbying we obtained funding to develop a cache of dressings, suitable for two patients with serious burns, at each of our RFDS bases. These supplies can now be deployed wherever patients are located across the state.

Kimberley Ultramarathon burns tragedy

It was 2 September 2011 and an extreme sporting event, the Kimberley Ultramarathon, was being held in very remote territory near Kununurra. The event involved a 100-kilometre run in temperatures in the high thirties. Tragically, a bushfire was approaching as runners entered Tier Gorge, and swept through the gorge causing serious burns to a number of trapped competitors.

We were able to task two turboprop aircraft to respond immediately and evacuate the two most seriously burnt victims to Darwin which, while not having a dedicated burns unit, was five to six hours closer than Perth. We subsequently sent our Rio Tinto LifeFlight jet from Perth to bring two more patients back to Perth.

It must have been horrendous for the victims: extensive burns, trapped in a remote area for a long time, with no communication, dealing with intense heat and lack of water to cool the burns or quench their thirst. Incredibly, all survived – a testimony to the fitness of the young athletes – but with subsequent serious disfigurement and years of ongoing treatment for two of the female athletes.

Lightening the load
Patient lifting and loading systems

When I first started as a flying doctor, we had four types of piston-engine aircraft: the Piper PA-31 Navajo, the Cessna 421B Golden Eagle, the Beechcraft Duke and the Beechcraft Baron. Loading a patient on a stretcher into each of these aircraft required three to five people – two on each side and one at the foot end – to lift the stretcher up to the floor sill height and then to push it into the aircraft.

All the aircraft had doors on the left-hand side aft of the wing, except the Barons, which were rarely used for patient transport in my time. On some aircraft there was an extra flap that could be opened to make the door space wider for loading patients.

The Navajo was the predominant type in the fleet and it had a single roll-on stretcher positioned on the right-hand side of the cabin. The stretchers and aircraft configuration were designed by Graham Swannell, the founder of Aeronautical Engineers Australia. They were a relatively simple frame with mattress, adjustable backrest, restraint harness and wheels.

Aft of this main stretcher was a platform extending into the tail. A second stretcher slid onto this and locked in place. This was a challenging load and would not be acceptable under modern occupational health and safety practices. However, in the 1990s and earlier, it was the best we could do to make the most use of the aircraft's capacity.

Outside the aircraft, the rear patient would be positioned on the rear stretcher, which itself was placed on the front stretcher. The whole combination was lifted up and loaded into the aircraft and the front stretcher locked in place. Then the pilot would somehow lift the foot of the rear stretcher up onto the rear platform and, with a great deal of grunting and heaving, slide it further aft until it locked.

In later aircraft the platform was replaced. As the tail of the aircraft swept upwards and the floor here was inclined, a stretcher was used that had wheels on long legs at the head end and short ones at the foot end. It saved weight and was slightly easier to load, but when positioned on the ground outside the aircraft it looked odd with the patient lying on a steeply inclined stretcher.

Clearly this was not an ideal spot for anyone who was big and heavy, or long, as his or her feet would hit the end of the cut-out recess that extended into the tail. It was also not very comfortable. There was no room to sit up and the foot well became very cold at altitude.

The Golden Eagle was even more interesting as the second stretcher was kept in the nose locker. When required, the backs of the seats on the left-hand side of the cabin were folded forward and the stretcher and patient lifted onto the top of these seats and secured. This was not easy to do, stooped inside a small aircraft fuselage. It meant that the patients were side by side in the cabin and there was no space to sit adjacent to either of them. Indeed, there was only one seat left in the cabin, so usually the doctor sat in the cockpit with the pilot, and the nurse in the small seat at the rear of the cabin.

All this manual loading was hard work, particularly in the hot weather, and a risk to our staff and patients. Fortunately, as one can see from photos of the era, the average person was considerably lighter than they are today.

Aircraft-mounted stretcher-loading devices

In the late 1980s, a clever aeronautical engineer in Adelaide, Peter Goon, established the company AFTS (Australian Flight Test Services). It was set up in a 'technology park' alongside a number of other defence-related businesses. He designed a loading system for the Beechcraft B200 King Air, which is still in use, with some modifications, twenty-five years later.

The AFTS loading system comprised a metre-long steel pedestal, roughly 100 millimetres in cross-section, which contained an electric motor, long screw thread and mobile 'truck' that moved up and down a track in the pedestal. The pedestal was hinged and attached to the aircraft floor, just inside the cargo door, where it could flop out when required for use. A folding platform was attached to the truck to hold the stretchers as they were lifted up and down (see photo).

It was an elegantly simple and effective solution, which was not too heavy and did not impinge on the cabin area much in flight. The RFDS Central Section (South Australia) began using these on all its B200 fleet. Our Victorian Section also introduced this loading system into two King Airs based in the Kimberley in the late 1980s, but unfortunately it was unsuitable for the smaller and lighter framed Navajos and other aircraft types used elsewhere in Western Australia. In 1995, when the three different operating sections of the RFDS in WA merged to form a single operating entity, we inherited two King Airs with the AFTS system in place.

Hydraulic scissor-lifters

In the early 1990s I felt we needed to improve our loading, particularly in places we visited frequently. I approached the School of

Design at Curtin University and they made this challenge a project for their final-year students. Though some interesting concepts were suggested, in the end a simple hydraulic scissor-lift platform was the simplest and most effective. It needed thick wheels to work on rough gravel and had to be resilient to being left in the weather at country airstrips and able to be locked down securely, so the hydraulic mechanism could not be stolen. A locking device was needed at each end of the platform to secure the stretcher against rolling off once loaded.

We then visited Howard Porter Pty Ltd, a well-known Western Australian manufacturer of truck bodies and other custom transport equipment. They tweaked the design and produced a standard model stretcher loader, which country towns could purchase at a fixed price. We promoted this system to all the country ambulance sub-centres and were delighted that so many agreed to fundraise and buy them. Subsequently, Aeronautical Engineers Australia, based at Jandakot, produced a similar device and offered some competition. The system substantially reduced lifting and the risk of injuries to staff when loading patients onto our different aircraft types.

There were many other attempts across Australia to develop a stretcher-loading system and new ideas continue to be developed to this day. The NSW Air Ambulance installed a system that used a series of rollers on a track and would allow them to push their stretchers up and into the aircraft. Like many innovative solutions, however, it was heavy and took a long while to set up and disassemble.

We also did some development work on an aircraft-mounted loader for the single Beechcraft C90 VH-FDT we inherited from the Victorian Section. It was a complex hydraulic-operated folding arm, mounted to the rear of the aircraft at the loading hatch. While an elegant piece of engineering, it was very heavy (adversely affecting the balance and payload of the aircraft) and cumbersome to use, so it had only a short life.

LifePort

In 1999 we found ourselves with an order for new B200SE King Air aircraft, with a different configuration of the cargo door, which was not conducive to the AFTS system used in the other King Airs. We had to adopt an aeromedical configuration developed in the USA by the LifePort company. Modules containing the essential medical services, such as oxygen, suction and electrical power, were installed on the floor of the aircraft. The stretcher litters did not have any wheels but high-density plastic glide pads, which would slide along a track on top of the modules and lock into place. A series of interlinking platforms was used to connect from the modules to a loading ramp that extended out the door of the aircraft.

The LifePort system was a clever design and could enable non-dedicated aircraft to be converted for medical transport relatively easily. The stretchers were very narrow and had cut-off corners, which assisted manoeuvring them around corners into the aircraft, but made them less than ideal for larger patients. An equipment arch was connected across the leg-end of the stretcher, over the patient, and used to secure all our critical care equipment during loading, unloading and during flight. A significant amount of lifting and heaving was still involved, however. There was no comparison with the electromechanical AFTS type of stretcher loader, which required no lifting at all.

In 2002 we purchased the first of our Pilatus PC-12 aircraft and proceeded over the next decade to move to a single aircraft type in the fleet. All the PC-12 aircraft have been fitted with the AFTS style of loading device and two identical stretchers, each of which can be loaded or unloaded independently.

I arranged to have the AFTS style of stretcher modified so it could take a LifePort equipment arch. This meant a standardised system for restraint of all our critical care monitoring equipment across each aircraft type during loading, unloading and in flight. I also commissioned the design of a new style of backrest, which had a gas strut attached, to provide assistance with raising and lowering. In a cramped aircraft the doctor or nurse are not well positioned to lift the backrest on the stretcher while the patient is lying on it, although this is necessary for patient comfort and care. Many patients can't lie flat. By adding a gas strut, which is compressed when the backrest is down, much of the load is taken by the strut; this protects staff from excessive straining and injury. As usual, additional effort was required to obtain aeronautical certification, particularly to develop a design that would not collapse in the event of an accident on take-off or landing.

Major incident communications
Gathering intelligence from mass casualty situations

There have been many times when the RFDS has been called to assist with a MCI (mass casualty incident). My first significant MCI event was the Ongerup football club explosion on 13 September 1986. Ongerup is a small country town about 400 kilometres southeast of Perth in the Great Southern region. There was the usual Saturday afternoon football match, after which the players were showering in the football club pavilion. Apparently, a pressure relief valve in the hot water system malfunctioned and the entire boiler exploded, causing bricks and hot water to blast out. Two children had been killed and many seriously injured with combined trauma and burns injuries. We had limited capabilities. A part-time RFDS doctor at Jandakot and I flew down to the town and started assisting with retrieval of the most critically injured to Perth. Volunteer ambulances from around the district responded, providing some initial first aid care and then road transport to surrounding regional centres.

Dr Bill Beresford, the Deputy Commissioner of Health who had previously been involved with the RFDS, came out to our modest Jandakot communications room to coordinate the transfers. This was the first time I had seen effective casualty redistribution occurring. With only two RFDS aircraft available and a significant distance to Perth, only the most serious patients were directed to the capital city. The remainder, based on the extent of their injuries, were distributed to locations including Albany, Katanning and Bunbury.

Communication in these settings is imperative. With no mobile phones at that time, once we had departed Perth on our aircraft, we had only VHF radio in the air for about 100 miles. Then there was HF radio for the remainder of the flight and for when we arrived on the ground. In an ambulance travelling to the country hospital we had no communication with Perth, and within the hospital there were only one or two landline telephones, which were running hot. It was difficult getting messages to and from my colleague and me, describing the situation and the number of casualties. Those involved were desperately trying to care for the incoming patients who were burned, had blast injuries and were in pain. More patients continued to arrive at the small emergency department by ambulance and by private vehicle, further overwhelming those working there.

In these circumstances, the last thing staff feel inclined to do is stand back and make a clear list of the names of the casualties, their injuries and vital signs, and to report them slowly and systematically to someone on a phone, hundreds of kilometres away. Yet, that is exactly what they need to do.

It is very difficult to ignore the compulsion to provide immediate care for the patients around you, yet the response of the health system and the additional resources it may be able to provide depend on having a clear idea of what is going on. In this case, based on the sorts of injury involved, patients could be moved to hospitals in surrounding towns, taking the pressure off the local hospital and leaving the RFDS the few critically ill needing long-distance aerial evacuation.

The local GP and nursing staff had done a sterling job although overwhelmed. Ultimately, we were able to provide some clearer information on casualties back to Dr Beresford in Perth, who then orchestrated the road ambulance distribution of casualties throughout the Great Southern region that night. We ferried the most serious patients up to Perth, then went down again that night and again the following morning.

In the 1990s I became involved in writing the *Australian Disaster Medicine Manual*, under the auspices of the Commonwealth Department of Health and Emergency Management Australia. There was a strong desire, after a number of major incidents, to improve and standardise disaster medicine training across Australia. The working group met at the disaster management college at Mt Macedon in Victoria and comprised a number of key individuals, including Brigadier Paul Buckley from the Australian Defence Force, Dr Richard Ashby from the Australasian College for Emergency Medicine and Dr Michael Cleary from Royal Brisbane Hospital. We produced an excellent manual and oversaw as faculty a number of week-long disaster medicine training programs at Mt Macedon from 1996 onwards. By the end of the decade, a shorter MIMMS (Major Incident Medical Management Support) course was developed from a UK program and adopted across Australia. Our program folded but it was a useful learning exercise and fun at the time. I learned a lot from researching the literature while writing the manual and gained a 'big picture' understanding of dealing with major events.

Subsequent incidents only reinforced my view of the importance of obtaining timely and accurate intelligence from the field, and the role of the first responders in providing very quick but effective triage of multiple casualties. In traditional emergency department situations, you identify the most seriously injured patients and focus your initial attention on resuscitating them. A true shortage of resources is uncommon.

However, imagine yourself as the first responder to an explosion with thirty victims, all with a variety of injuries. It is not easy to identify who needs assistance first. Often, those who are screaming and in pain have less life-threatening injuries than those who are quiet. If you were to attend to each patient in succession and spend only five minutes assessing them and providing very limited treatment, it would take 150 minutes (two and a half hours) to process them all – and some might die waiting. In these situations you have to resist the urge to care for patients as individuals and manage the entire group to achieve the best outcomes overall. One such method is to apply a triage tool sometimes called a 'sieve'. One of the first of these was called START (Simple Triage And Rapid Treatment). It is a simple but clever approach and works something like this.

You call out to the group and ask that all who can, move to one side of the area. This selects those who are less likely to have immediately life-threatening injuries: victims who are conscious, breathing and able to move by themselves, despite their injuries. They are a low priority for your attention.

You then rapidly process each of the remainder in turn. Are they breathing? If not, open their airway. If still not, they are dead or expectant. If they are breathing rapidly or very slowly, they are flagged as urgent. If they have a poor perfusion or a very rapid pulse, they are likewise urgent. If they are unresponsive or unable to follow commands, they are also urgent. Some methods include immediate control of haemorrhage but nothing more is done in this triage process.

With such tools, many patients can be quickly sorted into categories that identify those who deserve attention first. When more responders arrive, they can be deployed appropriately and more details obtained to assist in deciding where the patients should go and in what order. Knowing how many casualties there are is important for putting hospitals and other facilities on standby. In my experience, patients fit into a pyramidal pattern: a small number of seriously injured patients, a large group with moderate injuries and an even larger majority with minor problems. The latter group can be dealt with later or distributed to other locations so as not to clog up the urgent care needed for the most serious.

Derailment at Zanthus

In August 1999 we responded to a train smash at Zanthus on the Transline railway line, about 200 kilometres east of Kalgoorlie. There were twenty-one casualties. Fortunately, most had only moderate injuries but the nearest airstrip was at the remote Aboriginal community of Coonana, 40 kilometres away. We responded initially with one aircraft as there was no room for more aircraft to land and park on the dirt strip. Our medical team was taken to the accident by four-wheel drive, triaged the patients and started to ferry them back to the airstrip along the dirt tracks beside the railway line. There are no ambulances out there!

I had a phone call from the RFDS doctor on site, using a borrowed satphone. He provided some cursory information but not much detail about the number of patients or their injuries. He intended to provide more information shortly but this never eventuated. Unfortunately, sitting in our Coordination Centre at Jandakot, I was being called by Kalgoorlie Hospital, the main Perth hospitals, the Health Department, the ambulance service and the State Emergency Service. They all wanted to know more so they could be involved.

Ultimately, we transferred most of the patients using a couple of aircraft, ferrying back and forth to Kalgoorlie. The hospital sent some medical teams to the site using railcars but by the time they got there, we had moved all the patients with injuries and only the remaining uninjured passengers were left. The outcome of the incident was fine but it prompted me to become more proactive in pushing our staff to recognise the need for comprehensive on-site intelligence and reports. A number of medical staff attended disaster medicine training and we performed much better during subsequent events.

Boodarie HBI plant explosion

On 20 May 2004, four mine workers suffered extensive burns after an explosion at the hot briquetted iron plant near Port Hedland. A call came in at around 2.00 am and was handled by Dr Sally Edmonds, an experienced RFDS doctor based in Port Hedland at the time. The information about injuries was reasonably clear but what was needed was a response using multiple resources. Within twenty minutes she had obtained all the relevant details and ensured that four aircraft teams were being tasked from Port Hedland, Derby and Meekatharra to respond. She then proceeded to the hospital to assist with resuscitation of the patients.

The four seriously burned victims arrived in Perth progressively during the day, each accompanied by an RFDS medical team. It was a multiple-base response, achieved simply and cleanly with strong medical direction to begin with, based on the intelligence at hand. Our performance was ultimately recorded in the Hansard of the WA Legislative Council.

Airbus incident

In October 2008 a Qantas Airbus A330 suffered a significant inflight incident when it dropped hundreds of feet while in cruise mode down the coast of Western Australia. It was eventually discovered that the underlying problem was one of the three naviga-tion computers disagreeing with the others! A dozen passengers and flight attendants, who were unrestrained at the time, suffered serious injuries such as broken limbs. Many more passengers had minor injuries. The aircraft made an emergency unscheduled landing at the Learmonth Airport, a large ex-military airstrip near Exmouth.

Dr Angela O'Connell was on one of the number of RFDS aircraft we sent to assist. On arrival she was confronted with over 300 passengers who needed to be sorted to determine who had the most serious injuries. She did a remarkable job over a period of hours, quickly identifying those who needed care from those who were just badly shaken. It was relatively hot, there was an old airport terminal building and she had only a mobile phone with limited coverage. It was very difficult to provide an update to health authorities on all who were injured and to explain what the scene was like and what additional assistance was needed. For example, more shelter from the heat would have helped, as would more water and food for those with minor injuries. Additional support might have been provided by emergency response agencies if a better picture had been received of what the scene was like.

The RFDS team extracted a passenger list from the flight crew and systematically marked off everyone, categorising them according to their injury status, but it was difficult to convey this level of detail over a mobile phone, particularly when the battery started to run out.

In the end, we evacuated all the patients who needed to be, using four RFDS aircraft and another charter aircraft. However, it got me thinking. Wouldn't it be great if we had the capacity to provide a broadcast from such an incident site, just like a live TV transmission, which showed the scene in the background and enabled a senior doctor to report on the number of casualties and the situation in general? It would be particularly useful if this could be sent securely to key players such as the Health Department and police, fire and ambulance services. One broadcast, with all the information at once, from the scene to all the key participating agencies, and ideally a recorded transmission so it could be replayed. If it could be hosted on an RFDS emergency website, those with a password could view it and any subsequent updates.

It would be even better still to have a live streaming feed from the site, so all could see the progress of the incident, with the medical commander giving regular briefings.

Three weeks later another incident occurred at Manjimup when an RSL tour bus rolled over, resulting in one death and injuries to twenty elderly passengers. We also sent teams to this, with one doctor taking on the role of providing detailed updates on all the patients from the hospital. We were using only faxes and phones but were able to keep the incident command centre for the Health Department fully informed of the casualties and their injuries. They could then play their role and arrange hospital beds and resources in Perth.

RAVEN

An opportunity arose for sponsorship of a project by an energy company. Did we have any special projects they could support? I prepared a brief on what I had in mind. It seemed it would be so easy to set up a standard portable web camera mounted on a tripod, with a laptop computer and a satellite phone, at any incident and stream live from the site, whether we had mobile phone coverage or not. Developing the web interface that would make the images available to multiple other parties was a little more challenging. Mathew Turany, our IT Manager, found a company with a US product that appeared to do exactly what we wanted. It was a small portable computer inside a robust plastic 'pelican' case, which could connect to a variety of external inputs such as cameras and monitoring devices. It hosted its own web server, which was available for viewing by those with a password. It could connect to a simple satellite phone with A4-sized aerial panels and operate in areas without mobile telephone or data. It concurrently created a mobile wireless hotspot. Having internet connectivity meant that the responders could send email, search databases for information (for example, toxicology if there was a chemical spill), or transmit spreadsheets with patient numbers and their diagnoses.

I christened the project RAVEN (RFDS Audio Visual Emergency Network), which was quite apt as it was flown out to an emergency and was in a big black case. It took a while to develop due to some technical issues with the audio stream but ultimately we succeeded in producing a self-contained, battery or mains-powered system, with the camera and tripod all packed up nicely in a golf bag. I waited for the inevitable major incident...and none came.

In 2010, Apple launched the iPad. It was 'a magical and revolutionary device at an unbelievable price', according to the launch. In 2011 the popular video-conferencing and internet telephone application *Skype*™ became available on the iPhone and iPad. These provided a compact means of recording and live streaming video over the internet, if connected to the mobile phone network. We started to receive photos of injuries, taken on a phone or tablet, from rural responders at accident sites. We introduced a desktop video-conferencing system, Vidyo®, and this also became available on portable devices due to the implementation of SVC (scalable video coding) compression standards.

The RAVEN was a nice piece of work but I could see that, apart from when at very remote locations with only satellite coverage, we had been overtaken by rapid advances in technology in just a short period. It had been superseded by devices now carried in people's pockets.

Weighed down with big issues
Bariatric transport of the morbidly obese

There is no doubt that we have an ever-expanding population whose size and weight is becoming a big problem. In the early 1990s we might encounter a patient over 150 kg only once a year. In 2012/13 we had 200 patients over 130 kg and sixty over 160 kg. At least once a month we now have individuals over 200 kg to manage.

In the early days, loading onto most aircraft types was what I called 'mandraulic'. The patient would be transferred onto an aircraft stretcher on the ground outside the aircraft, then two blokes on either side and one at the foot end would do a coordinated lift: 'one, two, three, lift'. The head end of the stretcher would be placed onto the floor of the aircraft just inside the doorway. Here the flight nurse would grab it and start steering it into place, while those outside would continue to lift and push the rear end.

During the 1990s we adopted systems to reduce the amount of lifting (see earlier chapter, 'Lightening the load'). In 2004 it was clear that the problem of morbidly obese patients was getting bigger. It was not just the weight of the patients but also their size, particularly width, which made them too large to fit comfortably on our stretchers. Furthermore, the safe working load of our AFTS stretcher-loading system was around 180 to 200 kg. To move such patients in an emergency required us to remove all the stretchers

33. A de Havilland DH.83 Fox Moth VH-USJ airborne over the Murchison. The first aircraft owned by the Western Australian Section. Bought in 1941. Restored and still flying in 2015.

34. Cessna 180 VH-FDH and a portable dentist chair. Purchased in 1956 and initially operated out of Port Hedland. Restored by Jan Ende and still flying in 2015.

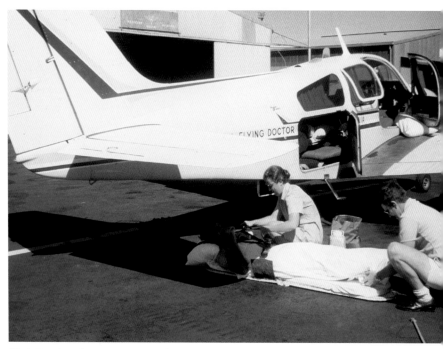

35. A Beechcraft Baron 95-A55. The first Barons were smaller and stretchers were loaded through a single door as shown. The Baron 58 model was longer with double doors into the cabin.

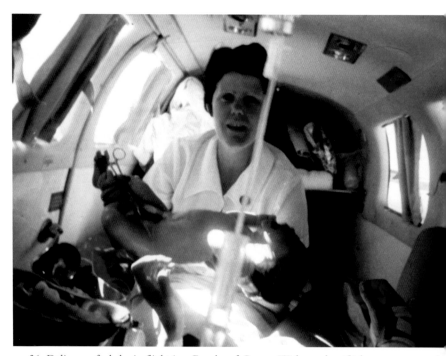

36. Delivery of a baby in flight in a Beechcraft Baron. With good preflight assessment and drugs to suppress labour, in-flight delivery is now extremely rare.

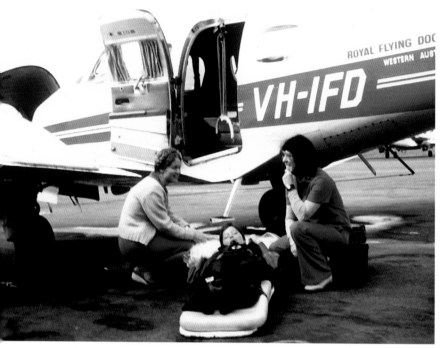

37. Beechcraft 60 Duke VH-IFD, the first pressurized RFDS aircraft, bought in 1972. Note the block and tackle arrangement to help lift the patient up into the aircraft. Two stretcher patients could be stacked, one above the other, in the aircraft.

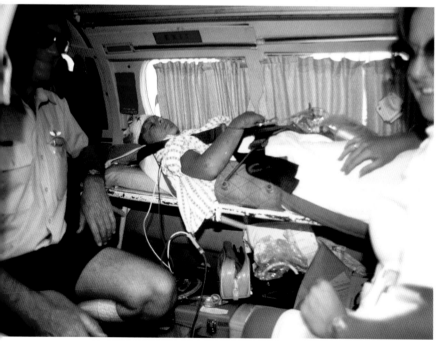

38. A patient on the top stretcher in the Duke.

39. Cessna C421B Golden Eagle bought in 1975. A larger pressurized aircraft used by the WA Section. The fuel tanks on the wing tips appeared to flap during turbulent flight.

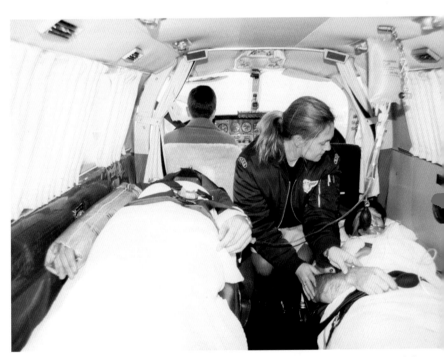

40. The Cessna 421B with two patients on board. The left hand stretcher was strapped down on top of the seat backs leaving only the co-pilot seat and a rear seat free. There was little space in which to work with two patients over a number of hours.

A Piper PA-31 Navajo landing in the Pilbara. First acquired in 1977 and the workhorse of the WA and Eastern Goldfields Sections until the 1990s.

42. Wreckage of Piper Navajo VH-DEE near Mt Augustus Station in 1982. The pilot and flight nurse miraculously escaped injury.

43. A Cessna C425 Conquest I VH-JEC 'Laverton" operated by the Eastern Goldfields Section from 1986. Shorter than the C441and with PT6 turbines. Re-registered as VH-EGS.

44. Captain Roger Waller, Chief Pilot of the Eastern Goldfields Section and Dr Elizabeth Green.

45. Cessna C441 Conquest VH–NFD in an early livery with the Cato logo. A fast pressurised aircraft to fly in.

6. Our 'wall-hung' bags seen here on the left side of the cabin, provided easy access to a range of consumables in flight, without the need to leave your seat. They could be unhooked, rolled up and taken with us when leaving the aircraft.

47. A Beechcraft B200C King Air VH–FDG at Derby in July 2002, offloading a patient.

48. A charter flight evacuation from a boat at Curi Bay in the Kimberley, using a Cessna Caravan on floats. (Photo Dr Simon Evans)

49. The final assembly hangar at Pilatus in Stans, Switzerland. VH-VWO, the 300th PC-12 manufactured, is seen here on the parquetry wood floors, together with PC-9 aircraft.

50. Captain Pete Smith and Chief Pilot Michael Bleus after ferrying Pilatus PC-12 VH-MWO from Switzerland to Jandakot Airport Perth in August 2001.

51. The first medical flight of the Pilatus PC-12 in WA. VH–KWO at Bruce Rock on 3 October 2001.

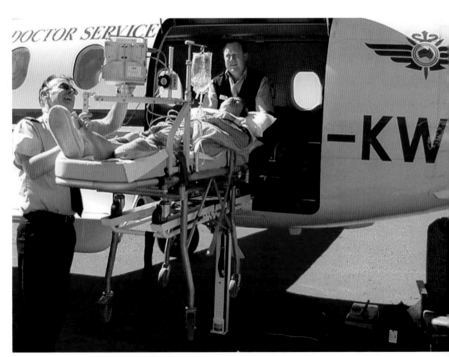

52. Captain Michael Bleus and Paul Ingram using the AFTS stretcher-loading device to lift a patient into PC-12 VH–KWO in 2002.

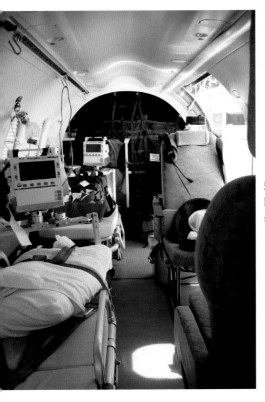

53. Interior of a Pilatus PC-12, looking aft. Two stretchers with monitors on the starboard side.

54. An RFDS Pilatus PC-12 dwarfed by an A330 Airbus at Learmonth Airport following an flight incident in 2008. Multiple aircraft and teams were sent to triage all of the passengers and evacuate a number of casualties. (Photo Dr Angela O'Connell)

55. The Rio Tinto *LifeFlight* jet, a Hawker 800XP VH–RIO, commenced in October 2008. The first RFDS jet in Australia with the capacity to carry two critically-ill patients with two medical teams, or up to five patients and two staff.

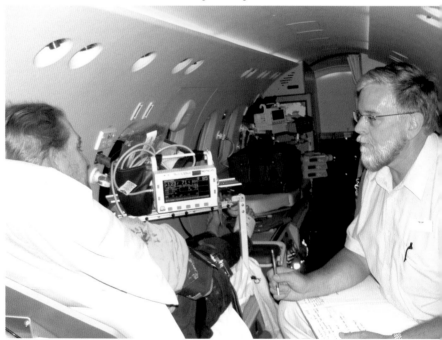

56. The first medical flight of VH–RIO on 16 October 2009. An opportunistic evacuation from a site near Kununurra to Darwin.

57. The 'Dash under the Ash'. Loading the neonatal cot into the Rio Tinto *LifeFlight* Hawker 800XP jet for an urgent flight to Melbourne. The dense ash cloud is visible in the background. (© West Australian Newspapers Limited.)

58. A Piaggio Avanti II at Jandakot in August 2010. One of the most stunning aircraft designs of recent years with 'pusher' turboprops and jet-like performance. PK-BVX on trial as maintenance cover for the *LifeFlight* jet service in August 2010.

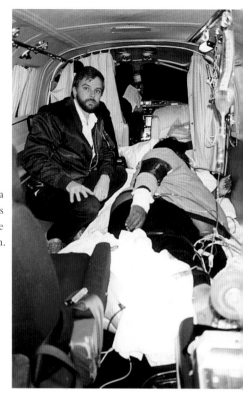

59. A morbidly obese patient in a Cessna C441 Conquest. A hospital mattress was placed on the floor of the aircraft and the patient physically dragged in.

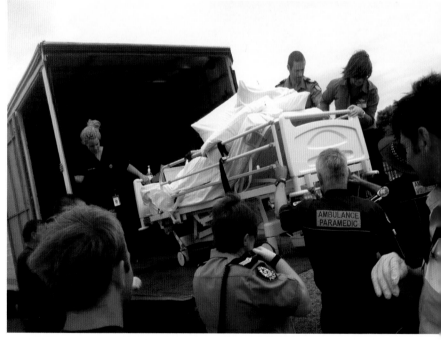

60. Prior to introduction of our Bariatric Transport System. A furniture removal van being used to transfer a large patient on a hospital bed to the airport. Getting them into the aircraft was a major challenge.

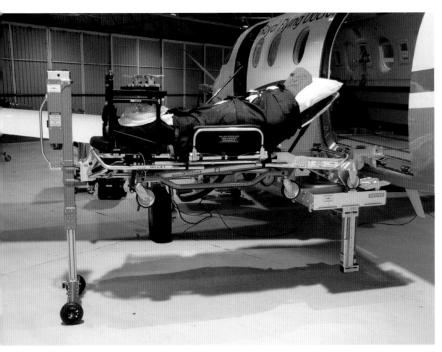

. Bariatric Transport System. A supplementary battery-powered device provides lift in addition to the aircraft mounted loading platform, enabling 400kg to be raised.

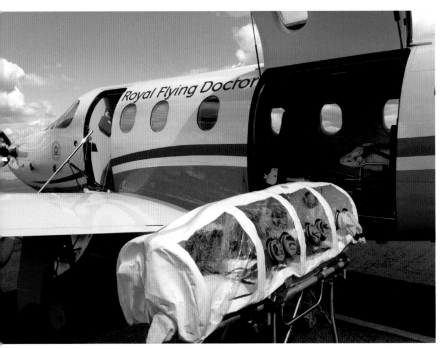

62. A modified Isopod, portable isolation unit, for carriage of patients with highly infectious respiratory disease. Developed after the SARS outbreak and uses HEPA filtration.

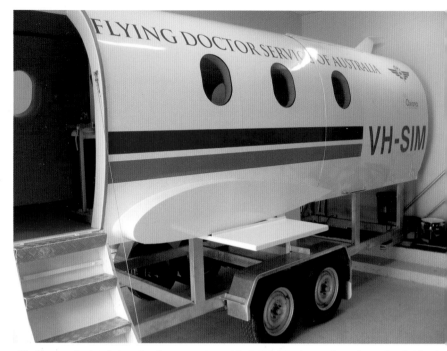

63. Our medical training simulator constructed in 2008. The internal configuration is identical to a PC-12 with medical oxygen, suction, two stretchers, cabinets and shelving just as in a real aircraft. Internal cameras enables recording of clinical training scenarios.

64. Eighty years of RFDS aviation history. DH.83 Fox Moth VH-USJ (foreground), Cessna 180C VH-FDH and Pilatus PC-12/47 VH-OWS. (Photo © Jon Davison, Photographer)

and brackets from the floor of the aircraft and to carry them on a mattress, effectively on the floor of the aircraft. As the patients were not properly secured, this required the pilot to declare a 'mercy flight' – a flight where due to medical requirements, aviation regulations were being breached.

To circumvent this problem I developed what we irreverently called the 'fat mat'. This was a vinyl-covered, high-density camping foam mat, integrated with a custom-designed restraint harness, which could be clipped into the floor tracks and safely restrain a patient of 250 kg. It was not ideal for patient care, as patients had to be dragged into the aircraft on a slide mat and lie flat during flight. Nonetheless, at least it complied with safety requirements and prevented us declaring mercy flights.

Unfortunately, it did not help with loading and many people were required to lift and drag large patients into our aircraft. Lying flat is not ideal either as these patients often have difficulty breathing. Many jury-rigged arrangements were made to try to provide some form of pillow or backrest support.

In 2010 it was apparent we needed to bite the bullet and design a special 'bariatric transport system' for large patients which would comprise a proper stretcher, so we could care for our patients adequately in flight, and a loading system, to minimise the risk of injury to our staff during the loading process. We were fortunate to receive the support of WorleyParsons, who wished to provide assistance with a project as a corporate engagement exercise. They had considerable expertise in engineering and project management, such as construction of oil rigs and mine sites, but this relatively small problem involving patient care, ergonomics and aeronautical engineering was an interesting and different challenge.

My initial desire was to use this as the impetus to design a completely new aeromedical stretcher: one which used all the latest in materials (carbon fibre, composites, new alloys) and new construction techniques, such as computer-aided machining rather than just welding or riveting numerous metal components together. The intention was that after designing a bariatric stretcher, we could use a similar, narrower design for standard stretchers. After our initial design phase, it became apparent that this approach would be a very expensive exercise – in the millions of dollars – and that we needed to regroup and be more pragmatic. So I opted to find a currently available commercially produced stretcher, which could be modified to meet our needs, and to develop an ancillary lifting device that could augment the AFTS system already on our aircraft.

We ultimately engaged a modest aeronautical engineering company in Melbourne, Five Rings Aerospace. The owner, Greg Hanlon, brought together ideas and products from Ferno Australia (one of the world's largest ambulance stretcher manufacturers) and Barker Tooling & Aerospace (the company making our current aircraft loading system) and set about the design and certification of all the components for use in aircraft and road ambulances.

The target we set ourselves was optimistic: a stretcher that could carry a patient up to 300 kg in weight, 1 metre wide and 2 metres long. Combining the weight of the patient, the stretcher and the medical equipment, we had a total of 400 kg to lift into the aircraft and take flying with us!

We achieved almost exactly what we aimed for, plus a number of useful design modifications. The backrest is adjustable, with gas struts so that there is limited lifting required by doctors and nurses to elevate the patient. There is a section under the knees which can be raised. This helps stop the patient from sliding down the stretcher during flight. The side rails are padded for comfort and can fold outwards to increase the effective width for the patient once in the aircraft. A large equipment bridge sits over the patient's legs and is used to secure our monitoring equipment during transport.

We purchased a special bariatric manikin to assist with evaluation of the concept and then initial training. Lovingly referred to as

Barry, the bariatric dummy weighs 180 kg, well short of our target operating load but still effective for training. What I somehow failed to appreciate when I bought him was that to lug a 180 kg manikin around and load it on a stretcher is no mean feat! A large number of people are required to lift him and he is not easily put in a cupboard. A forklift with a sling is a much better, if unrefined, solution for moving him.

To load the stretcher into the aircraft, a secondary mobile SLD (stretcher-lifting device) was developed by Barker Engineering in Adelaide. The stretcher is brought up to the aircraft-mounted lifting platform and then the mobile SLD is attached to the outboard end. Both lifters are used simultaneously to raise the stretcher to aircraft height, the stretcher wheels are brought up, then the stretcher rolled in and SLD disengaged.

Apart from the safe restraint of the stretcher in our PC-12 aircraft at 22G and the need to load up to 400 kg, we faced the dilemma of country ambulances. If the patient is too wide or heavy for our normal stretchers, then this is usually the same for country ambulances. We worked closely with St John Ambulance and Five Rings to ensure we produced a system that would enable the same stretcher to be used in the country ambulance. The same mobile lifter is required to load the rear end of the bariatric stretcher into the road ambulance.

This means that when we have to retrieve a very large patient, we land at the airport, put our special stretcher in an ambulance, go into the hospital with our team, load the patient onto the bariatric stretcher, then bring them out to the airstrip to load directly onto our aircraft. This all makes for a safer and more comfortable journey and prevents the risk of injury to everyone involved.

The entire project cost approximately $900,000 but fortunately was funded by the WA Country Health Service, so we could provide three mission-specific systems for use across the state. It went into service in June 2014 and before the year was out, had carried a 286 kg patient. It has helped with these 'weighty' problems ever since.

A big problem at Carnarvon

It was sometime in the early 1990s and Carnarvon Hospital called to see if we could transfer a patient with an acute abdomen to Perth for surgery. This man had presented with severe abdominal pain and, while the diagnosis was not clear, he needed a laparotomy to open his abdomen and manage whatever was going on. It was difficult to make a diagnosis and to treat him as he was around 160 kilograms or more and very wide.

It is really difficult to make a reasonable diagnosis of acute surgical problems in the morbidly obese. You cannot easily feel any masses in the abdomen below the patient's fatty apron and often the localisation of pain, which one can pick in a person of healthy weight, is unreliable. Moreover, even with a surgeon available, such patients are just too wide and heavy to manage on a narrow surgical table and there are very significant risks in trying to anaesthetise them. General handling and nursing care are a real challenge without appropriate lifting aids.

I flew up to Carnarvon with one of our 'can do' pilots, Captain Terry Richardson. Terry was a wonderful individual for whom nothing was ever really a problem. He was pragmatic and innovative and just got on with doing the job we needed done.

Once we arrived, it was clear that we had a problem. The patient was too large for the ambulance stretcher so they had put a standard hospital single-bed mattress on the floor of the ambulance and brought him out to the airport. There were half a dozen muscular blokes (or, like me, ones who thought they were) and we could see that we had little choice but to do the same in the aircraft.

Terry removed the front stretcher and the restraint frames from the floor of the Cessna C441. It left a nice flat floor down the starboard side. He secured the front stretcher on top of the rear stretcher using seatbelts and then we proceeded, with much straining and heaving, to lift this single-bed mattress and its occupant out of the ambulance and up into the aircraft. Occupational safety and health wasn't as highly developed then as it is today, but with plenty of grunt, we managed to secure the mattress on the floor of the aircraft, with the patient spreading across and occupying most of the floor space.

This was not ideal but then how else could we transfer this sick man to appropriate care about 800 kilometres south in Perth? It was not in our culture to say no to this sort of scenario if we could find a way of doing it, and when there really was no other option. In the end, the flight proceeded uneventfully and we repeated the heaving and manual lifting with the help of volunteers from the Fire Brigade at Jandakot Airport. The patient made a satisfactory recovery and we were all pleased with what we had been able to achieve that day.

Going with the flow

A similar problem arose only a year or so ago with another very large patient from the North West of Western Australia, before our bariatric transport system was completed. With our PC-12 aircraft I have always recommended that if we can fit the patient onto the stretcher, then we should use it and the lifting device, rather than risking injury by loading patients manually onto the 'fat mat'.

Some people can take my advice to extremes! One of our notable doctors in Port Hedland over recent years has been a Swedish graduate, Dr Catarina Widing. She has adopted the challenges of rural and remote Australia with gusto, a big heart and a willingness to always complete the job. Catarina had the patient on the stretcher all right but she described to me later that 'there was one buttock on the stretcher and one on my knee' for the duration of the flight! Still, we had a great team in the aircraft. Every ten to fifteen minutes the doctor would ask the pilot to execute a right bank, rolling the aircraft onto the starboard side. This meant that the patient rolled back so they were mostly on the stretcher, giving Catarina's knee some respite. Again, a successful transfer but requiring a degree of innovation to achieve it!

Isopods for infectious bods
Portable negative-pressure isolation units for infectious patients

In 2003 there was worldwide concern as the SARS (severe acute respiratory syndrome) form of atypical pneumonia spread around the world from Hong Kong, causing more than 8,000 cases of illness and over 900 deaths. The epidemic spread quickly and was notable for its high infectivity and fatality rate, and for being caused by a new virus not previously recognised. It was clear to those involved in the aviation industry and aeromedical services that carriage of these patients was very high risk. It became apparent that none of the aircraft commonly used for aeromedical purposes had internal air flows that could be filtered to make them safe. Indeed, in our aircraft, while there was a regular turnover of fresh air in the cabin, there was still significant recirculation, with air in the cabin being recycled and blown over the occupants.

When I worked for a term at the Fairfield Infectious Diseases Hospital in Melbourne (long since closed), there was a system in place to enable highly infectious patients to be evacuated by the RAAF while sealed in a large plastic 'tent' surrounding the bed. They could then be moved to a special high-security quarantine facility at Fairfield for treatment. Unfortunately, the foresight of medical experts in the 1970s was superseded by the bean counters of subsequent decades and we had no dedicated infectious disease hospitals or military transport options for these sorts of outbreak when SARS occurred.

When the fuss died down, I started looking for portable isolation units. I found a product from the USA that was intended to assist with containment of casualties from chemical or biological events. Called the Isopod™, it was essentially a compact, heat-sealed, vinyl tube with an internal frame, an air blower and a number of high-efficiency HEPA filters. It featured portholes with rubber gloves to attend to the victims, but it was not designed for transport, merely to provide an enclosure for contaminated victims in the field.

The best time to secure funding for disaster-related activities is immediately after a major event. With a small grant from the Department of Health, I set about a project to purchase and modify the Isopod to make it suitable for use in our aircraft. The plan was that in the event of another SARS-like outbreak or influenza pandemic, we would have some capacity to transport patients in isolation, at least as far as respiratory-borne viruses were concerned.

We set about redesigning the units to make them narrower to fit our stretchers and to install an appropriate harness to restrain patients safely in flight, while arranging certification for the restraint and power supplies in our aircraft. We made respectable progress and ended up with two working prototypes after a year or two of fiddling around. With SARS gone and many other priorities, the imperative to finish projects like this can take a back seat for a while.

I presented our work at a couple of conferences along with discussions about whether, in the event of a major epidemic, we should be transporting such patients at all; or whether they should be quarantined in the hospital to which they presented and not risk infecting many other people in the city hospital system. After all, in a major epidemic there may not be the resources to manage people as many health professionals, pilots and others become sick and unable to work.

The units sat at our base from about 2006 until the middle of 2014 when a large Ebola outbreak occurred in West Africa. I had my staff check the units and waited for the call to come from Dr Andy Robertson in the Disaster Planning and Management Unit of the Health Department about whether we still had those 'pod' things. Yes, we did, and in fact we were the only state to have such a device. Even the RAAF had no capacity to transport a patient in isolation. There ensued a number of months of anticipation as the outbreak spread and international health workers were affected. I received many calls about our units from other states, all keen to have a similar capacity. It took some time to convince others that the units were designed to minimise airborne spread of infection and that for patients with bloody diarrhoea and vomiting, they would not be as effective or safe as we would like. In such a situation, any contamination of the outside of the units could also contaminate the aircraft interior, such as furnishings and seats. We also had no clear idea how to decontaminate our aircraft effectively in this setting.

Many health authorities eventually purchased the basic units and made modifications similar to ours. Fortunately, with robust border control, no confirmed cases reached Australia. A further round of research and development is in order to prepare for our next infectious disease challenge.

Warming to new ideas
Resistive warming and chemical blankets

In RFDS practice, we are often dealing with problems of heat; trying to keep our patients and ourselves cool in the very hot conditions encountered in outback Australia for much of the year. In my first few years with the RFDS, I looked at how hot our aircraft became when parked on the tarmac. There is the so-called glasshouse effect which we experience in parked cars, where infrared radiation from the sun penetrates the windows and heats the interior so that it is hotter inside a closed vehicle than outside. Added to this you have aircraft parked on dark bitumen, which absorbs and re-radiates heat up to the aircraft and all around it. There are plenty of times when our shoe soles are sticky from the soft bitumen underfoot.

I left some 'maximum–minimum' alcohol thermometers in the aircraft to measure how hot they became inside, as I was concerned about leaving medical equipment and consumables exposed to such heat. When I returned to check the results, the thermometers had reached 60 degrees before bursting! I didn't pursue the study further, figuring that was enough to confirm that our aircraft became very hot. Indeed, as Robin Williams put it in the movie *Good Morning Vietnam*, 'Hot, damn hot!'

When I first started flying in the Piper Navajo, an unpressurised twin-engine aircraft, we were lucky that most of them had an air-conditioning system. It wasn't very effective and didn't work unless the engines were running, so it was no help on the ground while loading patients. We had to turn it off for take-off so that we had maximum engine power available, and then it took some time to help cool down an aircraft which was already heat soaked.

Not everyone would appreciate that there is a standard rate at which the atmosphere cools as we increase altitude. In what is called a standard atmosphere, the air cools by 2 degrees for every 1,000 ft of altitude. So in an unpressurised aircraft like the Navajo, the air would be 20 degrees cooler at the maximum flying altitude. On a nice, 'warm' 40-degree day in the Pilbara, the atmosphere was a much more pleasant 20 degrees at 10,000 ft. So most of the cooling of the aircraft came from this, not the struggling air-conditioner.

In our more modern pressurised turboprop and jet fleet, we can be flying at 25,000 ft, or even up to 41,000 ft in the jet. In these cases, the external temperature is well below zero even on the hottest days and, ironically, we need to have the heating on.

It is always cold down the back of the aircraft on our rear stretcher. While the pilot has a large windscreen with sunshine beaming in, and heat comes from all the avionics in the cockpit, the tail of the aircraft has few windows or other sources of heat. So if the pilot is comfortable, the rear patient is often cold.

A common problem in prehospital care is keeping patients warm. At an accident site, patients can be trapped in a vehicle for some time. It might be night, or cold or raining, with limited protection from the elements. Once the patients arrive at the hospital, their clothes are removed, they receive cool intravenous fluids and they lie still in an air-conditioned emergency department while everyone else is running around. It is therefore common for trauma patients to become cold. As well as causing discomfort, this fall in body temperature can have adverse physiological effects on patients.

In the back of an ambulance, helicopter or fixed-wing aircraft, it is difficult to correct hypothermia that has already developed. Yes, there is some internal heating but limited other opportunities to warm patients up. In a hospital setting, there are devices such as the Bair Hugger™, a blanket that blows warm air over patients to slowly elevate their temperature. It is also possible to provide warming of intravenous fluids. These devices are not suitable for use in an aircraft in flight and are either too bulky or use too much electrical power. So we investigated what we could do to help warm patients during transport.

Our first attempt was with a resistive warming blanket. These are composed of a carbon mesh which warms up when an electrical current is passed through. Essentially, they are an electric blanket but without the wires found in a household version. I noted them being used in Europe, such as in helicopter rescue of patients from the snow in alpine areas. The blankets or sleeping bag versions have a padded Dacron cover and plug into vehicle battery power with a solid-state temperature controller. Yet, try as I might to enthuse our staff to use them, they would forget to take them on a flight or would decide not to because of their bulk and storage limitations on the aircraft.

In 2013 we identified some very compact, lightweight chemical blankets being used in surgical practice. These are thin disposable polypropylene paper-like blankets with a number of pouches sewn across the torso area, each of which contain sachets of relatively inert chemicals (a mixture of active coal, clay, salt and iron powder). They come in a sealed airtight polymer bag. Once opened and exposed to the air, the sachets react with oxygen and generate heat. Each pad can reach 40 degrees and retains that temperature for hours. Some are produced for use in the operating theatre and others for remote environments. They are relatively cheap and can be used over the top of patients during transport. This means that we can easily and cheaply keep our patients warm and toasty, even in the middle of the night in winter, whether in the outback or south of the state. My staff are now warming to the idea of using them more routinely.

When you've gotta go
Toilet technology

I've had the privilege to meet two NASA astronauts at aerospace medicine conferences. They both told me that one of the most common queries they receive is, 'How do you go to the toilet in space?' So I make no apologies for the insight into this topic which follows. If you are not interested, move on; but if you have ever wondered how we deal with these bodily functions in flight, keep reading to learn about some low-tech innovations we have come to use and the risks of just popping behind a bush.

In Western Australia we need to fly very long distances, with patient transfers up to 2,000 kilometres within the state. We cover even greater distances when we fly to the Cocos Islands and Christmas Island. We don't have toilets in our standard aircraft and this can pose a problem for staff as well as patients.

When we were operating slower piston-engine aircraft, we usually had to stop to refuel after about three hours. The total flight time can be two to three times longer than this and in our current turboprops, we can fly non-stop for longer.

Our patients are usually on stretchers in the aircraft and when they can't hold on any longer, they need to use a bedpan or a bottle, just like in hospital. Our flight nurses are adept at managing this in cramped confines but dealing with the container afterwards, in a small aircraft, is not easy.

We have to be careful. While the displays for pilot instruments such as radios and navigation aids are on the control panel in the cockpit where the pilot sits, the actual radios and computers, which provide these essential functions, are often located under the floor panels in the main cabin. If we have a spill of urine, blood or other fluids, it can seep down and damage these electronic modules. Apart from the risk of moisture causing a short circuit, body fluids are a biohazard and can be corrosive to electric connectors, cables and the fuselage metal in general.

If we have a big spill, we have to notify our aircraft engineers. The aircraft is taken offline and, while wearing appropriate protective equipment, they need to remove the floor panels and clean out blood or other liquids that have seeped below them. Not a pleasant task and one we try to avoid.

The first breakthrough was in the early 1980s when we discovered the Spil-Pruf® urinal. This was a plastic urine bottle similar to that used in a hospital. The funnel section unscrewed, so it could be reversed and stowed inside the bottle to make it more compact. This was helpful with our limited storage space. However, the real innovation was the non-return valve built into the funnel. Once used, the contents of the bottle did not leak out. The risk of urinals splashing around in turbulence or during landing was solved!

Nevertheless, we still had a problem with bedpans. Whatever the contents, these were much larger to store and more open. The likelihood of a catastrophic event during severe turbulence or on landing was ever present. Fortunately for us, new products entered the market which we adopted early on. They consist of granules which can be sprinkled into a pan, or on any fluid leak, to rapidly absorb large volumes of fluid and form a more manageable gel. They work quickly and come in sachets with deodoriser or disinfectant. They can also be used to control the spread of other body fluids, which might escape onto the aircraft floor.

Certain patients on long flights need to have in place a urinary catheter: a soft tube that continues to drain the bladder into a collecting bag. It is essential for someone who is unconscious and other seriously ill patients on a long flight. It prevents incontinence during transfer and distress from a distended bladder. Sometimes the catheter bag can fill to nearly 2 litres during a flight. If the bag is punctured or the tubing disconnects, then suddenly all that urine is spreading across the floor of the aircraft. Battle stations! Throw down any spare sheets, blankets or pads to try to soak it up; if it is a smaller leak, use the absorbent sachets.

Similar problems occur when pregnant women rupture their membranes in flight; with patients who continue to bleed uncontrollably; and with patients who have extensive burns, where the volume of exudate from the burn area can be measured in litres.

As for staff, the lack of a toilet can be challenging. Working in hot conditions, it is important to keep up your water intake. We carry cold water and have the capacity to make a cup of tea or coffee from a vacuum flask of boiled water taken on each flight. Our aircraft team have to learn to pace themselves with drinks during a long journey – particularly female staff, as there really is no practical option for them. If desperate, men can use a urine bottle, though this is a humiliating exercise with little privacy available in the aircraft when airborne.

Not surprisingly, when we land or stop to refuel, there is often an urgent dash to the airport toilet or, at other airstrips, to the nearest bushes. Even this has been made more difficult with enhanced airport security fencing at some of the major airports, as the following tale demonstrates.

A bite on the backside

It was just before New Year and a cyclone was approaching. Our Port Hedland team were flat out on Sunday night, having been flying all over the Pilbara. As a final task, they landed at Karratha to evacuate a pregnant woman back to Port Hedland. It was after 3.00 am but if they didn't move the patient now, our day crew might have been grounded due to the worsening weather.

As usual, the crew took turns to use 'the bush' at the edge of the tarmac. Due to airport security measures, the RFDS was required to park the aircraft some distance from the terminal building to transfer patients. After hours, the gates were locked and the security fence effectively kept everyone marooned airside.

Our flying doctor had her turn in the shadows of the small bush, which was just out of sight of security cameras, the tarmac lights and the aircraft. As she went about her business, she felt a small bite on the side of her thigh in the dark. Presuming it to be from an insect or spider, she hurried back to sort out the patient and evacuate them to Port Hedland.

During the flight back, she was aware of the bite on her thigh but put it down to one of the many potential biting insects found in the Pilbara. Coming from overseas, she was learning of the many perils to be found in the Australian bush but had also adopted the complementary 'she'll be right, mate' philosophy. After handing over her patient, she went home to sleep, aware of an increasingly painful thigh.

This worsened to a severe headache, shakes and sweating with increased pain. She was feeling very unwell, so she attended the hospital at lunchtime the next day for advice on the painful inflamed area on her leg. All concerned put it down to being some form of sting, with secondary infection. Antibiotics, painkillers and going home to family was the plan as the town was now on a cyclone alert, with a major cyclone due to strike within twelve hours.

Our flying doctor was not well. She saw out the next two days at home with her family, feeling increasingly sick while the cyclone battered the town. A large dark area of dead tissue had appeared on her leg, surrounded by extensive inflammation. When *the cyclone had passed, she returned to the hospital where, after additional inpatient treatment for a day, the flying doctor suffered the ignominy of being evacuated to Perth herself.*

Sir Charles Gairdner Hospital provides a tertiary hospital toxicology service. It was now five days since the bite and while there was little to find on blood tests, it was clear to the panel of specialists that the flying doctor's symptoms were consistent with being bitten by a black snake! The doc had survived but required further treatment, including surgery to debride a large area of dead tissue on the leg. A number of weeks were spent in hospital and off work.

There are plenty of tales about snake bites and the flying doctor — but none where the doctor herself is bitten!

Snake bites are relatively common in our service, particularly in the summer months. In 2013/14 we evacuated seventy-four patients with likely or confirmed envenomation. With prompt correct first aid and modern treatment, the outcomes are generally good, despite the long distances patients are flown.

Section 4

Chests and clinics

Medical chests
A classic innovation, still going strong

With the development of the pedal radio and availability of radio medical advice, it became apparent to the doctors working for the new Australian Aerial Medical Service that treatment options were limited if the callers did not have a standard supply of essential medicines to use. In 1942, the concept of a standard medical chest was agreed. The dark green steel box, still used today, is a reminder that this initiative commenced during a wartime period when we had a 'can do' mentality. The rugged construction ensures that the contents are secure and protected. Inside the lid is a list of the items available, each of which has a numbered sticker so that users do not need to be able to read complex pharmaceutical names.

There are presently about 2,500 of these medical chests scattered across the remote parts of Australia, each containing about $700 of medicines and dressings, many of which are prescription-only items. I imagine that if we tried to initiate such an innovative program today, we would have difficulty circumventing the regulations and bureaucracy surrounding the supply of pharmaceuticals. Fortunately for the users, having worked effectively for over seven decades, it would be challenging for regulators to cease this vital service now.

The medicines are not extravagant, nor the latest and greatest. They are simple, effective and economical pharmacy items which have stood the test of time and are often relatively inexpensive to supply. A national committee seeks input from RFDS medical staff and modifies the contents every few years.

The review process takes into account the cost of items, their shelf life, tolerance of hot weather, the method of administration and other practical issues which might not be apparent to people living in the city. Apart from a few select items, it is not practical to refrigerate all the medications. So tolerance of storage in hot conditions must be considered. A short shelf life is also unhelpful as it requires replacement more frequently and increases wastage. While a couple of emergency drugs require an injection, in most cases oral preparations are preferred as these are more readily administered by untrained people.

A contemporary medical chest contains antibiotics to treat common infections for which it would be unreasonable to travel hundreds of kilometres to obtain. It also contains a potent injectable antibiotic for life-threatening conditions, such as meningitis. There are treatments for emergencies, such as anaphylaxis, severe asthma and cardiac conditions, as well as nausea and vomiting. Topical preparations are provided for common eye and ear infections, skin conditions and minor burns. Medium and strong pain relief is also included. When someone has been burnt, or has broken a leg in a remote location, one of the best things we can do is relieve their pain until help arrives.

Over the past decade some long-standing chest users have been disappointed at the removal of classic remedies, such as Magnoplasm® (for 'drawing' boils), Fryer's Balsam, calamine lotion and clove oil (for toothache). There has been a need to balance evidence-based medicine with the past 'art' of medicine and treatment options for patients at a distance. The 'morning-after pill' has been a necessary and important inclusion. Providing the latest technology in syringes, which have retracting needles, and sharps containers ensures we keep up with expected safety standards.

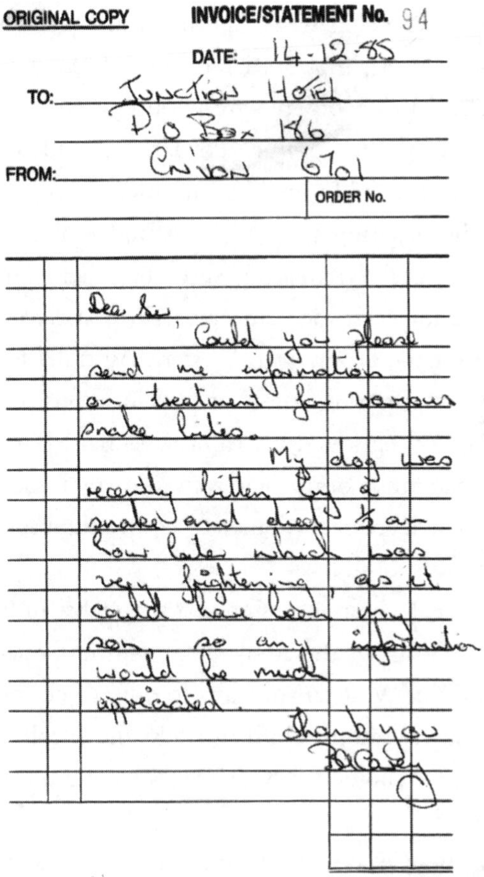

ORIGINAL COPY INVOICE/STATEMENT No. 94

DATE: 14-12-85

TO: Junction Hotel
P.O Box 186
C'n'von 6701

FROM:

ORDER No.

Dear Sir,
Could you please send me information on treatment for various snake bites.
My dog was recently bitten by a snake and died ½ an hour later which was very frightening, as it could have been my son, so any information would be much appreciated.
Thank you

Letter from medical chest holder.

Dear Sir,
Could you please send me information on treatment for various snake bites. My dog was recently bitten by a snake and died ½ an hour later which was very frightening, as it could have been my son, so any information would be much appreciated.
Thank you

When RFDS doctors undertake a remote consultation with patients, they prescribe treatment from the chest and furnish a code as a reference for the items that have been authorised for use. Over the following week, the medical chest custodians only have to complete a simple order form and fax it to the RFDS. New supplies will be ordered from our pharmaceutical supplier and freighted to them promptly. For families and communities in remote settings this will usually be at no charge.

While the ordering is simple, the underlying administration is done very carefully, making sure that there are appropriate authorisations for each medicine prescribed. I have held the poisons licence for the program in Western Australia for thirty years, covering pharmaceuticals in about 600 locations, none of which are in the care of registered health professionals! Being responsible for such a broad range of medicines in so many locations has necessitated a healthy level of flexibility to ensure the program operates efficiently but responsibly.

The medical chest is designed for use by individuals with no formal training. In the mid-2000s, we developed a weekend training course in Western Australia to offer to custodians coming to Perth for other reasons. Unfortunately, the enrolments were not adequate, but we subsequently created a simple online e-learning package instead.

Treating people at arm's length using the medical chest is a skill that takes time for new doctors to acquire. All the information you rely on has to be obtained by asking questions directly of the patient, or whoever is calling on their behalf. You can't examine them thoroughly, as would happen in a normal medical consultation. Doctors develop a sense of whether patients look really sick or not. Pallor, sweating and the way they walk, talk and breathe provides subtle clinical cues, which are missing over the telephone. RFDS doctors have to rely more on their experience in dealing with the populations and common conditions managed on clinics. This helps provide some statistical weight to our possible diagnoses. The patient's age, gender and past medical history are all factors that influence the likelihood of the possible diagnoses.

Abdominal pain, for example, can be a challenge. You are taking the patient's word on it without being able to palpate the abdomen and elicit the sort of tenderness one might find with appendicitis. The symptoms may be the portent of a serious problem requiring urgent surgery, or pain that is non-specific and may resolve. If it is mid-afternoon, you are under pressure to make a decision. If the patient ultimately requires an evacuation, this might not be possible once night falls and the number of suitable potential landing areas drops. So you are faced with evacuating the patient, costing thousands of dollars for what might turn out to be something insignificant, or delaying treatment and finding the patient ruptures their appendix and has a torrid outcome.

Much is made of the numbered body chart in our corporate publicity. It made it onto the Australian twenty-dollar note that acknowledges the Reverend John Flynn. In my time, however, I have never used it, nor met anyone who has.

Pain near Pullagaroo

I received a medical chest call from a woman in her late thirties on a station in the Murchison, hundreds of kilometres from medical care. She had dull but strong upper abdominal pain. She had put up with it for most of the day and tried remedies such as antacids and painkillers, but it was not improving. She had no previous history of gallstones, excessive alcohol consumption or any abdominal surgery. I couldn't put my finger on what the problem was. It was tempting to reassure her and see how she fared with more time. Yet, I had seen her briefly on a clinic in the past and her shy demeanour suggested to me that she would not have called if she were not genuinely unwell.

I arranged for an evacuation but the nearest practical destination was in Perth. I had to convince an assertive specialist in Royal Perth Hospital to accept a patient I had not seen nor examined, who was going to be flown over 400 kilometres. It was not easy to explain my gut feeling, the logistics of the evacuation and that if she was found to have a minor problem, she would have to travel a long distance home. It was one of those cases where you felt your reputation and that of the RFDS were on the line, yet I was not all that confident of my decision.

The flight eventuated using another crew and I did not even see the patient as I went out on a different aircraft that night. The next day I phoned to find that she had severe acute pancreatitis and was being moved to the intensive care unit. It's a dreadful condition but she had a superb outcome and I was so glad I had made the call when I did.

Flying clinics
Better care in the bush

Being a capable general practitioner and particularly a rural general practitioner is, in most respects, one of the most difficult jobs around. Firstly, you have to know a lot about a wide variety of medical conditions and can't rely on having a detailed specialist knowledge in just one narrow field. Secondly, you need the experience to be able to pick the few patients who have something important from the many with relatively minor illnesses who attend any clinic, day after day. Thirdly, you need a high level of resilience and self-confidence to work mostly in isolation, making challenging decisions and accepting criticism if you get it wrong. I admire and respect isolated rural GPs who live in small communities and can never escape from the responsibilities of their profession, twenty-four hours per day.

In a remote setting you need to use your clinical examination skills, experience and judgement to make decisions, without the benefit of multiple blood tests, x-rays or other investigations that are readily available in larger centres. This makes the RFDS flying clinics the challenge that they are.

Imagine having someone come to see you with a painful wrist, having fallen on their outstretched hand a day before. You examine it carefully and yes, it is painful to move and there are tender points; but from what you can feel, the bones of the wrist seem broadly normal. In a city practice, you can refer them for an x-ray and see the result later that day. In a remote clinic 300 kilometres from the nearest hospital, that is a little more difficult.

The patient can come back with you on the aircraft and have an x-ray completed in the base hospital. If there is a fracture you can go ahead and plaster it and you have achieved an acceptable outcome. But what if there isn't a fracture? The patient is now 300 kilometres from home, there's 'nothing wrong' with their wrist and they have to sort out how to travel home. 'Bloody useless doctor, dragged me into hospital for nothing.'

The alternative is not much better. You might recommend that the patient waits to see how things go over the next day or so and leave them behind when you fly home. A day later, you receive a call from the clinic nurse that the patient still has a really painful wrist, can't use their hand properly and something needs to be done. Do you fly out to bring them in or ask them to get a friend to drive them a significant distance to the base hospital for x-ray? 'Bloody useless doctor, couldn't tell my wrist was broken.' You are pretty much damned if you do and damned if you don't. It makes a nice bit of gossip around the town, which someone is bound to mention when you visit the following week.

Fortunately, most people living in remote areas are reasonably tolerant. If you have done your best and explained the options to them in the first instance, they usually understand. However, they do have long memories. I once attended a Pastoralists and Graziers Association meeting to discuss a few issues in an open forum. Once the meeting was in full swing and individuals stood up to ask questions, I was accosted by one pastoralist about 'the time when the flying doctor wouldn't come to pick up my fifteen-year-old daughter with a broken arm'. I politely responded that if he could give me more details I would look into it. 'Well, ah, she's forty-five now…so I guess that was thirty years ago.'

The same challenges arose for blood tests. There were no pathology laboratories at the places we visited, so if you took blood, you had to bring it back with you in the aircraft and take it to the hospital lab yourself. Unfortunately, we often ended up with erroneous results, particularly for electrolytes like potassium, as the blood specimens would be damaged during air transport. It almost made doing the tests a waste of time. Then there were delays in getting the results. This could mean that you had already treated the patient's ailment by the time the results came back.

Pharmacy was a similar problem. I used to write prescriptions then put them in my top pocket to take back on the aircraft with me. I would drop them in to the pharmacist who would prepare them and send them out on a truck over the next couple of days. It was not an ideal solution so we came up with a few tricks to help patients. They were probably not quite proper but they worked. We started to collect a small supply of the most common medications that patients were on and stored them in a small cupboard at the nursing post. Sometimes they were just spare repeats, or medicine ordered for patients who had left or changed their treatment. If someone saw me and needed to start a particular medication, we would dig out a box, write their name and instructions on it and give it to them immediately. When their script came in, we used it to replace our stock.

It really helped to have patients with common problems on similar medications. When I received phone calls that someone had run out of a particular pill, either we had a spare pack in our secret cupboard or I could suggest any one of a number of people in town to borrow from, until a replacement pack arrived on the truck. You had to be pragmatic!

Our visiting clinics provided medical care to the people living in remote communities who would otherwise have not been able to see a doctor. A great strength of the RFDS flying clinics, apart from the calibre of doctors, was consistency. In the 1990s we had a fundraising tagline, 'RFDS – always there'. The flying doctor arrived each week, other than in exceptional circumstances such as a cyclone or airstrip flooding. In one manner or another, the RFDS has, for example, provided a doctor to visit Marble Bar every week for the past eighty years.

Often there were multiple issues to deal with and you needed to spend as much time as necessary handling as many as possible on the one visit. So someone might come for follow-up of their high blood pressure. At the same time they might have skin cancers to review or cut out, or arthritis to manage; require a discussion about cutting back their smoking and drinking; then delve into problems with depression or some other personal mental health issues.

It is expensive to fly doctors out to remote locations, but the annual costs per patient can be less than for many city-based patients who attend their doctor many times throughout the year. As a society, we have an obligation to strive for equity and access to health services.

The RFDS did not bill patients on these clinics, so there were no pressures to pump patients through quickly. Instead, they received as much time as we could give them, which meant I was always running late.

A typical flying clinic day

On reflection, flying clinics were interesting, but at the time, they were also hard work. The day started at 7.00 am collecting pathology results and correspondence from the hospital in Port Hedland. There was a big cloth shoulder bag for each clinic site. It had been filled with results of the blood tests we had brought in from the clinic the previous week, plus radiology reports and discharge summaries. There were lists of patients who required follow-up for sexually transmitted diseases or immunisation from the Community Health team. Sometimes it contained reminders to pick up stocks of vaccines or consumables, which were needed urgently at the nursing post.

I would drive out to the airport, about 18 kilometres away, to be ready for the pilot to taxi at 7.45 am. There might be passengers on the flight, such as patients returning home after being in hospital. There might be an allied health worker visiting the town. It could be an occupational therapist doing an assessment of the living arrangements of an elderly person; the hospital pharmacist doing an audit of the drug stocks; a public health doctor doing disease screening; or the hospital electrician, coming out to fix a long list of overdue maintenance issues. Occasionally, we even took a flying blood bank; nurses would come out and bleed blood donors at Shay Gap, then take an Esky full back on the aircraft for processing.

In addition to our principal task of providing visiting medical care, the clinic flight was a valuable, reliable and efficient weekly conduit for communication, urgent supplies and essential visits to each remote site. This role is often forgotten when just looking at numbers of patients consulted on a particular clinic run.

After taxying and departure, we would head towards the main location for the day, usually about one and a half hours' flying time away. As we climbed away from Port Hedland, we could look down and see the railway lines and the massive ore trains snaking their way from the inland mines to the port facilities. I remember waiting at a railway crossing in Port Hedland once and counting about 200 carriages interspersed with a number of locomotives. Some of the privately operated railway lines in the Pilbara extended more than 400 kilometres, and even longer trains now run every day.

Gold for Australia

It was the first week of August in 1984 and the Games of the XXIII Olympiad were being held in Los Angeles. I was alone with the pilot on the day's clinic flight, so I was sitting up the front in the co-pilot's seat of our Piper Navajo as we headed out to Nullagine. The aircraft had an automatic direction finder navigational aid, which was used to locate non-directional beacons. You could also tune it to point to radio transmitters using the AM medium-wave broadcast band (531 to 1602 kHz), which are the frequencies used by commercial radio stations.

We tuned it to the ABC to see if we could hear what was happening at the Olympics. The signal was poor and getting worse as we flew further inland and we strained our necks to listen carefully. I can't recall for sure now what events we heard — it might have been Australia's silver medal in the men's 100-metre freestyle relay with Neil Brooks and team, or Dean Lukin's gold medal in the super heavyweight weightlifting — but I will never forget my sense of awe at the experience. Here we were, at 10,000 feet, flying across outback Australia and listening to a live event on the opposite side of the planet where our fellow Australians were doing our nation proud. What an uplifting and unique experience. I thought momentarily of my GP colleagues at their desks in the suburbs, seeing patients. It just further reinforced my view that this had to be one of the greatest jobs around!

By 8.00 am the balmy coolness of the night had already been replaced by the muggy humidity of the coming day. The two engines would be loudly throbbing at about 85 decibels and a combination of the air-conditioning and altitude would slowly start to take effect on the cabin. We would eventually reach our destination, join the circuit and come in to land on the dirt strip. The clinic nurse would be there with a Toyota LandCruiser 'troopie' — a four-wheel drive with bench seats and capacity for a stretcher in the back. There might be one or two kids who had come out for the ride and a dog or two. The dogs were clever, always settling down under the wing of the aircraft to avoid the heat of the sun. We would unpack the aircraft and put window shades up. The pilot would come with us as he was in for a long day, mostly catching up on paper work, as I saw patients.

We would drive to the small community where the clinic was held. Let's pick Nullagine. It took about twenty minutes, along a course that was often a sandy track rather than a proper road and included at least one river crossing. Sometimes I was allowed to drive and it was a real treat. I would roar over a concrete ford as we crossed the river, water spraying out each side of the Health Department vehicle, while the kids in the back yelped with excitement. This reinvigorated my dormant adolescent psyche and was often the highlight of the day.

We would get to the clinic, a shabby transportable building with a large verandah out the front. Patients would be hanging around and I would greet a few people, grab something to drink, then hurry to set up in the only office inside. The water in most Pilbara locations was unpalatable. You drank it really cold, with cordial, or as black tea, in an attempt to disguise the taste. I usually opted for black tea at most places I visited, as I figured having the water boiled would reduce the chance of becoming ill from bacterial or amoebic dysentery, without appearing impolite.

The clinic facilities were pretty ordinary even by the standards of the time. There was no hand-washing in the examination room so I had to use the toilet hand basin between each patient. Disposal of biological waste, such as dressings, was done by burning it in the incinerator in the back yard. Dogs would be running around outside and lying on the floor of the waiting room, waiting with the patients.

The nurse would arrange for me to see the patients she was particularly concerned about or we had decided to recall. Others would turn up as the day progressed. Sometimes we would hop into the four-wheel drive and cruise around the town and out to camp areas to try to locate specific individuals. In that sense, I did the odd 'home visit'.

Dying for dialysis

One visit I recall well was to a patient using peritoneal dialysis. This is a treatment for chronic renal disease, in which a catheter is surgically inserted into the abdomen (the peritoneal cavity). The patients infuse large bags of dialysate fluid into their peritoneal cavity every day, then let it drain out, extracting waste products in the process. It is used as a temporary measure for patients who are awaiting the opportunity to join a haemodialysis program or have a kidney transplant.

There was a lean-to made of corrugated iron sheeting at the back of a dilapidated house. The floor was dirt and in the middle was a small campfire surrounded by rocks. On the roof beams above were a couple of nails and the dialysate bag was hanging from these. I had a chat to my patient and asked her how she went about maintaining sterility when changing bags. She had been trained well in the regional hospital and given dozens of boxes of sterile supplies and dialysis fluid but her source of water for washing was the creek at the back of the property.

It was another revelation for a young doctor and explained why so many of these patients would develop peritonitis, a severe infection of the abdominal cavity, and need to be evacuated to the regional hospital regularly. Despite doing her best, it was unlikely at the time that the patient would get onto a haemodialysis program or receive a kidney transplant.

After a couple of hours in the clinic we would have a quick break for lunch, which the clinic nurse usually prepared. The pilot mostly spent the day in the nurse's residence, with the kitchen table covered in NOTAMS (Notices to Airmen) which he would be reading and replacing in his manuals. Otherwise, he would just go for a walk or read a book. As a bloke, I didn't appreciate at the time the efforts of the nurse in buying the food and preparing the meal for us all. It was a brief but important social encounter and a chance for her to have an informal debrief about the challenges of the job and gossip in the town, which she couldn't discuss with anyone else. Sometimes we would bring newspapers, magazines and even the occasional salad vegetables with us to the clinic. They were scarce luxuries in these locations.

The pilot would constantly ask how much longer we were going to be and remind me that he had to leave by a certain time to get home before he ran out of hours. He always brought the deadline forward to make sure we left on time. I knew that and understood what time he really needed to be back, so managed to keep working longer. It was like having a candle burning at both ends. You lost time at the beginning of the day travelling to the clinic and were pressured to finish early. Yet the people who came to see us needed as much time as there was available – and ideally more – if we were going to make inroads in health education and disease prevention, as well as dealing with acute issues.

When the last patient was seen, we would pack up our gear in a flurry and pile into the troopie. A few more kids would jump in the back for the trip back out to the airstrip. After saying our farewells, we would taxi down the strip and take off, heading back west into the bright setting sun. On landing, the pilot would refuel and pack the aircraft away while I collected the pathology specimens, my prescriptions and other correspondence and drove in to the hospital in Port Hedland. Sometimes I would bring back patients for admission, such as pregnant women near term, or people needing inpatient treatment. After dropping off the gear at the hospital, I could head home in the twilight, usually pretty exhausted, knowing that I was still on call until the next morning and wondering whether I would fly that night. A frozen steak on the barbeque and frozen chips in the oven was a quick and reliable meal for a single male doctor most nights.

The remote area nurses in these towns have a thankless job but provide an outstanding service, usually being available around the clock to attend to the expectations of the community. They deal with domestic disputes, drive the troopie as the local ambulance and are usually the first to deal with genuine medical emergencies. Tragically, in October 2012, the Nullagine nurse lost her life in a head-on collision at night, while driving to Marble Bar to assist with the evacuation of patients.

I visited Goldsworthy as it was closing, then Shay Gap, Telfer, Wittenoom, Nullagine, Marble Bar and, occasionally, Yande Yarra and Jigalong. Both Goldsworthy and Shay Gap were mining towns, built to provide accommodation for the families of workers at the adjacent open cut iron ore pits. When they were shut down, they were rehabilitated. There is little evidence of the towns – just a couple of very big pits full of water and the remnants of the railway lines that joined them to Port Hedland.

The very first clinic I visited was Shay Gap. It was the 1980s so I wore tight shorts, long walking socks and a short-sleeved white shirt. I also wore a tie. I decided that just because I was working in a remote location in hot weather, I was not going to let my standards drop. As the visiting RFDS doctor it was important to appear professional. By the end of the first day, with endless smirks and ridicule by patients and others, I decided the tie was not necessary! The shorts and walking socks remained. I subsequently learned from the nurse at Nullagine that all the Aboriginal patients called me the 'tall skinny fella with long socks'.

Dealing with Aboriginal patients was interesting, having had no experience treating them previously. The children were exuberant, as are all children worldwide, while the adults were generally more reserved and appeared shy. Their quiet nature concealed a wealth of knowledge of people and the land. When there was an opportunity, they could readily point out to me where to find water, what plants you could eat and a range of other useful information. It took a while for me to learn how to be more reserved in my consultations, taking time, minimising eye contact and just listening carefully. I learned that if you treated people with respect and just did your best to be open and honest, you would be accepted.

Many of the mob would visit Port Hedland and 'camp at Coles'. This meant hanging around, lying under the trees, outside the Coles supermarket in South Hedland. Groups loitering like this were usually treated with disdain by the many people coming and going who would ignore them, look the other way and scurry past. On occasions when I went there to shop, lots of yelling would suddenly come from the assembled group.

'Hey there, doc! Hey, you remember me?', they would shout. 'We're from Nullagine.' Some of the group would wander over, surround me and have a chat. It was a gesture of recognition, just like old friends, although the numerous passers-by seemed to view the exchange with suspicion.

I also started visiting Punmu, a new community which had been established on the edge of Lake Dora in the Great Sandy Desert, about 640 kilometres inland from Port Hedland and well past Telfer. The school facility was just a shipping container at this time. For a long period following a death in the community, the people all moved away and camped in bush huts. It was difficult to work with no proper clinic building and seeing patients outdoors. However, I respected their desire to live remote from the bad influences of alcohol, petrol sniffing, drugs and communicable diseases, as well as trying to pass on their traditional ways of living. I had to discuss with the elders if it was necessary to evacuate a patient: in particular, how we could get them back from hospital promptly without them succumbing to the temptations of town.

We also conducted episodic station runs where we would fly out and visit a couple of remote pastoral stations in a day to do some all-encompassing physical check-ups and provide an opportunity for counselling, health education or just a chat to these very isolated people.

While our clinics were for people, it was inevitable that the occasional animal would be brought along to be seen. I didn't profess to know anything about veterinary medicine but with time and advice from a local vet, I started to learn about some common conditions and, in particular, the drugs you shouldn't use in pets.

My predecessor in 1982, Dr David McDowell, was a frustrated surgeon. He loved any opportunity to keep his hand in and relished taking out lumps and bumps. Shortly before I started he had planned and undertaken a very significant procedure to try and treat a calf with an umbilical hernia. Apparently, he finished seeing patients at Nullagine that morning, then spent most of the afternoon with the sedated animal trying to put a nylon mesh graft in place on the abdominal wall. I never approached that level of surgical expertise but did manage to do a pretty good job on a dog at Wittenoom.

Wittenoom was a fascinating experience. The actual town that housed the employees of the closed mine was still occupied, although the population had diminished to only about fifty stalwarts who refused to leave. There was a nursing post, run by Terry Jordan and her husband Karl, based in what was once the large and well-equipped hospital. It was a delightful setting, in front of a hill and among the picturesque ranges which are now part of Karijini National Park. The old hospital building made for comfortable, free accommodation in the old wards for doctors and nurses from Port Hedland. If you were savvy, you could book a weekend stay and drive over to explore the Wittenoom Gorges.

Terry's pet dog was, as best as I can describe it, one of those little yappy dogs. It had been attacked by a dingo and had a number of nasty deep lacerations. She was upset and expecting him to die. I spent quite a bit of time stitching him up and was pleased to be able to review him on the next couple of clinics. Apart from the positive clinical outcome, most important was the gratitude and respect from the nurse. I enjoyed great morning teas every visit thereafter.

The remote area nurse at Telfer was Judy Kelly. She was a very experienced nurse and terrific to work with. One of my patients at Telfer had just delivered her third child in Port Hedland. I was fortunate to have been able to do the delivery and afterwards it was agreed with her husband that a vasectomy was in order. I'd done plenty before and the procedure is not hard except that the vas deferens, the tube you are cutting and ligating, is like slippery spaghetti and you need to be gentle when doing it under local anaesthetic. My first one in an RFDS clinic setting was a bit difficult as I didn't have exactly the instruments I was used to. Nevertheless, we got it done and the patient was 'firing blanks' in a month or two.

The remote area nurses at our clinic sites did it all. They provided routine child health checks and immunisation to all children in their communities. They attended any patients who turned up to the outpatient clinic each weekday and they managed emergencies after hours, helped by calling the RFDS doctor. They even drove the ambulance themselves. If there were an accident, they would go out, treat the patient at the scene, drive them back to the nursing post then call the RFDS for advice and to organise an evacuation. Sometimes they were confronted with multiple casualties or horrendous injuries but took it all in their stride.

When we flew in to Wittenoom, the airstrip was made of compacted asbestos tailings. You could see the fibres in the rough gravel surface and presumably, they blew throughout the town on windy days. I managed to visit the old mine site on a couple of occasions and at that time there were piles of old blue asbestos tailings just sitting in the open air. You could pick up handfuls of the silvery grey fibres and I can remember collecting a jar full. In hindsight, it was daft but I had an enquiring spirit.

Perth-based flying clinics
Keeping my hand in

When I moved to Jandakot Base, I took on the only flying clinics still conducted from there. It was a historical thing. In the late 1970s, a clinic circuit had been conducted from Jandakot, taking in towns such as Mt Magnet, Cue and Wiluna surrounding Meekatharra, and smaller communities such as Payne's Find, which was halfway between Meekatharra and Perth. This was continued into the early 1980s by Dr Rob Liddell, who had flown himself in a Baron on the clinic runs from Perth. After he moved on, my predecessor Dr David McDowell kept going to Payne's Find from Perth, while the other clinics were undertaken by our Meekatharra Base.

Payne's Find is a very small community on the Great Northern Highway, about 430 kilometres northeast of Perth and halfway between Dalwallinu and Mt Magnet. To say it is a small community is overstating it. The only visible feature is the Payne's Find Tavern, a roadhouse on the highway, with a couple of dongas (portable accommodation) out the back. There was a gold battery operated by the Taylor family for crushing ore — probably the last in existence in Western Australia. There were also stations in the surrounding area, with sheep, cattle, gold prospecting and tourism during the wildflower season being the main sources of revenue. The dirt airstrip was quite reasonable, with two crossed runways within half a kilometre of the tavern. This had strategic importance for us as a place to land for major road accidents along the highway. Just visiting every six weeks ensured the strip was kept graded by the shire.

Many of the families in the area were related and their various predicaments, trials and tribulations would fill a book on its own. I had the privilege to be the visiting GP for most of the community for about thirteen years, until a restructuring of our clinics allocated them to our Meekatharra Base. During that time, I didn't always relish the long days and the low-key nature of the clinics. But in hindsight, it was an eye-opener to the complexity of trying to manage multiple chronic medical problems and the inter-relationships between people, their families, their illnesses and their physical environment. This was a great revelation to me and doing the occasional rural GP clinic reminded me of the harshness of life on the land. I kept myself fairly regularly exposed to the dust, the heat, the flies and long bumpy flights, so I could continue to identify with the work done by our rural base doctors on a daily basis. It makes me now admire even more those who can practise rural medicine well.

When I first visited the clinic, I was collected by Rosemary Fogarty, a wiry country type who coordinated the clinic visit. She had an uncanny ability to drive a car, carry things or talk to you with a roll-your-own cigarette almost permanently dangling from her lower lip. I spent a decade trying to convince her to give up smoking, without success. She organised the clinic every six weeks, making sure everyone was aware of the date and collecting the pilot and me from the airstrip in her ute. On the first visit, she explained to me that she was grateful to my predecessor for picking her up when she had been shot in the chest the previous year. 'This is an interesting place', I thought. According to her story, she was outside walking around the homestead when a stray .303 bullet, probably from some shooters miles away, penetrated her chest, causing a collapsed lung. She called the RFDS – as one does in these circumstances – and we flew in and evacuated her to a hospital in Perth.

My clinics were initially held at the tavern, out the back in an old bedroom with a table and a bed. It had the pressed-steel ceilings and walls of a century ago: the type which were quick to erect and were impervious to termites and the wet. The waiting room was the bar, which caused some problems. As the day wore on, the level of noise increased and the sobriety of the patients diminished. I learned to work as quickly as possible.

While I was busy in the room doing my best to see patients thoroughly and with discretion, I am sure that everyone outside was discussing their ailments and what treatment I had given them, and guessing the circumstances of the few who were not willing to share their medical problems in public. Some customers of the tavern could be heard to encourage others to come and see me.

'Let the doc have a look at that skin cancer on your face.'

'Show him that lump you've got.'

'How about letting the doc check your blood pressure?'

While the community was quite generous, I refused regular offers to have a beer while I was seeing patients. So did the pilot.

In the middle of the 1990s, a government grant was used to build a community centre midway between the tavern and the airstrip. It was a community hall, with kitchen area and an office down one end, which we provided with an examination couch, some resuscitation equipment and a desk so that it could be used as a consulting room. This was a much better environment for seeing patients, although I probably missed the opportunistic consultations I could have with patrons in the bar who otherwise would not see a doctor.

One of my remarkable patients was Ruby, a small but tough elderly woman with hands swollen and gnarled with osteoarthritis after years of servitude on the land. She had been born and brought up in the region and, despite being elderly and in significant pain most days, was still active around the station. She cared for two others: an elderly sister who had an intellectual disability from a childhood accident, and one of her own daughters, now in her late forties, with Down syndrome. Nevertheless, she was always cheery and happy to see us as she turned up to every visit in her band of three. I marvelled at how she could cope with no opportunities for respite care for roughly fifty years. Both her charges were happy individuals, well accepted among the local community. Her main concern apart from her arthritic pain was how they would be cared for when she was no longer able to do so.

There were some funny stories mixed among the adversity. At one clinic visit, I showed her some forms which we needed to fill in. She asked if she could take them home to complete and I suggested we just do them now so I could sign them off. She hesitated for a while and then explained to me that she couldn't read. I was gobsmacked. She said she had received little education growing up on a remote station and got by without reading. I did not appreciate at the time that adult illiteracy even existed, nor that someone could survive in the contemporary world without being able to read.

'How do you read the instructions on your medicines?' I asked. She explained to me that she had someone read the instructions to her and then she just remembered them, based on the colours and shapes of the pills. It was another real eye-opener and I learned a lesson about the risks of pharmacies supplying generic brands of medications, with different colours and shapes, for those whose compliance with treatment was based on 'a little blue pill and a pink one'. I also learned to not assume things and be more careful in my explanations in future.

On another clinic, she announced loudly, with a grin across her face, that she had finally received her driver's licence. I was a bit stunned for a moment.

'Haven't you been driving everyone to the clinic each time I visit?' I asked.

'Oh yes, I've been driving since I was eleven!' she replied.

'Then what do you mean that you've only just got your licence?'

'Well, I've been driving for over fifty years but I just never got around to getting a licence. However, the Dalwallinu cops told me I better get one or I'd be in trouble, so I did!'

A final recollection of this remarkable lady was the day she announced she had a washing machine.

'Huh, what do you mean? What have you been using up until now?' I asked.

Apparently, she had been washing clothes by hand for decades but this new washing machine was an indulgence. However, things are not as easy in the bush as they are in the city. Despite now having a washing machine, there was insufficient water pressure from their tank to fill it, so she had to use a bucket. Then, when it was ready to go, she would start up the diesel generator in the shed out the back to provide the power for it to wash and spin dry. I wondered then, as I do now, whether contemporary young couples in the suburbs would cope with this sort of arrangement for long?

Life on the land can be beset with tragedies. One has only to read gravestones in country cemeteries, and Payne's Find was no different. Ruby had a son in his late forties who had worked hard, doing physical work all his life. He rarely came to the clinic but when he did, it was because of severe chronic low back pain. He had been referred repeatedly to Perth for spinal fusion and specialist advice but, with the work he did, he was never going to make a complete recovery. He was coy the few times I saw him and I gathered from others that he liked his drink. It took away the pain and he regularly came home late from the tavern.

At one clinic I arrived to be told that he had died the week before. He had come home late at night from the pub and blown a hole in his head with a shotgun, just outside the house. He was found by his wife and children the next morning. I struggled with self-reflection on whether I could have prevented it, with better treatment of his back pain or undiagnosed depression. In the end I realised that the best I could do was to provide a listening ear to his wife and children on clinic visits over the coming months.

The other tragedy engrained in my mind relates to a telehealth call about Rosemary's husband.

Collapsed at the pub

I was at home one night when a call came through from the Payne's Find Tavern. A man in his late fifties had collapsed with severe chest pain and breathlessness. Apparently, there had been a young bloke playing up in the bar and he, a large man, had confronted him and sorted him out. Shortly afterwards, he developed severe pain and was described to me as being on the floor of the tavern, sitting up against the wall and looking terrible. He was clearly having a heart attack. I immediately phoned our operations coordinator on another line and told him this was a priority one flight and we needed to move fast. I would be on my way as soon as I had given them some medical advice.

I returned to give advice to the tavern staff on using items from the RFDS medical chest. We had a treatment for angina pain, the common tablet taken under the tongue. We also had narcotic pain relief and some other drugs which might help. I discovered that the patient was the husband of Rosemary, who diligently organised our clinics and often helped others with drugs from her RFDS medical chest. People had tried to contact her but she was not answering the phone on her property.

I gave some advice then jumped in the car to drive to the airport. I had barely left when the phone rang again. The patient had collapsed unconscious and they were trying to do CPR. I pulled over and spent twenty minutes trying to provide support to someone on the phone in the bar. It was to no avail. Without a defibrillator, a patient most likely in a ventricular fibrillation cardiac arrest could not be resuscitated. We didn't even manage to launch. The tragedy to me was not just the death, but that a woman who had committed herself to organising clinics, attending accidents and helping others with the medical chest, was not there at the tavern, only a couple of kilometres from the homestead, to be with her husband in his last minutes.

I spent time later that night talking with her and again on our next clinic. It reinforced the importance of our telehealth service in providing rapid emergency advice, on the end of a phone, even though in this case we were unable to save a life. It is easy to ignore the isolation of many rural and remote communities, and to underestimate the comfort of being able to phone at any time and have a reassuring ear on the end of the line, able to provide medical advice, with some appreciation of their circumstances.

Some people have a misconception that only the emergency flights of the RFDS save lives. This completely overlooks the vital importance of regular visiting medical services to those who otherwise would have access to none. Our clinic patients often had multiple medical problems and usually far more genuine physical disease than their city counterparts did. Picking up a serious medical problem in a clinic, such as early heart disease, or cancer, or a problem in pregnancy, can also be life-saving.

Eradication with vaccination
The impact of vaccination on infectious disease

Quality general practice and routine preventive health measures, such as immunisation and selected screening, are not considered as exciting as our emergency work, yet our clinic services prevent suffering, improve quality of life and, indeed, save lives. I will discuss screening in the next chapter but first I want to focus on immunisation.

In the 1980s it was not uncommon to see cases of a serious disease called epiglottitis. The epiglottis is a small flap that covers the opening of the larynx and windpipe when you swallow so that food does not go down the wrong pipe. Bacteria called *Haemophilus influenzae type b*, widely found among all the other bugs in children, can infect the epiglottis. When this happens, the child becomes very sick with a fever but, more importantly, the epiglottis can swell up and become a large swollen ball sitting just over the larynx. This can ultimately cause obstruction and suffocation of the child if they lie flat.

I had seen a number of cases on my paediatric terms before joining the RFDS. It was certainly a nasty disease and it was important to differentiate these cases from the hundreds of children who were brought in with high fevers, runny noses and a host of other viral illnesses. If the diagnosis was made, the patients needed to be in an intensive care setting, where staff could intervene if the child developed an obstructed airway. In many cases, patients were taken to the operating theatre and electively intubated (a tube put down into the lungs to ensure they could not obstruct). This itself was a difficult procedure as the anaesthetist was often navigating around a large swollen epiglottis in the throat. For aeromedical transport, it was imperative that the child was intubated prior to flight, as it was considered too risky to move them without this protection. If a problem arose in flight, it would not be possible to intubate the patient successfully in the aircraft.

Whenever such a case arose in any of the hospitals around Western Australia, we would transport them to the Princess Margaret Hospital in Perth but we needed to have them intubated by an expert to make the journey safe. The RFDS had a small panel of anaesthetists who helped us out. The most prominent of these was Dr Barney Cresswell, a specialist anaesthetist at PMH who was also in private anaesthetic practice. Barney subsequently became a member of our board, chairman of our board, and national chairman of the RFDS.

The specialist panel was an informal arrangement. The doctors were often not paid, but if a case arose at 2.00 am on a Sunday morning, I could call them and they would come willingly on what might be a six to eight-hour round trip to perform a risky procedure and oversee the safe transport of the child to PMH.

On one occasion, the referring hospital in Carnarvon had managed to intubate their patient themselves and so, with some advice from Barney, I did the flight myself. Once the tube was in place and the airway safe, it was just a matter of dealing with the intravenous fluids and antibiotics, and making sure the tube did not come out! It was in my first few years as a flying doctor and about fifteen years later the parents of the young boy brought him out to say thank you. His mother had accompanied us on the aircraft and remained grateful for all who had helped save her young child's life.

Now he was a tall robust adolescent. We had a nice chat, showed him an aircraft and took some publicity photos.

The point of this discussion is to highlight the amazing impact of immunisation. Before the introduction of the *Haemophilus influenzae type b* (Hib) vaccination in the late 1980s, we saw not only epiglottitis but severe forms of Hib meningitis and pneumonia in infants. After the vaccine was introduced into Australia, epiglottitis almost vanished, as did Hib as a cause of the other serious diseases. There are now two generations of young doctors who have probably never seen a case, nor are likely to. The disease virtually just stopped. We need to remain vigilant with immunisation if we wish it to remain that way.

Anyone who has seen a baby with paroxysms of coughing, or gasping to breathe due to Pertussis, commonly called whooping cough, should be concerned at the recent resurgence of this illness, which appears to be due to waning levels of immunity in the population. Measles and mumps are not benign conditions and can cause serious illness and complications, such as meningitis. The viruses are still prevalent but reduced levels of immunisation and natural immunity leave us vulnerable to significant outbreaks in the future. I have evacuated two patients with tetanus, a disease most people know they should be vaccinated against but know little about. The cases were both elderly patients with little or no previous immunisation. They suffered severe spasms in their jaw and difficulty breathing and the diagnosis could have been missed. We need ongoing vigilance in our society to ensure that initial immunisation and booster doses of vaccine are widely administered if we are to avoid slipping backwards in preventive health care.

The role of Robin Miller-Dicks in providing immunisations to remote communities is well known in the history of the RFDS in Western Australia. As a descendant of the Durack pastoral dynasty on her mother's side and MacRobertson Miller Aviation on her father's side, she was both a pilot and nurse. She flew to numerous remote Aboriginal communities to administer tens of thousands of doses of Sabin oral polio vaccine, given on sugar cubes. It resulted in her legendary status and nickname of 'Sugarbird Lady' in Aboriginal communities. Her work was a great reflection on people within the RFDS who see a need and find an innovative solution to resolve it. A replica of the last aircraft she flew, a Mooney VH-REM, has been proudly perched on a stand across from our offices at Jandakot. It is something I have looked at unconsciously almost every day since I first started. It reminds me of our role in remote medical care and the need to strive for ways to overcome challenges in the work we do, to serve a population in need.

In subsequent years, vaccination of children in remote settings has been more formally structured through the Department of Health, Community Health or Public Health units. Since the 1980s, the RFDS has mostly been an opportunistic provider on our clinics, when individual gaps in immunisation have been identified. In the 1980s and early 1990s we used to do occasional station runs when we would spend a day flying in to a series of remote pastoral outstations, as was more common in our earlier history. This was always a nice change: having time for a yarn with the station people, checking the medical chest, doing some simple health screening and ensuring basic immunisations were up to date. Similar opportunities existed with some of the country race meetings we also attended, for example the Landor Races and the Rawlinna Nullarbor Muster. Unfortunately, fiscal responsibility and the need to justify the cost-effectiveness of every flight ended these ad hoc visits in the late 1990s.

Over the past couple of decades, many conditions have been radically modified by developments in immunisation. Hepatitis A and B are good examples. Viral hepatitis is inflammation of the liver, one of the body's most vital organs, resulting from infection with one of a variety of different viruses. As the viruses were discovered, the microbiologists just started adding different letters to the name to identify them. Hepatitis A is spread through the faecal–oral route, meaning it is prevalent in areas with poor hygiene, while hepatitis B (and C and others) are blood-borne and spread by needles, injections, tattoos and through sexual contact. Recent outbreaks of hepatitis A in Australia from infected imported foods have highlighted the importance of hygiene in the food chain and that these diseases are still prevalent.

Hepatitis is characterised by severe jaundice: a yellowing of the eyes and skin from high levels of bilirubin in the body, and is accompanied by being unwell for weeks. Though there is still no cure, in the 1980s and 1990s vaccinations became available which could provide some immunity and mitigate the effects of being infected.

A jaundiced view of things

In 1986 we had two doctors working in Meekatharra. It was a tough job as they ran the hospital around the clock, did our flying clinics and covered emergency calls twenty-four hours a day between the two of them. Hepatitis B carrier status was prevalent in at least 10 per cent of the population, which meant that if you suffered a needle-stick injury or had a splash of blood on a mucosal surface, such as the eyes or mouth, you could be infected. This made management of obstetric and trauma cases particularly risky.

General hygiene around the community was not ideal and there were occasional outbreaks of viral hepatitis A. Unfortunately, being at the forefront of the medical system, our doctors both con-tracted hepatitis A at the same time. They were really crook, with severe fatigue, nausea, vomiting, abdominal pain and jaundice. It was just like having severe influenza but lasting for at least four weeks. While they convalesced, moping about at home, we flew in relief doctors to help in town.

This situation would not arise today. We introduced hepatitis B and hepatitis A vaccination to our staff as soon as it was widely available. We have always tried to practise proper techniques to prevent transmission of blood-borne diseases, but hepatitis A could be picked up by any of our staff living and working in areas with poor sanitation and hygiene. Again, we are thankful that we no longer see what was once a more common illness.

Other 'old-fashioned' infections are still found in rural and remote parts of Australia and particularly in Aboriginal communities. Rheumatic fever is an illness following streptococcal infections, which can lead to permanent damage to the heart valves. With the invention of penicillin and widespread use of antibiotics, it is rarely seen in metropolitan areas. Indeed, it was a disease seen by the generations of medical practitioners before me. Yet, if you work for the Royal Flying Doctor Service, you will still come across cases, together with a related disorder, post-streptococcal glomerulonephritis. This is an acute inflammation of the kidneys, immune-based, following certain strains of streptococcal infection. There are episodic outbreaks in remote communities, such as in the Kimberley, every few years. No vaccine exists, unfortunately, so we have a low threshold for using antibiotics in remote medicine and high-risk populations.

Prevention is better than cure
Routine care and screening on remote flying clinics

Those who have a superficial view of health care often do not appreciate the genuine benefits of visiting the doctor. Emergency care is exciting but the truth is that we save more lives in Australia through quality medical care, screening and treatment of chronic diseases. People have a right to access medical services and an expectation that paying a Medicare levy should give them a minimum level of health care when they need it. There is a vast array of evidence-based guidelines on the regular age-based checkups and screening that should be done to detect and manage common diseases.

Much of the work on flying doctor clinics is dealing with acute medical problems. Patients come in with lacerations, sores, broken digits, rashes, infections and the like, which need immediate attention. They also turn up for ongoing management of chronic conditions, such as arthritis, asthma, heart disease and diabetes. This is one of the key reasons the RFDS started and has flourished: to meet the medical needs of people in the most remote parts of the country. As part of a general practice consultation, there is an opportunity and an expectation that we check for common diseases and ensure early treatment is provided to prevent some of the long-term complications.

A good example is the Pap smear to detect early changes which can lead to cervical cancer. It is an easily diagnosed condition but the consequences of missing the diagnosis can result in an awful cancer, which can subsequently lead to death. It is easy for women to put off having a Pap smear because they are busy, can't attend a doctor easily, will do it soon, and a raft of other excuses. In remote areas where it is much harder to see a doctor, it is even more important that the RFDS ensures opportunities are provided for this basic screening to occur.

The same goes for many other cancers, such as skin cancers, breast cancer, bowel cancer and prostate cancer. If we don't offer such services during our limited regular clinics then a significant number of people miss out. The same goes for health education. The rare visit to the flying doctor for many patients is an ideal opportunity to provide education and advice on other important health and lifestyle issues, such as alcohol consumption, smoking, diet and obesity. Evidence shows that health education provided by a patient's doctor specifically targeted to their needs is far more effective than broad publicity campaigns. Thus, at every clinic the flying doctor may spend much longer with each patient, giving them a year's service in a single visit and particularly trying to ensure that a variety of health problems are addressed.

Telehealth is not a substitute for face-to-face and hands-on clinical medicine. It can be helpful for sorting out short-duration ailments and assist with ongoing management of previously diagnosed chronic illnesses. However, if you are not able to physically examine a patient, a chunk of important information can be missed.

With telehealth you cannot palpate an abdomen to feel the enlarged liver or a cancerous mass. You can't do a rectal examination or Pap smear, to detect prostate or cervical cancer. You can't manipulate the painful knee joint to determine if there is a ligamentous tear or cartilage injury which will need further referral. Doing procedures such as excising skin lesions is not possible and counselling patients is not the same as in a considered face-to-face consultation in the privacy of the consulting room.

Rural Women's GP Service

In 1999 the Commonwealth Government announced a program to support female general practitioners visiting rural areas to give patients a choice of gender of doctor. The story goes that the Commonwealth Minister of Health was harassed by members of the Country Women's Association, which resulted in an announcement soon afterwards on Budget night. The RFDS applied to operate the program across Australia and was successful, so each of the sections had to implement it in their areas of operation.

I remember at the time thinking this was going to be interesting! Most country doctors are reasonably protective of their turf and their patients. After all, they are running a business. The idea of the RFDS trying to push a visiting female GP into towns with a single male GP was going to be challenging. I anticipated it would be received in the same vein as, 'Hello, I'm from the government and I'm here to help'.

We were allocated a certain amount of funding and given criteria for the locations that would be eligible, then set about trying to implement the initiative. Our first job was to recruit some female doctors willing to visit country areas for a couple of days every month or two.

Most active quality GPs were already working flat out in their own practices, so this was potentially a problem. The next issue was to convince the country GPs to accept the visiting practitioners and the third issue was to work out the logistics of getting them there and back efficiently.

I managed to recruit Dr Christine Marsack, a very capable doctor who had worked as an RFDS flight nurse with me in Port Hedland prior to gaining mature-age entry to medical school. I knew she would be suitable and had an affinity for country people.

We then approached our first target, Dr Anthony King, a solo male GP in Kojonup, to see if he would accept this visiting arrangement. It meant allowing another doctor to come and work in his town, so he would potentially take a cut in income from those patients who saw the visiting doctor. However, I convinced him that if he would allow the doctor to visit and use his practice, it would be a good deal all round.

It would provide an option for his patients to see a female doctor, but to do so in his practice, not undermining him as many state government visiting services often did. He would need to provide consulting rooms, consumables, arrange bookings, provide access to his medical record system and provide follow-up. This would ensure continuity of care in the weeks when the visiting doctor was not there. 'Look on it like a free visiting locum for a day or two', I suggested. 'It may indeed increase the patients visiting your practice or give you a chance to take half a day off.'

A sticking point was government insistence that the visiting doctor had to bulk bill Medicare and was not permitted to charge the same fee as the doctor in the town. This meant they were offering a 'cheap' service and undermining the normal fees that country doctors had to charge to meet their practice costs, but our concerns were disregarded in Canberra.

Nevertheless, the doctor agreed and the program took off, first in his town, then in many others around the state. We determined that rather than flying the doctors to the towns, it was usually more economical if they drove despite the extra time involved. Having a car gave them transport within the town and far more flexibility with travel. It was quite a new way of us providing additional services in rural areas and has proved to be an exceptionally popular and stable service since then. As a result, thousands of patients, mostly women, have attended general practices in rural towns where previously they were uncomfortable doing so.

Hospital nurses, practice staff and women from surrounding areas have had their cervical smears done, when otherwise they would put it off. Likewise, some blokes who were mates with the town's GP could see another doctor to discuss a personal problem they were otherwise too embarrassed to deal with. Improved screening and routine medical care ultimately benefits the entire community. The presence of a visiting doctor also enabled some collegiate support to be given to the solo country GP.

The Rural Women's GP Service has been a very positive program all around. It is fully government funded, however, so it continues to be at risk from the usual whims and uncertainties of budget cuts in health.

P'aps next time

It was the remote town of Nullagine in the Pilbara and one of the locations I flew out to weekly. The clinic was a hard slog. After a bumpy one and a half hour flight, we would travel over dirt roads and cross a river to get to the nursing post. The clinic was just a transportable and was not intended to be a permanent facility, though it had been in place for more than a decade and showed the wear and tear of a building that had suffered flooding from a number of cyclones. There was no hand basin for hand-washing. The phone and air-conditioning often did not work and there was an assortment of dogs and sick children piled up in the waiting room on arrival.

It was a physically tiring day: the long travel time each way, the heat, the airsickness, the flies. In addition, it was professionally frustrating, with trying to find information in disorganised patient records and communication challenges with people who were often shy or could not explain to me clearly what their problem was, while trying to be patient and culturally sensitive. To do the job properly took time and yet I was often under pressure from the pilot

288

to see everyone in the busy waiting room within a certain period, so we could get home on time.

A young Aboriginal mother came in or, more accurately, was pushed in by the dedicated nurse at the clinic, Philomena Woods. She needed to have a Pap smear and Phil had convinced her that this nice young doctor had done lots of women's health and could do it today. She had not had a cervical smear for about five years, since around the time that she gave birth to her last child. She was an articulate and well-presented woman who worked part time in town. Her marriage and family situation were stable and not disrupted by alcoholism and violence, as was often sadly the case. She just kept putting off having a smear test.

I proceeded to do a routine internal examination, chatting away to try to put the patient at ease, when suddenly my jaw dropped. You have a sort of motor memory in your fingertips which is used to feeling what it should. All of a sudden, my fingertips connected with my brain and told me I was feeling hard nodules where otherwise a smooth small cervix should be. I stopped and looked at the nurse while the cogs started whizzing around in my brain. It was one of those moments which probably lasted only a few seconds but seemed to be much longer. I stood there with my hand in a delicate position. What am I going to do, what am I going to say? This poor woman must have extensive invasive cancer of the cervix, yet surely it couldn't be? I had never seen such an advanced case in my metropolitan training.

I completed the cytology sample and then asked the woman to go and bring her husband back from work to see me. I told them what I suspected and arranged for immediate referral to specialists in Perth. I was shell-shocked for the rest of the day and in fact for days to come, self-doubting and denying that I had discovered what I had and hoping it was something benign. Unfortunately, I was right. Our patient had an extensive invasive cancer of the cervix. Despite all the best surgery and radiotherapy, she suffered a torrid

course and died during that year, leaving her caring husband and
children behind.

There continue to be many other patients in remote areas who present late with serious diseases. It is our job to ensure we offer a readily accessible service to them. We also need to be proactive, ensuring that, as best as we can, everyone receives the level of medical care that citizens of a wealthy country such as Australia deserve.

Gail Freeland deserves special mention here as our RFDS primary health-care nurse in the Kimberley. For over three decades, with RFDS and the Health Department, she has regularly visited the most remote communities in the region, ensuring that patients have all their required medications and their illnesses are properly monitored and treated. Her care has ranged from the youngest of infants through to the oldest in every community, trying to ensure they don't fall through the cracks in the health system.

Technology in primary care

There have been a few technological advancements that have benefited our clinic patients. Portable spirometry, dermoscopy and electronic medical records have helped us to improve our remote medical care. When I used to fly out on clinics in the 1980s and 1990s, lung function testing required a large bellows-type machine, a Vitallograph®, which was far too large to take on clinic flights. Patients had to blow into the device and it would chart the rate of exhalation over time, helping with the diagnosis and management of asthma and other chronic lung diseases. From the 1990s onwards, small, compact, handheld devices using electronic flow-measuring circuitry replaced these bulky machines. We could start taking them on clinics to do our own lung function testing, rather than sending patients hundreds of kilometres to the regional hospital to be tested. With time the devices were refined further so that they could be integrated into a notebook computer and electronic patient record system.

We always carried or had a portable 12-lead ECG machine with us, as diagnosis of heart disease and dealing with patients with chest pain on clinics was common. Again, with time, these became ever more compact and integrated into notebook computers and medical record systems.

We also introduced dermatoscopes to our clinic service to assist with diagnosis of skin lesions. Not surprisingly, there are many skin lesions in our patients who spend a lot of time outdoors, though most of these are benign. The dermatoscope provides a highly illuminated and magnified view of skin lesions to help differentiate potentially serious melanomas from more benign lesions. This can be done as part of any clinic visit by staff trained in their use.

The development of computerised medical record systems has the potential to improve patient care significantly by helping organise the myriad of investigations, results, referrals and treatment which patients may receive over many years. Electronic records also have great potential for itinerant individuals who move between many different locations. Unfortunately, we are still frustrated by lack of standardisation across the health system for patient medical records.

We have used computerised records since 1994 in some RFDS clinic locations, yet there is still no standardised method of transmitting an encrypted record of a single consultation, or entire patient medical history, to another professional in the health system. A method for importing or exporting confidential blocks of clinical information across the health system still needs urgent work. Combined with this are the challenges of ensuring strict privacy with health data and ensuring the consent of patients regarding who views their data. In some health services, these issues are overlooked by otherwise well-intentioned providers. A final challenge that we have faced, particularly in the RFDS, is that in some very remote clinic settings, there is still no reliable internet connectivity, which would enable access to central databases and transmission of files.

Regrettably, sexually transmitted infections are quite common in remote communities and can be a challenge to eradicate. We need to get the patients to turn up to the clinic, ensure the diagnosis is correct (as more than one type of infection can be present) and facilitate proper treatment. Making sure treatment is complied with and that contact tracing occurs takes a considerable effort. The remote area clinic nurses do most of the hard slog with support from regional public health units, but everyone involved has to manage these problems diligently to minimise ongoing spread. Patients forget to take their full course of medications if they are tablets, but when injections are offered, they are even less willing to come in for treatment. One of the least pleasant chores I had on some clinics was to go to the police lock-up and do a set of swabs on men and women to help manage these conditions.

This sort of medicine is not exciting to most. Yet, picking up a sexually transmitted disease and preventing its spread to a dozen members of a community is arguably more valuable than evacuating someone with a broken leg – especially when you consider the impact on so many people and the long-term health consequences of these conditions.

Not just an aeromedical service
Variety and innovation in caring for the community

While the RFDS has always provided the three core services of telehealth, flying clinics and aeromedical evacuation, this has not precluded us from extending our services in a variety of directions when the need has arisen. For example, while our original telehealth service was only to people living, working and travelling in remote outback Western Australia, we have, over the years, extended it to vessels at sea around the Australian coastline, oil platforms, hospitals without doctors and even the occasional Australian stranded in an international location. The service started by using radio, then progressed to predominantly using telephone. In recent years, dedicated video-conferencing and internet-based conferencing have been available, although not widely used.

Likewise, in our clinic services, we have principally provided high-quality visiting general practitioner clinics but our activities have also brought visiting medical specialists (paediatricians, obstetricians and general physicians) or we have facilitated their travel in some way. In addition, we have maintained a long-standing primary care nurse servicing remote communities in the Kimberley and provided transport for a variety of other allied health professionals to visit remote populations. The RWGP (Rural Women's

GP Service), which we ran between 2000 and 2015, was another style of visiting clinic service.

Most of our visiting services have been undertaken using aircraft due to the travel distances involved. However, in some places, travel has been and continues to be by road where it is more cost-effective or efficient. As an example, our clinic visits to Yande Yarra community in the Pilbara are by four-wheel drive, while our RWGP doctors have travelled on international airline flights to service Christmas Island.

Our evacuations have mostly been on our own fixed-wing aircraft, although we have provided a critical care retrieval service using road vehicles (from utes to ambulances), other fixed-wing aircraft (from small charter planes to corporate jets) and rotary wing aircraft (from mustering helicopters to large offshore oil and gas company assets).

A health service, not an airline

A mantra among clinical staff of the organisation nationally is that we are a health service, not an airline – although it is very hard to not be captivated by the allure of shiny new aircraft, nor focused on the significant capital and operational outlays they represent. It is interesting to note the insightful comments of a past president of the WA Section, Professor Desmond O'Connor, in an address he made to the Victorian Section in 1987.

> When I first came on to the Federal Council I expressed amazement at the amount of time devoted to arguing about money for aeroplanes and communications, while medical services were rarely mentioned. I am pleased to say that the situation seems to be improving and that we are seeing ourselves more as a medical service.
>
> My experience has been that when you focus on money and technology at the expense of the missionary aspects of

the service, it becomes sterile and gamesmanship triumphs over ideals. The experience of my own Section has been that employment of your own doctors and nurses is the best thing you can do for the Service.

Further, an official history of the RFDS, commissioned and published by the RFDS Federal Council in 1990, states that:

Radio and aviation are vital, but they are a means to an end. That is, to provide communications between outstations and the flying doctor base and transport for the doctor.

Take away the flying doctor and the service loses all meaning.

It has always been clear to me (and I think to most health professionals) that if your primary focus is health care, then leadership and innovation in your core business has to come from those health professionals. It is unlikely that you will achieve significant improvements in patient care if you rely on non-clinical managers and aviators to drive the agenda. There are, unfortunately, some organisations where medical staff are just contracted in as technical experts to fly on the aircraft. Without ownership of the service, commitment and the opportunity to influence decision-making, the achievement of any significant and relevant changes is elusive.

I recall once a communications expert proposing how they could install an expensive system in our aircraft so that we could 'talk to the top neurosurgeon in London' if we needed to. I politely asked him, 'Why would we want to do that?' Not only is the advice unlikely to be particularly relevant to a doctor in an aircraft at 25,000 feet, but the interventions possible in that setting depend on the clinical skills of the medical team and the equipment on board. It would be much more beneficial to spend the money on well-trained staff and appropriate medical equipment. The proposal was enthusiastic but lacked insight.

Flying dentists

When I was working in Port Hedland, we had a government dentist in town. His name was Adrian Longworth and we would sometimes windsurf together off the spoil bank. In addition to offering public dental services in Port Hedland, he would fly out with us occasionally to locations such as Shay Gap and Telfer and provide dental services from a beaten-up government dental caravan on site. I am aware from old photos of portable chairs under the wings of aircraft that dentists have flown with the RFDS intermittently over many years. The most successful and sustainable service in recent times has been that operated since 1998 by Dr Lyn Mayne from the Broken Hill Base.

In the years from 2008 to 2011 there was increasing enthusiasm in Australia about expanding and improving primary care. The recently elected Commonwealth government promised to 'end the blame game' in health and take greater responsibility for primary care services. Grants became available for a range of programs, including rural and remote oral health. There was a growing mood in the RFDS that expansion of our general practice services to include more allied health professionals, such as dieticians, psychologists and dentists, was going to be a priority growth area, where we could do more for patients in remote areas. Numerous surveys had shown that lack of dental services was a major issue for most people living in the country and needed to be improved.

In early 2010 I prepared a briefing paper for our CEO, Tim Shackleton. I found numerous reviews highlighting the poor state of rural dental services which would have formed a pile a metre high. Action was needed, not more surveys.

I investigated some of the funding grants being offered but they all seemed to be for infrastructure: buying dental equipment. This was a safe option for federal bureaucrats as they only had to commit to spending money once, rather than 'recurrent funding' to pay for service delivery, where they would be obliged to keep paying for a number of years. I was stunned to find how many locations already had dental equipment. Even some of the most remote Aboriginal communities had new equipment, still in original packaging. What they needed were dentists to come and use it.

I proposed that we take some of our donors' funds, say $200,000, and use them to 'do good work' – as seed funding to pilot a new dental service. I was conscious of Flynn's maxim that 'if you start something good, no one can stop it'. I was confident that if we established a dental service, it would work and we could obtain additional financial support later on. I even digitally edited an amusing new logo. Instead of our national fundraising tagline 'The furthest corner, the finest care', I proposed 'The furthest molars, the finest caries'.

There were plenty of locations that we considered low-hanging fruit, such as Meekatharra or Newman, where the dental equipment was present but the state government dental services were unable to visit often enough to meet the community's needs. The program did not need to be free either, with many people willing and able to pay to see a dentist if one was available. All we had to do was find a good dentist, pay for travel on commercial flights to a couple of locations on a regular schedule and provide the consumables.

Our primary care team was fortunate to employ a terrific experienced dentist, Dr Brett Abbott, who started the program off in a pragmatic manner. After a trial in 2011, rather than pick the easy targets, he took on more challenging remote communities such as Warburton and Wiluna, doing an enormous amount of work on every visit. Subsequently, with a five-year sponsorship from two resource companies, we commenced a road-based mobile dental clinic through the Mid West.

Apart from the variations in traditional services mentioned earlier, we have had other involvement in the health system at various times. It was normal practice up to the end of the 1990s for RFDS doctors to admit their own patients from clinic sites to the regional hospital and provide continuing inpatient management. When I was in Port Hedland, I valued the opportunity to admit and manage pregnant clinic patients. It was not without difficulty and I needed backup from other hospital colleagues in case the women went into labour when I was on a flight hundreds of kilometres away. However, I was able to deliver a number of babies, which was very satisfying, and to follow them up at the remote clinics afterwards.

In subsequent years, our doctors dropped out of obstetrics but kept up emergency department visits for patients who had come in from clinics and also provided anaesthetic lists in the hospital. It has been a source of minor frustration over a long time that we have never had a sufficient critical mass of doctors to enable regular participation in some hospital roles such as anaesthesia, surgery or emergency medicine. We need our doctors to maintain their clinical procedural skills but the rostering is always so tight that every day they are paid to be working, they have to be performing RFDS duties such as clinics or evacuations. This means that most ongoing attachments are done informally in their own limited time off.

Meekatharra Hospital

In Meekatharra we had a completely different and flexible approach. From 1985 to 2014, we provided the complete suite of hospital medical services, effectively running the hospital medical service for all that time. The background to the arrangement is interesting.

In 1985, I was working at the Port Hedland Base. It involved emergency flights almost every day, even when I was on clinic days. I did not fly on all evacuations, delegating appropriate cases to our flight nurses but giving them guidance and support by radio when needed. Yet, many nights were spent handing over seriously ill patients to a doctor who had flown up from Perth to meet with us at Meekatharra. As described elsewhere, the flight time from Port Hedland to Perth was about five hours in a Piper Navajo, plus refuelling stops. After flying out to pick up a patient, it was not possible to then fly all the way to Perth and to subsequently return within the pilot's permitted duty hours. So whenever possible, we would fly our patient to somewhere like Meekatharra, midway down the state, and hand over to a second crew which had come up from Perth. We came to call this a 'Meeka meet'.

I would do this at least two nights every week (as well as working every day), getting home by midnight on one night and getting home closer to dawn on the second. It was frustrating that while we had an informal arrangement for the government doctors in Meekatharra to be the 'flying doctors' on a voluntary basis, they rarely wished to do so. This limited our capability to use our aircraft, pilots and nurses there to do the more complex cases.

We also used to hear adverse feedback from people in the region about our service. On a couple of occasions, we had complaints from the Pastoralists and Graziers Association in the Gascoyne and Murchison regions. The general manager and I attended public meetings where a few speakers had the chance to have a go at us. It was done respectfully but they made their point of view very clear. After all, they lived in these remote areas and the RFDS was an important lifeline for them.

The station people needed to have confidence that if they called the RFDS, we would come. The concerns they raised were mostly about aircraft not being sent from our Meekatharra or Carnarvon bases, both of which used volunteer hospital doctors to make the decisions. RFDS General Manager Terry Jorgenson was a large man of formidable stature who had a long history of working in rural areas. Together with me as the 'doc', we defended

299

our service at these public forums but took home the message that we were being held accountable for decisions being made by hospital doctors, who were not clearly responsible to us for their judgements and performance.

I had another concern: that the skills and competency of some of the hospital doctors employed in Meekatharra was not at the level appropriate for our emergency service. It was a bit of a hardship posting in terms of medical employment and there was significant turnover in medicos. The town is, of course, famous for being labelled 'the end of the earth' by Tamie Fraser, wife of the then prime minister Malcolm Fraser, when their aircraft was diverted there during the 1977 election campaign.

We arranged a meeting with Dr Bill Roberts, the Commissioner of Health. Dr Roberts was an eminent physician who had worked extensively in the Goldfields as a flying doctor and had risen to become the head of the Medical Department, subsequently renamed the Health Department. He was, from my relatively junior perspective, a benevolent autocrat, who had a clear mandate to rule the health system with authority.

Occasionally, there might be a problem with a town where a doctor had left. Dr Roberts would call the RFDS and ask us to provide visiting medical clinics for a short while. When asked how we would be paid for this, it was very much along the lines of 'Don't you worry about that'. The issue would be sorted with a phone call and reliably reconciled at the end of the financial year. It is a great shame that this clarity of decision-making, integrity and trust no longer exists in the complex world of health funding. Bureaucrats developed relationships lasting decades; nowadays they change deck chairs on the *Titanic* regularly.

We explained to Dr Roberts that we were not happy with the quality of the doctors provided in Meekatharra Hospital and that their refusal to send the RFDS aircraft out to a case, or to travel on it, was adversely affecting our reputation. Likewise, in some cases their clinical skills were not up to scratch for the serious emergency patients we managed.

Recruiting for Meekatharra was obviously challenging and on a par with Roebourne and Halls Creek at the time. I was expecting to be offered a commitment for the doctors to provide a better service to us. Instead, to our surprise, he turned to us and exclaimed, 'If you don't like the doctors in Meekatharra, YOU employ them'.

What an interesting idea! We agreed it was challenging but we could do it, so we set about recruiting our first two doctors for Meekatharra RFDS and Meekatharra Hospital. These were Dr Nigel Jones and Dr Alastair Reid. They started in February 1985 and provided a twenty-four hour service to the hospital in addition to twenty-four hour cover for the RFDS roles. It was a tough job but they worked very hard at it and our service improved dramatically. Over subsequent years they were followed by a number of doctors, too many to mention, but including notably Dr Alastair Currie, Dr Jack Wearne, Dr Ann Ward, Dr Paul Crouch-Chivers and Dr Tania Wallace. In more recent years, the most noteworthy have included Dr Chips Thelander, Dr Rosalind Reid, Dr Christine McConnell and Dr Ron Dobson.

Our services in the hospital over the past twenty-nine years are a reflection on the changing face of rural medicine. Originally, we provided obstetric care for selected cases, had a visiting surgeon a couple of times per year and did some minor surgery when required. Sick children and adults were admitted and managed in addition to aged care in the hospital. We effectively provided a general practice for the entire town and a surrounding community of people living up to a few hundred kilometres away. On top of all this, our doctors managed medical chest calls, the RFDS flying clinics to surrounding small towns and nursing posts, and emergency evacuations.

Over the years, rural obstetrics has been shut down, there are no longer outreach surgical services and inpatient admissions have been curtailed. Doctors who are well trained to undertake procedural medicine are unlikely to go to work in towns where they cannot exercise these skills, and are voting with their feet by staying in the city or only moving to major regional centres.

Dr Christine McConnell deserves special mention. She joined the RFDS in 1995 when we were merging to form RFDS Western Operations. At the time of publication, she is approaching twenty years of continuous service in Meekatharra, a remarkable effort for a single female doctor in an isolated town such as this. There are few towns or country hospitals in Western Australia that have had the calibre or tenure of doctors that the RFDS has provided in Meekatharra over this period. Likewise, few towns have had regular access to a female GP for most of this time.

Regrettably, this holistic model of care, the variety of clinical roles and the synergies achieved from having the same doctors cover a range of duties were ceased in September 2014 due to a government funding issue. The RFDS and its fundraising had been effectively subsidising a service for the Health Department, which we could no longer continue to do. The hospital medical services and all the town GP services were handed back to the Department of Health. Our RFDS doctors living in Meekatharra now concentrate entirely on aeromedical emergency services and outreach clinics, while the townsfolk rely on a succession of locums, rotating through the hospital, for their medical care.

Other hospitals

At other RFDS bases, RFDS doctors provide clinical services in hospitals depending on needs and local arrangements. When I worked in Port Hedland, in addition to my other around-the-clock commitments, I was the duty doctor for the Port Hedland Regional Hospital emergency department every alternate Friday night on a voluntary basis. The deal was that if I had to go flying for the RFDS, my first priority, I would need to leave. Otherwise, I did the shift through to Saturday morning and, in return, the hospital senior medical officer would provide a doctor to cover me for a couple of rare weekends off.

We have had some very skilled staff giving formal anaesthetic lists at locations such as Port Hedland, Derby and Kalgoorlie, working in the emergency departments. In the 1990s we set up an itinerant 'flying surgeon' service from Port Hedland to towns like Newman in the Pilbara. Similar flying surgical programs existed in Queensland well before this. The general surgeon would fly out on our aircraft to operate, while the RFDS doctor would provide the anaesthetics. In the afternoon, past patients would be reviewed and new patients for future surgical lists assessed. Dr Jim Flynn was the driver of the program and it worked well for a couple of years until it became too resource-intensive for both the destination hospitals and us.

Dr Jim Flynn (no relationship to the Very Reverend John Flynn) also deserves special mention as one of our longest serving flying doctors. He served in Port Hedland for eleven years and then continued at Jandakot Base, making a total of seventeen years. Stability of staffing and continuity of care are critical for ensuring effective services and relationships in rural areas. Jim had a passion for anaesthetics but eventually completed training to become a specialist emergency physician in Perth, which just reinforces the calibre of the people the RFDS has employed over this time.

The point of this chapter is that you need to be flexible and keep looking at different options all the time. It is easy to become stuck in a rut doing things the same way when there may be other alternatives. In the past we have constantly evaluated our objectives – to provide equity and access to health care to those in remote areas – and been able to experiment a little with different projects.

Unfortunately, the funding chains, which shackle us with increasing weight and ever more micro-management, make it far harder to be as flexible as we previously have been. In the 1980s, if there was a town where RFDS doctors reported an increasing demand for medical services, we just increased the visits and cut back elsewhere where it was quieter. Today, we need months of planning internally and a year of negotiation with our Commonwealth funders to make such a change. Bureaucracy stifles innovation and adds to an increasing level of visible and concealed costs under the guise of accountability. I often think we need to reset back to the frugal but 'can do' mentality of post-World War II Australia. Our behemoth of a health-care system unfortunately makes that an improbable eventuality.

Learning the lingo
Managing the Aussie idiom

We are fortunate to employ an eclectic group of medical practition-ers from across Australia and a variety of international locations. During my time in the RFDS, I have employed many doctors from countries such as New Zealand, the United Kingdom, South Africa and Germany. We have also employed a few from Canada and the United States. Our recruiting efforts know no bounds, however, and I have also recruited and relocated doctors from such diverse locations as the Falkland Islands and Sweden.

With such a mix, it is easy to overlook the challenges of the Australian idiom for international practitioners, without even getting into the complexities of indigenous languages. Australian colloquial language – Aussie slang – has always fascinated me, having been brought up to accept with indifference many common Australian phrases as just normal speech. They add to what I con-sider to be a rich twentieth-century Australian culture, which deserves to be acknowledged and preserved, including regional variations between states. My daughters censure me when I rile against linguistic threats to Australian English – cookies instead of biscuits, candy instead of lollies or sweets, fries instead of chips – which are progressively invading our culture from *Sesame Street* in infancy to today's advertising by fast-food outlets.

Language is of course dynamic and always changing, but many phrases will be here for a long while yet. To help our new doctors from overseas, I set about preparing a set of training notes on Aussie slang. Many of our colloquialisms relate to vulgar or socially taboo topics involving certain anatomical areas and bodily functions. Therefore, as doctors who discuss such matters with patients, it is important we are familiar with the variations of terminology used. It can also be quite fun to learn of the many innovative descriptive words that have been concocted.

My set of notes slowly expanded. Initially I collated a very wide range of words used for anatomical areas and bodily functions, then broadened it further to include descriptions of occupations, personality types, states of health, terms of endearment and various forms of abuse. It has continued to evolve.

Doctor, I'm crook

Dr Catarina Widing had arrived from Sweden. She was doing a remarkable job during our orientation program of understanding the Australian way of speaking, mixed with the perverse pronunciation of vowels by a staff member raised in New Zealand. Even the term 'feeling crook' was foreign to her. I gave her the set of notes with some case examples of Aussie slang in clinical encounters, such as the following.

> 'Doctor, I'm crook. I was really knackered after work yesterday and felt like spewing. I had awful heartburn last night and thought I was going to cark it, so I had to take a sickie today. Of course my knees are stuffed and my back is buggered from farming. Now the gearbox in the car is rooted, so I had to walk here, which really gave me the shits.'

Note: this patient may have ischaemic heart disease, peptic ulceration from his anti-inflammatory drugs, or another illness. He has taken sick leave, his car is not working and he is unhappy about having to walk to the clinic.

During her first week in Port Hedland, Catarina did a flying clinic out to Marble Bar. I received an excited call at lunchtime.
'Hey, there! Guess what? My first patient came in and told me he was crook...and I knew exactly what he meant!'

Section 5

Evaluation

Crunching the numbers
Implementation of medical records and data analysis

In my early paediatric and obstetric posts where I worked as a senior resident medical officer, I was expected to present cases and tutorials every week. I expended quite a lot of time in the medical records department, chasing up patient records and trying to obtain data on the number of cases with specific diagnoses which we had treated over a particular time period. I became familiar with the ICD (International Classification of Diseases) and how medical records were coded and classified, something which was not well covered in our undergraduate medical course. I also had time to pursue my folly with computers and programming, writing short sequences of code to pull the data I was looking for from the hospital computer system.

Together with a few friends, I had been enthused by the new breed of 'personal computers', typified by such systems as the Tandy TRS-80, which were more business-like than the Atari and Commodore game machines of the time. In 1982 the IBM Corporation released its first personal computer, the IBM PC, which revolutionised our world. It was too expensive for me but before I moved to Western Australia I settled on a Cromemco CP/M machine. What a beast it was. It cost 20 per cent of my net annual salary. It had dual quad-density 5-inch floppy drives able to store 1.2 megabytes of data each and a whopping 64 kilobytes of RAM. Those who know about computers will appreciate the sarcasm. An average portable drive at the time of publication can easily store one million times the amount of data of my floppies.

I also spent two weeks' income buying a copy of *dBase II*, the first of the serious relational database systems for PCs. I set to writing applications, such as a personal accounting package and catalogues of books and medical articles, as a hobby.

When I commenced with the RFDS, I was a little surprised that there was no computerised register of patients we had transported, nor any useful clinical information such as their diagnoses. These were still the days of mainframes and the RFDS had a 'dumb terminal' going to a large computer at the TAB. It was used for accounting purposes mostly, with a modest customised program to keep track of aircraft flying hours, but that was about it. The RFDS did not bill patients so there had not been any need to record these details for accounting purposes.

Standardised records

I also found that our inflight medical records were not as detailed as they might have been. When I got to Port Hedland, the flight nurses and I developed a better structured record, which was comprehensive but easy to use and provided opportunities for data collection. Working in an aircraft is not like a hospital or clinic where you can have files and many different forms for various purposes. There is limited room, you may be caring for three patients at a time in flight and you need a system that can record all the important information in one place. This includes patient demographics (name, age, sex and address), their diagnoses and condition on handover, their vital signs in flight, fluid balance, drugs given and other specialised observations in certain cases. We came up with an A3 pad, with a carbon duplicate, which was large enough to see all the key observations at once, but easy to use on your lap in flight.

Most ambulance services have 'tick the box' forms where, because of the short transfers and limited care, only a few basic parameters are recorded. In contrast, we provide hospital-level care in the air, often for many hours at a time. We need a system where the treating doctor and nurse can make ongoing comprehensive observations and notes about the patient during a long journey. These observations are not just for our benefit – to record care for medicolegal purposes – but are also to inform the receiving hospital about the treatment patients have received from our staff and our overall assessment of their illness or injury.

In most places, hospitals receive a poor-quality carbon copy of the original record and barely look at it. I took a more radical view that if the information recorded was important, the treating hospital should receive the most legible copy so they would read it, and we should retain the poorer quality carbon duplicate. We have continued that philosophy to this day and I am pleased when I am given feedback about patients that the RFDS record was often the most legible and comprehensive summary in the patient's notes.

Our A3-sized paper pads still offer many benefits in the field, despite the availability of compact electronic tablet devices. You can drop a paper pad in the dirt, stand on it, sit on it, spill water on it and the record is still there! They are cheap to buy, the battery doesn't go flat and you can see a substantial amount of information on such a large sheet, with a single glance. You can hand it over to another health professional to read and it is far more conducive to recording comprehensive notes than trying to type in flight. While it is inevitable we will transition to some electronic device in the future, I suspect it will be more expensive and less reliable than a well-designed paper record.

Medical data

As an adjunct to implementing an improved medical record across our service in 1985, I wrote a database application in *dBase II* to record key fields about each patient. I spent time analysing what was core information and the minimum data fields we must record to provide meaningful reports. I did not want to burden our nurses with unnecessary detail. For the first eighteen months, I was the only person coding the diagnoses and entering the data – usually each weekend – using the PC I had brought with me.

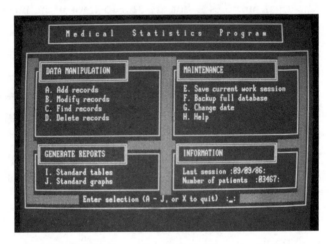

Medical statistics program created by the author in 1985.

Our operation is not as simple as flying out and bringing a patient back. Sometimes we fly out to pick up a patient, divert via another location for a second case then drop the patients at a location such as Meekatharra, where a second aircraft and crew may take them on to Perth. We could pick up an additional patient on the way home and have changed aircraft during the handover. So where patients go and where aircraft go can be different. The staff caring for a patient may also vary if they swap aircraft at different locations.

I reported my initial findings on our work out of Port Hedland during 1984 in an article I wrote for our fiftieth anniversary publication. Of 801 patients we had attended, 41 per cent were suffering from traumatic injuries, 15 per cent had complications of pregnancy and labour, 13 per cent had acute gastrointestinal and surgical problems, 12 per cent respiratory disease and 10 per cent cardiac conditions. Interestingly, 27 per cent of trauma cases had head or spinal injuries and 36 per cent were primary evacuations from pastoral stations, nursing posts or Aboriginal communities where there was no doctor at all. At the time, 42 per cent of patients were transferred to Perth.

I subsequently expanded our data collection across all WA Section bases, starting in 1985, and factored in the various permutations and combinations of aircraft and staff so we could track patients rather than aircraft movements. Analysis of the sort of cases we were managing helped to highlight the skills and equipment we needed for our emergency service, based on information rather than gut feeling.

Our General Manager, Terry Jorgenson, and WA Section Council could see the benefits of what I was doing and I am grateful they supported me in it. They made the big decision to agree to purchase the 'medical' computer. This was an IBM PC AT, the second generation of IBM PCs. It had a hard-disk drive (wow) as well as floppy disks and a colour CRT (cathode ray tube) monitor. Our annual report in 1986 showed a photo of this PC which, with printer, cost approximately $17,000.

In hindsight, this single machine made a significant difference to our service. We started to collect patient data formally, established a database to monitor use of our medical chest drugs and commenced 'word processing', which was also a new concept.

Before this, if I wrote a clinical guideline or protocol, it had to be typed on a typewriter. It would be corrected, then retyped from scratch, with the occasional minor error rectified with white Liquid Paper® correction fluid. Maureen Prime, our secretary, was very good but production of large manuals was very time consuming and the layout, in a basic typewriter typeface, not visually appealing. With our medical computer capable of operating as a word processor, we were able to be much more productive and create the first of our clinical guidelines for patient care in our aeromedical service. I bought the newly released *PageMaker®* desktop publishing software, which dramatically improved the layout of printed material, and we really took off. Our current comprehensive RFDS Clinical Manual, now twenty-five years on, has its origins in this early work.

It is sometimes hard to comprehend having no network, no email and no internet. If I had a document to share with someone in the office, it had to be saved on a floppy disk then physically given to them to copy onto their machine. I put in a fledgling peer-to-peer local network using *LANtastic®* on DOS. It worked well among a few in our medical group until we moved to Microsoft® *Windows®* about 1993 and, a little later, established a company network. Our data was stored on floppy disks, then on servers and now is disappearing into the 'cloud'.

Using the data

A conference paper I presented in 1990 provides an interesting insight into our services at the time. In 1987 I reviewed 5,000 evacuations by the WA Section over sixteen months. The principal diagnoses were coded according to the *International Classification of Diseases, Ninth Revision.* When grouped into ICD chapters, the following pattern emerged. (A comparison with twelve months in the 2013/14 year for Western Operations is also shown.)

In the 2013/14 year, our doctors handled over 10,000 evacuation requests in Western Operations, which resulted in 8,846 aeromedical transfers. It is of interest that the proportion of our work from trauma (injury and poisoning category) has decreased. This is undoubtedly due to a greater focus on road safety, particularly driver education about seatbelt use, speeding, drink driving and fatigue, combined with improved vehicle safety. In addition, occupational safety and health is a much higher priority in both mining and farming enterprises, resulting in fewer serious industrial injuries.

ICD9 Category	WA Section (only), 1985–86	Western Operations, 2013–14
Injury and poisoning	30%	24%
Obstetric	14%	5%
Circulatory	11%	23%
Ill-defined	10%	10%
Gastrointestinal	7%	11%
Respiratory	5%	6%
Musculoskeletal	4%	2%
Neurological	4%	2%
Other	10%	14%
Mental health	3%	3%
Perinatal	2%	1%

Table 1. Comparison of diagnostic categories of patients evacuated in 1985/86 and in 2013/14

In contrast, there has been a significant expansion in the number of patients transferred with heart disease (circulatory category). This is due to improved diagnostic tests over the past decade, which means that more patients with chest pain are accurately diagnosed and being evacuated to specialist care in Perth, resulting in much better long-term outcomes. The number of women with complications of pregnancy has remained relatively constant but, as the workload from other conditions has increased, their proportion overall is falling. Over the past decade, evacuations for acute mental health problems have actually increased in number such that they remain the same percentage of our workload.

The figures also differ from my early data analysis of our work out of Port Hedland in that this focused only on the northern region, which included vast remote parts of the Pilbara with fewer hospital facilities than are found in the southern half of the state.

At the conference, I reported on the composition of the national RFDS fleet at June 1990. This is shown in Table 2 and compared with our fleet at 30 June 2014.

National RFDS	1990	2014
Beechcraft B200 King Air	7	15
Beechcraft C90 King Air	5	–
Cessna C441 Conquest II	4	–
Cessna C425 Conquest I	2	–
Piper PA-31 Navajo	14	–
Piper Chieftain	2	–
Piper PA-31P Mojave	1	–
Beechcraft B80 Queen Air	2	–
GAF Nomad N22B	1	–
Pilatus PC-12	–	31
Beechcraft B200C King Air	–	11
Beechcraft B350C King Air	–	3
Cessna C208 Caravan	–	2
Hawker 800XP jet	–	1
Total	38	63

Table 2. Aircraft types in use in 1990 compared with 2014

Apart from the increased number of aircraft overall, there have been significant changes to the types of aircraft operated. The Pilatus PC-12 is now the most prevalent type and there are no piston-engine aircraft owned and operated (although many chartered clinic flights are still on older piston-engine types).

In the year to June 1990, the national RFDS fleet flew 7.9 million kilometres. In the year to June 2014, Western Operations alone flew 7. 7 million kilometres and the national organisation 25.6 million kilometres.

National RFDS	1990	2014
Sectors*	23,979	71,274
Hours	24,816	78,788
Kilometres	7,916,565	25,617,353

* *A sector is a flight leg, or take-off and landing*
Table 3. Aircraft activity in 1990 compared with 2014

The three sections of the RFDS operating in Western Australia merged into a single entity, RFDS Western Operations, in 1995. As part of the restructuring, under new CEO Bruce Rathbone, we looked carefully at the number of aircraft we owned and the distribution of our bases across WA. It was reports from our clinical database that enabled me to show the distribution of patients across the state and the locations to which they were being moved. I taught myself to use *SPSS*® software and used it for data analysis across all our bases from 1995 onwards.

It became clear from the data that there were almost equally distributed numbers of emergencies in the Kimberley, Pilbara, Mid West and Goldfields. This aligned well with retaining and expanding our bases located in Derby, Port Hedland, Meekatharra and Kalgoorlie. In the south of the state, there were double the number of emergency calls but generally much shorter distances and this fitted well with the resources of the Jandakot Airport base.

I rewrote our first database in a better *dBase* compiler called *Clipper* and it served well in recording all our patient records until 1997, when I employed some young IT professionals to rewrite it in the new database program Microsoft® *Access*®. I christened the software Hermes, after the Greek god, in the knowledge it would become a messenger, showing us the work we did and the demographics of the patients we carried. We had a very basic computer network across our bases at that time and we tried to have our clinical staff code the diagnoses and do the data entry at each base at the end of a flight. It was a flop. The quality of coding and data entry was compromised by many staff who at that time were relatively computer illiterate. Reliability of the data replication across each of our remote bases every night was exacerbated by regular issues with power failures and poor modem connections after hours. The old saying 'garbage in, garbage out' rang true and we returned to centralised coding and data entry.

Our current information systems are much more robust thanks to the incredible expertise of our Database Administrator, Helen Bartholomew, whom we were fortunate to lure from the University of Western Australia. Our patient data is still based on the core fields I established in 1985 but with many more linkages and greater robustness than before.

Streamlining the system

With our inflight medical records sorted, I moved to streamline our processes for receiving flight requests and prioritising them. We had a fledgling system for taking calls, originally derived from the receptionist answering the phone during the day, supported by an after-hours person who had a mixture of roles including answering the phone, tracking aircraft movements and providing security to our building during the night. In the 1980s most bases self-tasked, that is, a call would come in to the regional doctor, who would decide that an evacuation was necessary and who would notify the base radio operator or the pilot and nurse directly.

General Manager Terry Jorgensen, or 'Jorgo', was amenable to developing a more professional operations centre, having been a committed RAAF Reservist and appreciating the need to maintain awareness of aircraft operations. I was most interested in providing a reliable, professional medical interface for callers. I designed a referral form for country hospitals and nursing posts which specified all the core information we would like when we received an evacuation request. I based it on my experience in Melbourne when calling the neonatal retrieval service NETS, where I would be asked to methodically go through each of the items on a form they supplied to obstetric units. The idea was that if you encouraged people to acquire all the relevant information about the patient in advance, in a standard manner, and your own staff followed the same structured approach, you could convey a lot of clinical information correctly and efficiently and then have a discussion about the priority of the patient and any special requirements.

We printed and distributed to all the common referring locations hundreds of standard pads, which contained the core non-clinical information (name, weight, source, destination) and the essential medical information (diagnosis, vital signs, drugs and other treatment). Then we designed a similar pad for the non-clinical information for our operations coordinators, and a pad for the clinical information, in a similar format, for our doctors. My goal was to make referral of emergency cases as streamlined as possible, with callers only needing to call one number and make only one phone call. Our operations staff would take the basic details then pass the call on to the duty doctor in the region for the more detailed medical discussion.

The one-stop shop

There was a little more technology needed to make this work. First we needed a 1800 number so that anyone could call from any phone for free. We set this up properly in 1992 with a memorable number, 1800-625-800, that was directed to the single RFDS Operations Centre in Perth. It meant that every call to the RFDS was properly logged and would be acted upon. It was far superior to callers trying to contact a regional doctor directly.

However, once that single referral call had been made, the problem was that our doctor in the region was notified and had to call the referring location back. Often the original caller was busy, either on the phone or sorting out the patient, so we wasted a lot of time trying to contact them to obtain and discuss essential medical information. We eventually managed to install telephone technology which enabled transit switching; that is, an incoming call could be put through to our staff on either an internal extension or an external number at any time of the day. This meant our 'one-stop shop' would now work.

The final step was to try to record the calls into our Coordination Centre. We obtained some second-hand tape-recording devices from the Civil Aviation Authority and initially used them to record all incoming calls. They were archaic and it was difficult to locate a call retrospectively. What I really wanted was for the call that was switched out to the RFDS doctor to be recorded also. Eventually we adopted a Red Box® recording system, as used by the WA Police. The system records all incoming phone calls on operational lines and all calls out to our doctors, as well as inflight radio communications. This is done in a digital, time-stamped format. It has become a great asset for quality assurance and follow-up of problem cases.

We have worked assiduously to educate health professionals around the state about how to contact the RFDS for emergencies, as well as those remote patients seeking telehealth medical advice. For a number of years, a professional and user-friendly booklet has been published and supplied to hospitals to explain our processes and how users can best obtain assistance from the RFDS. There is no other state with such a clear and simple process for arranging emergency evacuations

The flight to electronic records
Establishing electronic medical records

Patient records have always been a challenge for us in remote medical practice. There can be a variety of clinic sites using different systems. We undertook clinics at mine sites, Department of Health nursing posts, Community Health facilities, Aboriginal Medical Services and locations which only the RFDS visited. At each clinic the records were different. I can recall wasting a lot of time trying to find things in Community Health notes. While the records were comprehensive, every provider used different pages in different sections of the folder. The system had a structure but it was still confusing to try to find everything. If I had a child with a chronic ear infection and I wanted to find the immunisation details, they were in one section. What the paediatrician thought on a recent visit was in another section, as were details of audiometry, the recent ear-health screening team notes and the pathology results for recent ear swabs. It was mostly handwritten, which made it just that bit harder. I am sure many practitioners relied only on their memory of the patients and so some of the work done by other health workers was overlooked or forgotten. This was in places with proper structured records. At other sites, we inherited the old 7-inch by 5-inch card system, which usually had a few illegible scrawls on it for each consultation and not much else.

Around 1994, computerised medical records were starting to emerge in Australia, especially to help doctors with the burden of managing prescriptions. The most prominent was software called *Medical Director for Windows*, written by Dr Frank Pyefinch, a GP in Bundaberg, Queensland. I met him at a medical computing conference and he showed me how his program had streamlined the chore of managing repeat prescriptions. Comprehensive medical records were not the primary aim of the software at the time but a useful secondary benefit. Another product called *Rx Healthcare ProfDoc* used a database compatible with other *dBase* records we were accumulating. The company had an office in Perth and a medical advisor, Dr Rob Hills. I was acquainted with him from my involvement in the Royal Australian Navy Reserve and he was willing to listen to the specific requirements we had for our remote clinics and receive feedback on the ease of use of the program.

In 1996 we were offered a generous donation to support a project which I labelled with the acronym CARE (Clinic And Remote Consultation Evaluation). It enabled me to purchase a couple of Toshiba laptop computers so that we could establish a portable electronic medical record system on our clinics. The laptops were the fat clunkers of the time, about 3.5 kg in weight, 6 cm thick and with a colour LCD screen of about 11 inches and SVGA resolution of 800 by 600 pixels. They had floppy disks and a hard-disk drive. We loaded *ProfDoc* software and set about using it on our clinics. Dr Jim Flynn was an enthusiast in Port Hedland and managed to encourage our other doctors there to try it out at Marble Bar and Nullagine. I took the laptop to Payne's Find and gradually converted our paper records to the system.

It was a new paradigm. As doctors, we were used to talking to patients and making the odd note on a pad, but most of the time we were engaging them with eye contact and listening carefully. We now had a computer in the middle of the desk and had to learn to talk and listen while trying to find our way around the screen and type notes in the right place with some accuracy. It was not an easy transition for us, nor for patients. I think it made them feel like they were at a bank or travel agent, with attention divided between a screen and their genuine issues. Still, we persevered.

At the time there was no connectivity. We took a portable computer out on the flight then brought it back and backed it up. Fortunately, we had only one doctor doing a clinic flight on any day; otherwise, we would not have been able to synchronise the changes made on multiple versions of the software. While it was theoretically possible to set up a dial-up modem over the phone line, the phones themselves were unreliable and the speeds were in the order of 28.8 kilobits per second. In the present era, data is easily transmitted at 100 to 1,000 times that speed, even over a mobile phone, and that will undoubtedly continue to increase.

We continued to press on, ahead of many city general practices, using the program as well as we could and waiting for software vendors to develop better synchronisation across multiple devices. Regrettably, metropolitan practices were their main customers and this was not a particularly important feature for their fixed clinic sites.

Another issue we faced was that when we finished a clinic and took the computer with us, our medical records went also. While it was important for RFDS doctors to have access to patient records between clinics to do recalls and follow-ups, it was also important for the remote nurse to have up-to-date patient records on site. They needed details of our consultation, investigation results, the treatment plan and the medicines prescribed. We therefore had to do a print dump after each patient so that there was a paper record to file in the notes kept at the clinic.

If other health practitioners visited, what record system were they to use? Did they write in the paper notes or use their own and separate electronic record system?

We eventually converted to *Medical Director MD2* software when *ProfDoc* folded and subsequently, on a national basis, have trialled many alternative programs. None of these have met all our requirements, particularly the synchronisation of multiple devices or ease of using the data for analysis and reporting.

Over the last couple of years, there has been optimism that a government program to establish a national electronic health record will enable the RFDS and many other providers to share electronic patient records, with the patient's consent. So far, progress has been frustratingly slow.

A robust and accurate system, which provides doctors with reliable information on past investigations, diagnoses and treatment, would genuinely improve patient care in rural and remote areas. It would prevent unnecessary repetition of expensive investigations, minimise errors in prescribing, reduce pharmaceutical wastage and help avoid important past history and diagnoses being missed by clinicians.

Care will be needed with privacy to ensure that patients' most personal details are kept highly confidential and are available only, with consent, to the health professionals they nominate. While there is much to be done, many benefits will ensue. Unfortunately, it still appears to be a long way off.

Championing our challenges
Research and publication

Doctors in the RFDS work in a distinctly different environment to metropolitan medical practitioners or those in tertiary hospitals. It requires a much broader skill set and provides challenging clinical situations, which need flexible and innovative approaches. As an example, when managing a complex trauma case at a dusty remote airstrip, decisions need to be made based on basic clinical examination skills, without the benefit of x-rays, pathology or a variety of specialists on hand to provide advice. Patients have minor surgical interventions done in the field, are anaesthetised and then transported hundreds, if not thousands, of kilometres to tertiary care, direct from the accident site, without any further investigations.

Trapped on the Nullarbor

A large truck was carrying a 17-tonne cherry picker across the Nullarbor on the Eyre Highway. At about 9.00 pm, it veered off the road near Madura and jack-knifed, the huge load on the back coming loose and sliding forward onto the cabin, partly trapping the driver. The accident occurred about 700 kilometres from Kalgoorlie. There are no ambulances out there and it takes hours just to reach the site by road. At 11.50 pm the Madura Roadhouse was notified and sent volunteers to the scene. The Kalgoorlie Base received a call and Dr David McGuire, a pilot and flight nurse headed off and landed on the road nearby the accident at about 2.30 am. This landing in itself was a significant feat.

The driver was in a serious condition, with a 'degloving' injury to his thigh. Much of the thigh muscle had been stripped from the bony femur below. His lower leg was crushed and he was trapped in the cabin. The RFDS doctor was able to obtain intravenous access to provide resuscitation fluids and analgesia.

To extricate the patient required the cherry picker to be lifted off the cabin and this needed another equally large crane to do so. It was going to take at least twelve hours to drive it from Kalgoorlie to the accident site by road, so our team stayed, giving fluids, pain relief and a blood transfusion. At daylight, the first pilot and nurse departed and a second aircraft flew in during the morning. By about 3.00 pm the mobile crane had arrived and extrication of the driver was achieved by 5.00 pm. Patients like this can deteriorate quickly once the crushing load has been removed. However, once the driver was freed, the medical team controlled further bleeding, effectively anaesthetised him on site and then commenced the evacuation.

The flight was from midway across the Nullarbor directly to Perth, about 1,000 kilometres away. There was no point in stopping en route, as even Kalgoorlie Hospital could not have provided the specialised care this patient needed. Ultimately, the doctor and patient arrived at a tertiary hospital at 10.00 pm, twenty-five hours after the accident occurred! There are few places in the world where primary evacuations of major trauma patients over such distances would be undertaken, with no radiology or laboratory investigations but just sound clinical assessment and care. The patient survived. The doctor had a well-earned rest after more than twenty-four hours on the job. He has subsequently become a specialist anaesthetist.

Primary evacuation from Pardoo to Perth

One day in October 2000, at about 2.00 pm, a four-wheel drive vehicle with two adults and five children under eight years of age rolled on the highway, 150 kilometres north of Port Hedland. It was a straight road so the driver was probably going at around 110 kilometres an hour and may have veered off the road due to fatigue, or to avoid livestock. The Pardoo Roadhouse, only 15 kilometres away, was notified and called the RFDS and road ambulance in Port Hedland.

Our medical team responded very rapidly, landing on the road at 3.40 pm, with the ambulance arriving at 4.30 pm. Both adults at this time were deceased and one six-year-old died shortly after arrival at the scene. The remaining children had multiple injuries. A five-year-old ejected from the vehicle had a serious head injury, fractured femur and other trauma, while an eight-year-old also had a fractured shaft of femur, fractures to other limbs and a closed head injury.

Dr Jim Flynn, a very capable and long-serving RFDS doctor in Port Hedland, was on the flight. He intubated and anaesthetised the five-year-old at the scene and put him on a ventilator. It was a challenging case. Triaging children whose parents have both been killed is difficult enough, but Jim also had a young son of a similar age to those injured. It would have been hard not to think this accident could have been his own family.

The two most seriously injured children were evacuated directly to Perth, the only location with neurosurgical and intensive care facilities. The RFDS was able to offer a 'direct from scene' primary retrieval to a neurosurgical centre which was 1,750 kilometres away by road, or 1,350 kilometres in a straight line by air. Again, there was no hospital in between that could offer an appropriate level of care. The patients arrived direct from the accident site in a little over three hours. The remaining children went by road to Port Hedland

329

*Hospital, where they had secondary aeromedical evacuations later
that night.*

Given the challenging circumstances in which our doctors
operate, and the innovative approaches that may be required for
different problems, it is important to encourage research and
publication of our experience. It is fascinating to examine a draft
constitution of the Australian Aerial Medical Service, as discussed
in October 1933:

> '7. That isolated doctors should be furnished with
> facilities to devote part of their enforced leisure to
> medical research: and that provision should be made
> for those who have faithfully completed terms of
> service, to engage in adequate postgraduate studies
> before resuming practice elsewhere.'

There is very little 'enforced leisure' in a contemporary RFDS
doctor's workload. While a short period of sabbatical leave is available at five-year intervals, formal opportunities for research are still
sadly lacking.

Research can be elusive

It has always been a challenge to encourage research and publication activities within the RFDS. The average flying doctor does
not sit at a desk with a computer all day. They are out flying or
doing other clinical work, day and night, often coming home late.
There is no formal administration time, no funded research positions and few, if any, opportunities to obtain financial or academic
support for research. Just getting time to collate data, analyse cases
or discuss with a statistician requires considerable motivation and
takes longer to achieve when based in rural locations. In addition,
many of the doctors with strong clinical skills who gravitate to an

RFDS position don't have the same passion for research activities. We have therefore struggled to publish much in formal medical journals over the years.

When we have, it has been striking. For example, our approach to the transport of women in premature labour is unparalleled elsewhere in the world. Western Australia has a very centralised health system with many specialty services only available in Perth. When it comes to obstetric emergencies, while there has usually been one obstetrician in each region who is able, for example, to do a caesarean section, the neonatal intensive care facilities to manage the baby once born are not present in rural regions. We have therefore developed an approach that ensures the majority of patients end up in a tertiary hospital before the baby is born. This means flying many pregnant women long distances while in labour, or bleeding, or with some other complication – a scenario not found in many other developed nations.

Our circumstances provide the opportunity – indeed, require us – to try radical approaches to certain problems, which would not be contemplated in a metropolitan setting. This need for unique, alternative solutions also offers us the prospect to research and publish the results of our different approaches to care.

The drugs we use to suppress labour, based on thirty years of clinical experience, are not usually used in tertiary hospitals, because they have no need to move patients in aircraft across half a continent. In 1988, under the auspices of Professor John Newnham, our experience on long-distance transport was published in the scientific literature. The research was repeated and published in the *Australian and New Zealand Journal of Obstetrics and Gynaecology*, with equally impressive results, in 2012. Few people would consider it sound clinical practice to put a woman in labour into an aircraft for a flight lasting a couple of hours. Yet, this is exactly what we do. In our hands, women in active premature labour can be transferred long distances by air without delivering in flight. This means that they reach the best tertiary obstetric and neonatal facilities in the state before delivering, which provides the newborn baby with the best chance of a successful outcome.

Our performance in managing patients with major trauma is equally impressive. In the 2000s, Dr Dan Fatovich, with the support of the late Professor Ian Jacobs and me, reviewed nine years of our major trauma data for his PhD study. The results were impressive and published internationally. Patients with major trauma (defined according to a special score as having severe injury to multiple body systems) who were injured in the metropolitan area took an average of 59 minutes from the time of accident to reach sophisticated trauma care at Royal Perth Hospital. In contrast, patients from rural and remote areas took an average of 11.6 hours from the time of accident to reach specialist care! This included the 'time to discovery' (it may take hours before the victims of an accident are found on an isolated road), the time for volunteers to take them to the nearest medical or nursing facilities, and the time for an aeromedical retrieval team to fly out, stabilise them and then transfer them all the way to Perth.

Nevertheless, the results were remarkable. The mortality rate (death rate) was lower for patients transferred by RFDS than in the city. It can be argued that some patients die in rural areas before they can be evacuated. When the number of deaths from trauma in rural areas is added to the RFDS outcomes, they become the same as in the city.

In simple terms, despite the huge distances, long times and limited resources, if patients with major trauma are retrieved by the RFDS, their outcomes are as good as if they were injured in the city. I see this as vindication of a carefully developed aeromedical service, with sound decisions and effective clinical coordination by experienced medical staff, combined with treatment by capable retrieval teams in well-equipped medical aircraft. The benefits to the population in general, and to employees in our resource industries, are inestimable.

Patients with mental health problems are also an interesting group. There are few countries where acutely disturbed violent or psychotic patients are put in a small medical aircraft and transported very long distances to the nearest specialist psychiatric hospital, certainly not at levels of two hundred to three hundred cases a year. Despite the risks of this practice, the RFDS in Western Australia was a leader in establishing regular aeromedical transport of mental health patients in 1982. We apply simple processes, which include a careful assessment of the risk by an RFDS doctor, minimal restraint and sedation, and an appropriate crew. These patients with severe illness, who need the benefits of care in specialised secure facilities, have a relatively quick transfer by air in a respectful manner, with the minimum interventions necessary to ensure air safety.

We have studied our performance with a number of clinical audits and internal reports to the Department of Health on aeromedical transport of acutely mentally ill patients, as well as conference presentations, but I am still to publish openly in the medical literature on the topic. Our approach to these cases is another example of innovation in clinical care and how difficult situations can inspire effective solutions.

Section 6

Education and training

Simulating the situation
Advances in aeromedical training and simulation

When I joined the RFDS, I was offered three days of orientation at our Jandakot Base. It was organised by our Flight Nurse Supervisor of the time, the late Gaye Richardson. She was a nuggetty, determined stalwart of the service who had the respect of her nursing staff while imposing very high expectations on them in terms of clinical care and checking of equipment.

Gaye showed me around on the first day and outlined the program for the next few days. At the end of that time, the general manager handed me the keys to a Holden Gemini, a small 1500cc car without air-conditioning, and told me I needed to drive it up to Port Hedland. It was an 1,800-kilometre trip along the Great Coastal Highway, as the Great Northern Highway up the middle of the state was still not sealed all the way. I was allowed one night's accommodation in Carnarvon so I could make the journey in two days. I was also told to take care and not hit anything, such as kangaroos! It was an eye-opening journey and reinforced, for a city boy, just how great the distances were and how isolated you were if you had a breakdown or medical emergency.

Working in an aircraft environment and in remote areas is not the same as working in a hospital or city general practice. You must know the aircraft medical configuration well and the location of all the essential items you might need in a hurry. You must also understand aviation safety.

In most of our aircraft over the years, the doctor and nurse have sat on the left-hand side of the cabin, facing each other, with the first patient on the right side of the cabin, maybe 30 centimetres away. That's an A4 sheet of paper between you and the patient for hours, while knocking knees with the flight nurse for the duration of the flight. It is cramped and there is limited stowage space. It would help if you were an octopus so you could reach everything you needed without leaving your seat.

We would carefully plan where everything was stowed and ensured that we took out, in advance, anything we were likely to need in a hurry in flight, as we might not be able to remove our seatbelts and leave our seats. For example, we would need to draw up emergency drugs beforehand, rather than be rummaging through a drug box trying to find the correct ampoule when in turbulence. Nearly all the aircraft fleet was unpressurised so we were limited to flying relatively low at 10,000 feet, where it was still hot and bumpy.

I believed it was important that we trained in emergency resuscitation inside a real aircraft, not just on a hospital trolley or on the floor inside our base building. A cramped aircraft in flight is a completely different situation to a spacious room and you need to work through where you will position yourself, how you will do things and what is in reach. So I started a program for us all to do CPR and defibrillation training in our aircraft out on the tarmac. We had a basic Laerdal Resusci Anne® training manikin. New nurses, doctors and I would go through simulated cardiac and respiratory arrests. I purchased an ECG rhythm simulator so we could then run through different cardiac rhythms and practice realistic defibrillation on the manikin.

After returning from completing a Diploma of Aviation Medicine in the United Kingdom, I expanded our orientation training to include more aviation medicine, and to transfer more of our collective corporate knowledge of how to do aeromedical retrieval properly. From the early 1990s I was helped by Dr Glenda Wilson, now an emergency physician, who also took to conducting resuscitation training in our aircraft with great enthusiasm.

There was considerable work in setting up a training session in a real aircraft. After identifying one that was not going flying, we lugged the manikins and other gear out to the aircraft and dragged out power cords across the tarmac to operate the rhythm simulator. We would be all ready to go when a flight would arise and the aircraft was needed, so we would have to disband and put off the training to another day. This was frustrating and costly in terms of medical and nursing staff time wasted.

I pondered whether we could buy an old aircraft of the same type, perhaps damaged from an accident, and use the fuselage as a training platform. Most airports have a few old airframes used for fire-fighting and emergency exercises. However, we would need to acquire exactly the same model of aircraft – a Navajo, a Conquest or subsequently a Pilatus PC-12 – to make this realistic. A seriously damaged airframe is hard to come by and still valuable, so I started thinking about other options.

In 2007 I was in the foyer of a company where they had a model of an offshore oil rig. It was of exquisite detail and made to scale, something like 100 to 1. I started thinking, 'What if we could have a model aircraft interior built, but on a scale of 1 to 1?' Peter Northover, at that time our Regional Manager in Perth, scouted around and found a model maker, Graeme Coleman, based in Bibra Lake near the airport. We brought him out to see what he could do.

Yes, it was possible. Exact dimensions of the aircraft were not available from Pilatus for commercial reasons, so he made multiple measurements throughout the interior and developed a three-dimensional plan for the project from that. We did not need a cockpit as that only complicated the proposal and made the simulator longer in length. We decided to build it on a trailer base so it could be moved around and occasionally taken to special events for training or promotion. But the primary goal was for simulation training of clinical staff in a realistic environment, without the hassles of trying to use a real aircraft for the role. I decided we should give our new non-flying aircraft the registration VH-SIM.

We were fortunate that a mining company, Oxiana, was looking for a project to donate to at the time, and this was ideal. We used their funds to pay for construction in the first half of 2008 and had the interior fitted with spares of real stretchers, real seats and a real stretcher-loading device. The 'aircraft' has medical oxygen, suction and a communications panel which enables the occupants to make calls to the 'ground'. We have inbuilt cameras so scenarios can be recorded for playback and review. We have taken it to medical conferences to show country doctors and medical students what it is like in our real aircraft; this is an opportunity to promote the service, explain the challenges of what we do and to sometimes undertake a bit of recruiting at the same time.

The SIM is housed in a renovated engineering workshop in a building next to our main Jandakot Airport hangar. This has led to the establishment of an adjacent simulation space, where our staff can rehearse clinical handover and perform emergency procedures in an imitation country hospital emergency department.

We have added adult and paediatric training manikins and ultrasound models, and can practise a variety of airway and vascular procedures. We have also acquired the iSimulate training system, which uses an iPad to replicate the front of a critical care monitor. The instructor holds another iPad and uses it to change the settings of the vital signs, ECG trace and other parameters. Simulation is clearly going to play an increasing role in medical education in the future, rather than practising on real patients.

You can be as innovative as you want, but without people willing to support your vision, you get nowhere. I am grateful for the opportunity to use donations to underwrite new ideas and not just to support general revenue. The entire medical simulator cost us around $65,000 and, in hindsight, that has been fantastic value. Every new doctor and nurse completes resuscitation training when they join us and regularly throughout their employment. In a recent collaboration with Edith Cowan University, some of our staff are learning how to make simulation training more effective. In return, we expect to offer university nursing students the chance to experience the challenges of simulated inflight nursing in VH-SIM.

Ahoy, me hearties!
Medical care for ship masters

For someone who works in an aviation environment, it probably seems odd that I love the water and the sea. I joined the RAN (Royal Australian Naval Reserve) in my second year as a doctor and had the opportunity to do some time at sea in ships and submarines, and to participate in some excellent training courses. Completing a Diving Medicine course at the HMAS *Penguin* in Sydney was helpful, not just because of my own interest in scuba diving, but also in understanding the correct management of patients with decompression illness ('the bends') and the implications of moving them by air.

NBCD (nuclear, biological, chemical defence), now more commonly referred to as CBR (chemical, biological and radiation), medicine was fascinating, opening up a completely new field to me which few doctors are familiarised with in their undergraduate training. It provided a solid foundation for understanding toxicology and disaster management.

I was fortunate to complete the RAAF Medical Officer's Aviation Medicine Course at RAAF Point Cook, which, as a private pilot, was also fascinating and helped me to gain my placement on the highly regarded Diploma of Aviation Medicine program at RAF Farnborough in the UK.

I was privileged to do an abbreviated RAN Staff Course as a Reservist in the early 1990s. This introduced concepts of formal service writing, which has helped me in establishing policies, procedures and operational documents. I was also taught how to produce an appraisal, a formal proposal which addressed a particular issue and outlined the appropriate course of action. At the time, hepatitis B immunisation had only just become available and it was expensive. I used the time on the course to research the subject and produce a recommendation that all service personnel should be offered hepatitis B vaccine using a technique of sub-dermal injection, which might make the program less expensive. I felt quite strongly that our service personnel could be exposed to blood-borne viruses in the course of their duty. Whether in combat, or from tattoos or sexually transmitted diseases in foreign ports, we had a duty to protect them if possible from preventable diseases. I was pleased a few years later to find that this policy had been implemented.

To feed my desire for more knowledge of all things maritime, I enrolled at the Fremantle TAFE in a Diploma of Applied Science in Fishing. I thought this would be a great opportunity to learn about marine engines, coastal and celestial navigation and nautical regulations, which would help me with my boating aspirations. The idea of earning the qualification 'Dip Fish' was also appealing. I did all the units but was unable to complete the practical require-ments of so many months at sea in watch-keeping roles to achieve the basic Master certificate. I did meet some interesting people, however. Captain Richard Grono was one of the course instruc-tors who, together with a few of his cronies, convinced me to run an update program in Medical Care at Sea for many of the experienced maritime officers who now occupied desks.

I put together a two-day training program that featured an update on common emergency topics, infectious diseases, giving injections, suturing wounds and the like. Slide shows containing images of traumatic injuries and sexually transmitted infections always provoke interest in such courses and keep the candidates awake. They were shown how to give each other tetanus booster shots, to practise giving injections, to stitch up lacerations in pig-skin and other procedures. Overall, it was great fun.

The course was successful and I was coerced to take on pre-paring and overseeing a formal two-week training program which all ship masters are required to complete to obtain the top Master certificate. The program is directed at captains of large vessels, such as international freighters and tankers, who may be remote from all medical care for many days and need to deal with emergencies on board. There is a formal requirement for them to do this in accord-ance with a syllabus meeting international maritime standards.

At the time, the TAFE was trying to provide the training using specialist doctors from a nearby hospital. If you want to teach a layperson how to manage a head injury, probably the worst teacher is a neurosurgeon. The same applied to cardiac and most other medical conditions. Here at the RFDS, I had a cadre of doctors who were down to earth, used to dealing with people with limited medical knowledge and could explain how to manage a variety of emergencies in a pragmatic manner. We were used to remoteness and to providing advice over the radio or telephone. So I wrote up a course program and, as they say, the rest is history.

We started the 'Medical Care for Ship Masters course' in the early 1990s and since then have been the only organisation providing this recognised emergency training to ship masters in Western Australia for over twenty years. The program is well established: we recover our costs and provide vital instruction to mariners who will be confronted by various medical emergencies during their careers. To top it off, it enhances our doctors' skills in instructional technique and it is fun, too!

Opportunities online
Introduction of e-learning

I do not have a formal professional background in education but after surviving ten to fifteen years of undergraduate and postgraduate training, and some experience in other areas, I think I have a reasonable feel for some of the concepts of instructional technique and adult learning. I have continued to develop our orientation program for new doctors and nurses over a very long period, seeking feedback as we go to try to improve what is covered. As time has passed the volume of information and complexity of the job has increased significantly.

It was not an uncommon occurrence that three months down the track, a new doctor would ask something and I would explain it and then follow with, 'Remember we covered that during orientation?' Ah yes, a light bulb moment! We had covered the material but it just hadn't sunk in with the massive amount of new information we had to instil in new staff in their first few weeks at the RFDS.

A significant amount of the knowledge we try to impart to new staff is factual. Basics of aviation physiology, our aircraft equipment inventory and layout, the operation of each item of biomedical equipment, our communication and coordination procedures, clinical guidelines on air transport plus safety in and around aircraft. The list goes on. It is really too much to absorb in one to two weeks and most new staff are reeling by the end of their second week.

What I wanted to do was to infuse some of the core knowledge into new doctors and nurses prior to them starting with us. If they could do pre-reading or have a little instruction in advance, then their time in the first few weeks could be spent partly revising and, more importantly, using the factual knowledge for problem solving. Furthermore, it is not appropriate to provide extensive training if you don't assess the understanding and retention of the knowledge afterwards. Medical education is quite poor in this regard, often cramming masses of information into young doctors and just expecting them to absorb it all. 'Yeah, I covered that.' 'They know all about that.' But did they? There is often no sound assessment process to round off clinical training in many situations. In fact, a common adage in medical training is 'See one, do one, teach one!'

With limited educational resources, I started looking around in the mid-2000s for ways of delivering interactive training using computers. My thoughts were that structured assessments online might provide more variety and be more efficient. Some fledgling quizzing programs existed but were too simplistic. There was only so much you could do with banks of multiple-choice questionnaires. I tried writing a questionnaire database myself but could see that it was going to be too labour-intensive.

Then, during the 2009 Christmas holidays, I discovered the *Articulate*® suite of software. This was revolutionary. It enabled me to relatively easily produce fully narrated training packages with audio, embedded images and video. As trainees worked through each module, it could be programmed to branch to different scenarios depending on the choices made. It was linked with another quiz-making application, which enabled quizzes of various formats to be constructed. These could also be written to provide different feedback and to branch according to the answers. Hosting was available on an internet site in the USA, so all you had to do was send a new staff member a link and they could start working on the material prior to joining us.

In early 2010 I put up a proposal to Geri Christie, the CEO of the Victorian Section, who had been looking for innovative projects to pitch to large philanthropic groups. We had already made some applications together to large pharmaceutical companies to sponsor a fellowship position, a secondment for a specialist in training, and to sponsor a customised Emergency Management of Severe Trauma course for RFDS doctors across Australia. These had been unsuccessful but then I proposed a project which I called RITA. It stood for 'RFDS Interactive Training and Assessment'. I was hoping to have an administrative position funded to produce the content and manage training for our doctors and nurses. Unfortunately, it did not get up – so I just went ahead and did it anyway.

It was like an epiphany. The opportunities for e-learning appeared unlimited. During 2010 and the following years I managed to produce a suite of in-house modules dealing with a variety of realistic emergency clinical scenarios in remote settings in WA. They required the doctors completing the modules to think about both clinical and logistical issues. They had to make decisions about what advice should be given to the callers, the urgency of the flight, how the illness or injury should be managed and where the patient should be taken. For doctors coming from interstate or overseas, the scenarios highlighted common problems but also gave them insight into our vast distances in WA – a hospital was not just around the corner.

These were followed with some direct instructional modules and other purely quiz-based assessments of information taught during our orientation program. We proceeded to enlarge our offering whenever new training was required, such as on new equipment.

I produced one module on basic medical terminology so that our coordination staff and some other non-clinical office staff could learn about the medical terms we often used. This e-learning package was put up on our national RFDS website. To my surprise, I started receiving feedback from a variety of users around the country. One large government insurer contacted me and asked if their staff could use it. They had been running a course for their claims assessors, to give them basic medical terminology, but found my program was quicker and more comprehensive!

We continued to expand the suite of modules with no specific funding or staffing. Most of it was done in my spare time as a bit of a hobby. I am convinced that multimedia interactive e-learning will have a major role to play in the future but even at this early stage in development of the art, it is apparent that it needs to be done well. It must be short, sharp, fast-paced, interactive and relevant. Otherwise, it becomes just as bad as 'death by *PowerPoint*'.

Our e-learning applications can cover core material in a concise and consistent manner and then assess understanding of that knowledge. It leaves the precious one-on-one time with a medical educator for more intense problem solving and discussion of the complex clinical and logistical decisions required in difficult cases.

Our e-learning modules have also been added to the resources we provide as part of our Aeromedical Retrieval training partnership with Edith Cowan University.

Clinical education
Aviation medicine and hypoxia training

In 1988, after returning from studying aviation medicine in the UK, I was keen to set up a training course in Aviation Medicine for RFDS doctors to utilise the knowledge I had acquired. I compiled a condensed one-week program which, as well as lectures and discussions, included a trip to the Air Force hypobaric chamber at RAAF Pearce. Most doctors come to the RFDS with little or no knowledge of aviation physiology or aviation medicine – even those who might have a private pilot's licence. It is important as a professional organisation transporting thousands of patients by air each year that we have that expertise in-house and that our medical and nursing staff are properly trained to ensure they can manage various conditions.

I was again fortunate to have the support of our general manager, Terry Jorgenson, and our Medical Advisory Committee, particularly Dr Barney Cresswell, who was ex-RAAF, and Dr Harry Oxer, who was ex-RAF. We were allowed to have a week to run the course. In a relatively small, not-for-profit organisation it is commonplace to be challenged in doing new and innovative things because of lack of time to do them. There is an expectation that doctors should be doing clinical work 100 per cent of the time, which leaves no room for creative ideas, program development, equipment evaluation, teaching or just writing and reviewing protocols. These days, in tertiary hospitals, medical staff are allocated a significant component of their time for non-clinical duties.

After preparing the course, I was able to muster registrants from all RFDS sections across the country. This in itself was quite a triumph: being able to meet with other flying doctors from other states and find out what they did and how they did it. Not surprisingly, we had many practical issues in common and it was great to be able to share our approaches with them.

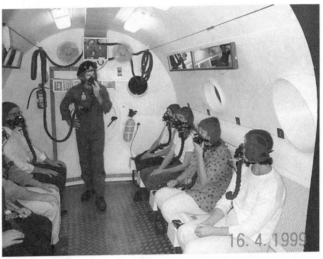

Doctors and nurses in the RAAF hypobaric chamber undergoing hypoxia training.

The RFDS Introduction to Aviation Medicine course went well. On that course was a young female doctor, Elizabeth Green, recently from Melbourne, who had just joined the RFDS Eastern Goldfields Section in Kalgoorlie. We struck up an acquaintance and ultimately married a few years later, but that's another story.

The doctors had the opportunity to spend time in a hypobaric chamber to experience altitude hypoxia and depressurisation. While hyperbaric chambers provide increased pressure and are used for treatment of decompression illness, hypobaric chambers provide a reduced pressure and simulate the effects of altitude.

In conjunction with the senior medical officer at RAAF Pearce, our group of RFDS doctors from around Australia went up to Bullsbrook for the day. They were given a briefing, had a cursory medical and then a run in the hypobaric chamber to 25,000 feet, equivalent to almost being dropped near the top of Mt Everest.

In these exercises, you wear a military pilot's oxygen mask. You experience the rush of a depressurisation to 25,000 feet, clearing your ears as you rise and watching balloons expand. Then, in groups of two, you remove the mask and do some simple exercises such as drawing five-pointed stars, subtracting seven from one thousand repeatedly or other simple arithmetic challenges. All the time you are becoming fuzzy in the head and watching your colleague become bluer in the lips as they become more hypoxic.

Once you have clearly recognised you are hypoxic, you put the mask back on and feel the rush as you suddenly become more alert and the fuzziness disappears. Very rarely, some people with an underlying predisposition can have a seizure with hypoxia and unfortunately that was the case with this group of doctors. One of them collapsed on the floor of the chamber and had a short seizure. It lasted only a few seconds but, nevertheless, was a bit of a surprise to the RAAF doctor leading the exercise.

I don't think it was this episode that caused a problem but over the following years the Australian Defence Force became less willing to provide training to non-service personnel due to perceived public liability issues. We ran a couple more visits, the last of which was in 1999, then they stopped. Since then we have acquired a different way of training pilots and others in hypoxia recognition. It involves the subject wearing a mask and being given a hypoxic breathing mixture, that is, air that has less oxygen in it than normal. While this does not demonstrate the effects of gas expansion at altitude, it does enable our flight crew to experience hypoxia and recognise its symptoms so that they can take emergency action if it occurs to them in flight. All our RFDS pilots in

Western Australia and most of our flight nurses and doctors now complete this training.

National collaboration and *Best for the Bush*

The 1980s was a period in which there was a greater sense than previously that we were all part of a single iconic organisation and should be trying to do more as a national entity than as disparate state-based outfits. Each state had a Medical Advisory Committee comprising a number of senior doctors and specialists with an interest in rural and remote health or aeromedical work. They advised each section's council on appropriate policies and priority areas in health and provided a representative to an equivalent national Medical Advisory Committee.

There was a growing resolve to try to develop a comprehensive suite of services for people living and working in rural and remote Australia, and that each section, despite individual state differences, should be offering an equivalent range and level of care. The first national CEO was appointed: Allan Thomson, a seasoned corporate warrior who had previously run a major publicly listed company, Howard Smith Ltd. He was energetic, diplomatic and, in an appointment that was supposedly more a transition to retirement, he made significant strides in concentrating on health care as a priority rather than aircraft, and holding different sections accountable.

I was fortunate to be involved in a small medical working group to develop a simple framework of what we believed were key issues for the RFDS at the time. We focused on our core services of telehealth, primary care and aeromedical, and the issues of workforce attraction and retention, training and education, and quality and standards. Subsequently Allan led the organisation to engage a consultant, Mick Reid, to work with every state and develop a comprehensive report, *Best for the Bush*. (Mick subsequently became the Director General of Health in New South Wales, then later in Queensland, and is currently a national board member of the RFDS.) This was a tremendous piece of work, which reviewed our health services nationally, was evidence-based and proposed a comprehensive national health strategy for the RFDS.

RFDS medical symposia

We started to run an annual RFDS Medical Symposium in 1985 at which RFDS doctors and nurses from around the country would congregate for a weekend of upskilling, presentations from invited experts, and sharing of case reports and other topics relevant to us all. Dr Barney Cresswell, who chaired our Medical Advisory Committee, was instrumental in pushing the other sections to run with this. The first time we held the symposium in Perth was outstanding. We produced such a comprehensive program that it was of interest to a much wider rural medical and nursing audience, and we had 200 registrations. This was great for the reputation of the RFDS within the health system and brought many of the players in the rural health system together. The energy and hours needed to run such events is substantial and, unfortunately, with only me and one part-time doctor in Perth at the time, it couldn't be sustained. Nevertheless, the concept of an annual internal RFDS symposium continued during the late 1980s and 1990s, strongly supported by the national Medical Advisory Committee.

It is regrettable that with time, this strong clinical guidance at a national level has withered. The pendulum has swung to where each section is mostly focused on its own turf, and innovative and successful national collaboration has slowly diminished. In the last few years that we held the symposium, it was in conjunction with a national conference. This was a radical idea in which board members and administrative staff of each section actually met in the same venue where medical and nursing staff presented on key health issues affecting our patients. The revelations about what needed to be done in rural health, and why, were enlightening.

Tertiary collaboration
A university-level aeromedical qualification

I am proud of the quality and skills of our people. Our pilots are well-trained professionals and I have always felt safe when flying with them because I know that our chief pilot and training captains do not cut corners when training and check-flying. Likewise, our medical and nursing staff are experienced and capable individuals. In addition to the skills and experience they bring to the role from previous appointments, we work hard to provide in-depth, structured training when they join us, plenty of opportunities for study leave and upskilling, and regular review of their skills and performance.

Over the course of twenty years, I expanded and refined our medical orientation program to at least eighty hours of rigorous instruction and supervised duties. It seemed to me a shame that this in-depth training was not better recognised. We expect people to bring skills and knowledge to the service but I have long believed they should leave us with additional skills and knowledge to what they came with.

As much as we would like long continuous service from staff, when working in remote areas we are always going to have a reasonable turnover, with few people prepared to stay for the long haul. Often the clinical work is appealing but career progression, education of children and lack of employment opportunities for a spouse take their toll. As such, we have to think of ourselves a bit like the Defence Force: a conveyor belt, taking in capable people and giving them valuable professional experience, which they take with them to other roles when they leave.

University partnership

In 2013 we made two modest but significant steps for the organisation in improving our academic credentials and ability to support and encourage research. The first was my appointment of Professor Russell Jones, a professional educator, to our staff part time. My initial goal was to improve the quality of our medical training syllabus: to better define the knowledge and skills provided to our staff and look at alternatives for delivery of the training in accordance with principles of adult learning. We worked hard on it, coming up with ideas to make our training more efficient and interesting at the same time.

The second goal, which followed, was to develop a relationship with a university. I wanted to obtain recognition of the extensive training we were providing to our staff and give them the opportunity to receive a tertiary qualification if they completed our rigorous program and additional assessments. With Russell's assistance, we identified and formed a partnership with the School of Medical Sciences at Edith Cowan University in Perth in 2014. The university has a reputation for flexibility, innovation and commitment to teaching, which aligns well with our values in the RFDS. I was privileged to receive an appointment as an adjunct professor with the School of Medical Sciences and to be able to take much of the training material I had worked on over the years to seed new courses. This has led to the RFDS in Western Australia now being able to offer tertiary qualifications to clinicians in aeromedical retrieval, with the expectation we will expand our offering and opportunities for research in the future.

The newfound affiliation offers the potential to seek out research grants and support for studies and publications focused on the clinical services we provide. Joint grant applications from the RFDS and a tertiary institution are more likely to be successful than from us alone. These opportunities range from primary care, telehealth and Aboriginal health through to aviation medicine, emergency medicine and other critical care disciplines. The partnership we have established has many exciting possibilities.

Guardian angels
Collaborating with the Kalgoorlie mob

In 1988 a young medical graduate from Melbourne commenced with the RFDS Eastern Goldfields Section in Kalgoorlie. There were three separate divisions of the RFDS in Western Australia at the time. The Victorian Section managed all of the Kimberley and was administered from Melbourne. The Eastern Goldfields Section was based in Kalgoorlie and covered the Goldfields region, including the Nullarbor Plain across to the South Australian border and the Central Lands region up to the border with the Northern Territory. The Western Australian Section, for which I worked, operated over the rest of the state.

Accepting the appointment was fate for this doctor. She had seen an advertisement and was dared by a friend to apply for it, while a concurrent application to a general practice in rural Victoria went astray in the mail. By the time she had been offered the Victorian job, she had already said 'yes' to the RFDS in Kalgoorlie.

The young doctor completed the small team of three doctors in Kalgoorlie: Dr Peter Carroll, Dr Justin Johnston and herself, Dr Elizabeth Green. The base was made up of many notable characters, including Syd Winchcomb (General Manager), Lorraine Winchcomb and John Flower (radio operators), Captain Roger Waller (Chief Pilot) and some dedicated nursing staff, among them Anne Judd, Margaret Gordon and Sally Wilson.

The RFDS was a relatively small organisation and while there was healthy rivalry between sections, we got on well together if the opportunity arose. Each section worked independently but we saw a bit of the Kalgoorlie mob as they regularly brought patients to Perth and came through our facilities at Jandakot Airport. I started up an RFDS doctors' newsletter one year, to try to keep each of us more aware of what was happening around the country. Like most newsletters, it stopped due to lack of input and the energy to keep it going. Our contacts with the Kalgoorlie staff remained frequent and strong, however, and we knew the doctors, nurses and pilots pretty well.

While flying around day and night, in all weather and in remote Australia is risky, the service has a very good safety record. Nevertheless, there appears to me to be many times when a guardian angel was looking after Elizabeth. The following stories are not so much about innovation but blind determination to be of service to the community and get a job done, even when there was personal risk involved.

Trapped underground

There was an underground collapse at a mine site near Menzies. A man was trapped in a rock fall, deep underground, with only his head and upper chest free. The police took young Dr Green by road from Kalgoorlie, at high speed, direct to the mine site, while the RFDS aircraft flew to the nearest airstrip at Menzies. And if the road journey was not frightening enough, without hesitation or, dare I say it, careful thought, Elizabeth agreed to go down the mineshaft and be led to where the miner was trapped. She tells me that she was with a bunch of blokes who were as concerned as she was about the potential for another collapse, but desperate to save their mate.

After scrambling up rocks and a ladder at the scene, deep underground, one of the victim's arms was freed. With deep subterranean rumblings in the background and the occasional shower of small rocks, she inserted an intravenous line into his free arm under the light of a headlamp, to administer resuscitation fluids and intravenous pain relief. All the while, the trapped miner was reassuring her that the rumblings were distant but he would warn her if they were closer and she needed to leave.

The victim clearly had crush injuries and, after being underground for what seemed like an eternity, Elizabeth told his colleagues that he was unlikely to make it unless they could dig him out within the hour. Despite enormous personal risk, they went to work frantically and he was eventually extricated from the rubble and brought to the surface. After transfer to the waiting aircraft, the miner was evacuated by air back to Kalgoorlie where he underwent initial surgery. Then, later that night, the same RFDS team flew him to Perth for further management.

I am not sure if this sort of situation would occur in the modern era with so many restrictions on staff safety. A large basket of flowers was sitting on the doorstep of the doctor's house the next morning when she awoke. It was a courageous although frightening episode which gained the admiration of the workers and added to the rich tapestry of RFDS folklore.

Careful flight planning and safety are always at the fore, particularly when contemplating very long flights across outback areas at night. Before GPS, remote area navigation was done by dead reckoning. You set out on a track using radio aids and ground navigation for the first 100 miles or so. When the radio aids were out of range, you kept going with the same offset for cross winds and the like, in the hope that you would stay on course as you crossed the dark desert. The odd light may have encouraged you that you were in the right place, but it was difficult to be sure in the dark. However, you looked forward to seeing the runway lights and other lights at the community you were heading for.

Lights out at Warburton

One night, Elizabeth received a radio call from a nurse at Jamieson, a remote Aboriginal community in the Central Lands, about an infant having seizures. She assessed the case and gave the nurse emergency treatment advice but it was clear that they needed to evacuate the child that night. The child would have to be driven by the nurse to Warburton, quite some distance away, as this was the nearest airstrip suitable for night landings. While normal practice was to call the community to advise them of the flight, the team couldn't get through. Rather than wait, they embarked on the mission, expecting that in the more than two hours to fly there, the base radio operator would be able to make contact.

When the pilot, 'Drew', arrived in the vicinity, there were no runway lights showing. Only a couple of feeble house lights could be made out to confirm that the aircraft was indeed over the community in the otherwise black, featureless landscape. The aircraft circled, waiting for the lights to come on, but nothing happened. They knew the child they were coming to evacuate was very sick, otherwise they wouldn't have flown out this far in the middle of the night. So they kept buzzing the community at the lowest safe altitude, hoping to attract attention. It was now well after midnight. Eventually you reach a point when you will not have enough fuel to safely return home or go somewhere else. If you can't land, you must leave and fly directly back to base or to a designated alternate airport.

The time ticked away and continuous attempts were made to call the community to have the lights put out. Radio Operator John Flower convinced one of the TV channels broadcasting in the

360

region to put a banner message on their transmission, but that did not raise anyone. You would think that in a very remote location late at night, someone would have noticed an aircraft going around overhead in the dark, but it was not to be. Finally, with minutes to spare, the nurse from Jamieson arrived in her troopie and set about waking people to come and help set out the airstrip lights. It was a lucky break for the team as well as for the sick child.

On a few night flights, the Kalgoorlie crew would use a portable reflector landing system. It was often a struggle for people to put out lights at night when an RFDS aircraft was coming. Many locations used flares – dirty black pots filled with diesel or kero – set up along each side of the runway and set alight. There could be errors in putting them out straight and at the correct spacing, which is important for the pilot to judge the aircraft approach for landing. Sometimes they did not have enough fuel for the flares, they might be locked away or couldn't be found, or they didn't have enough people to help put them out. Excuses were common.

Reflector landing system

In a cleverly designed innovation, the Eastern Goldfields Section, led by Captain Roger Waller, developed a reflector landing system to use instead of flares for night landings. Roger was a remarkably committed and experienced pilot who served the RFDS for decades. The system comprised reflective panels about the size of A4 paper, which were hung on wire frames set into the ground in an A-frame configuration at 100-metre intervals. When mounted properly, the slanting panel would face the oncoming aircraft at the correct angle and the landing lights of the aircraft would be reflected back to the pilot. There were also three pairs of flares identifying the ends and middle of the runway, which could be seen when circling and lining up the approach. An extra flare was placed at the approach end, signalling the wind direction.

Pilots needed skill and practice to use the reflectors to land as it was only during the final approach that the runway layout became clearly visible. The benefits were that they were relatively inexpensive, compact, required little fuel and could be pre-positioned so they were relatively easily set up at night. They are still available for use today.

Road landing sites

Another significant Eastern Goldfields Section innovation was formalising emergency road landing areas. With the Eyre Highway, the longest piece of road in Australia to cover, they managed to have selected segments of road built wider and clear of obstructions, to enable a fixed-wing aircraft to land on them. This work included painting 'piano keys' on the bitumen and erecting signs to identify the landing areas. This system continues to be used in various locations across Western Australia.

Engine failure

Despite diligent maintenance, aviation remains a risky business. About 1990, Elizabeth – whom I was now quite friendly with – was departing Jandakot with Captain Yvonne Dobinson to return to Kalgoorlie. Yvonne was the first female RFDS pilot in Western Australia and remained the only one for a long while. She worked at Meekatharra and subsequently at Kalgoorlie. The Eastern Goldfields Section operated twin-engine aircraft and the pilots regularly rehearsed emergency procedures in the event of an engine failure. You never expect that to happen, however.

Shortly after take-off and while heading out from Perth, an engine failed on the Cessna C425 Conquest. As a consummate professional, Yvonne corrected the yaw of the aircraft, shut down the failed engine and feathered the prop, then proceeded to turn back to Perth. If mishandled, these sudden engine failures can cause loss of control of the aircraft but Yvonne nursed it back to Perth on one engine and the emergency services were alerted for her landing. I was called out to come and see, in case the aircraft had a bad landing and they needed medical assistance. Then I realised that my girlfriend was on the aircraft! The guardian angel was on duty again. As hoped, the pilot made a safe landing and all were well. The failure was attributed to a mechanical fault in the engine. Things break, despite the best maintenance and the expectation that they will not.

I felt it was my duty to improve collaboration between the two adjacent RFDS sections and eventually Elizabeth and I married. I have been privileged to have a soul mate who has understood the importance of the RFDS to the bush, had experience of the service over a couple of years and was subsequently willing to put up with the long hours and challenges of my role and its impact on our family over nearly a quarter of a century.

Connections and coincidences
Fortuitous findings

It is a strange coincidence, but my wife Elizabeth spent a portion of her early childhood in Wyndham and Kununurra between 1965 and 1970. Her father, the Reverend Barry Green, was the first Anglican priest in Kununurra, as part of the Ord River Mission with the Bush Church Aid Society. He covered his parish of 20,000 square miles by road. After being severely bogged once in a remote area, his congregation bought a radio for his vehicle so that he could contact the RFDS radio base in Wyndham. It highlights the vital importance of the RFDS as an emergency communication service at the time.

Elizabeth had also stayed on the famous Argyle Downs Station. While the homestead was moved, the rest of the station eventually found itself at the bottom of Lake Argyle when the Ord River Dam was constructed.

When researching this book, I received from Elizabeth's parents a collection of books written by the Rev. S. J. Kirkby, the Rev. T. E. Jones and the Rev. L. Daniels (see the bibliography).

The Reverend Leonard Daniels was arguably the first 'flying padre' in Australia and had been her mother's parish rector. He was a pilot in World War I and then an Anglican missioner to the Far West of New South Wales, based in Wilcannia, from 1923. It was fascinating to read that he commenced an appeal to purchase an aircraft in 1926 to help him in his work and eventually took delivery of a new Cirrus Mark 2 Moth, *Far West*, in Melbourne in February 1928. His flying ministry spread across vast reaches of western NSW for at least four years, being able to cover considerably more ground than by car. He recounts meeting with Flynn of the Inland and providing advice to him based on his experiences in the Far West. They discussed Flynn's vision for bases across Australia, including Broken Hill, which was near Wilcannia. He also describes how his flying exploits provided the idea to the Reverend Kirkby, which underpinned the establishment of a flying doctor service at Ceduna in 1938.

The BCA (Bush Church Aid) society formed its own Flying Medical Service with a DeHavilland Fox Moth VH-AAA in January 1938. The aircraft was constructed in England at the same time as an equivalent aircraft was being built for Dr Fenton, a notable doctor who flew from Darwin in this era.

The BCA medical aircraft was based out of Ceduna from April that year, operating across 450 miles to the Western Australian border. This supported a hospital in Ceduna built by BCA in 1925, a new hospital built in Cook in September 1937 and nursing posts at Koonibba and Penong. At this time, the RFDS – then the Australian Aerial Medical Service– had only just started in Broken Hill in 1937. The first independent base of what was called the SA Section at that time, commenced in Alice Springs in 1939, serving the north of the state.

Flair with fundraising
Friends far and wide

Innovation is not limited to how we provide our health services. Over the decades, there have been many supporters and fundraisers for the RFDS who have come up with novel and very clever ideas for raising money for the organisation. Some ideas have been very clever, while others so unusual that we could not support them.

I wish I could list the thousands of people who have come up with great ideas over the past three decades but I just can't; indeed, I wouldn't know where to start. To all of them, the organisation and the people we serve thank them. A couple of innovations in particular stand out in our recent history. The first of these is the Flying 1000. This group of women came up with the idea in 2002 of encouraging 1,000 women to each pledge $1,000 dollars to the RFDS over four years and thereby raise $1 million. They organised many networking and social functions. At the time of publication they have well exceeded their original target and raised in excess of $3 million for aircraft fit-outs and vital medical equipment for the RFDS in Western Australia. The group has a large number of members with a core committee that has been leading it for over a decade. They are terrific people, generous of time and spirit, and with strong links to Western Australia's proud pastoral and grazing history.

One of the other unusual or innovative ideas that I recall was the Dog in a Ute challenge. Not satisfied with simply breaking a world record in 1998, the organisers from Corrigin smashed the world record again in 2002 with a convoy of 1,527 utes, each with dogs in the back, raising money for the RFDS.

In 2012 another ingenious activity, labelled Operation Strato-Bear, raised awareness of the RFDS and resulted in a popular online video. A cuddly teddy bear in pilot uniform was attached to a weather balloon and ascended from Donnybrook to 105,000 feet. The journey was recorded on camera all the way, including his rapid descent back to earth when the balloon burst.

Less high profile, but nonetheless creative, is a group of women who quietly and continuously knit hundreds of woollen teddy bears for the RFDS every month. Every bear they make is unique and important. We carry a couple on every aircraft so that our flight nurses can give them as a gift to young children on board who are sick or injured.

The Buy the Sky concept is a recent novel idea that enables donors to purchase a sector of sky on one of the common flight routes taken by the RFDS. It is an Australia-wide project and donors can view an online map, showing the part of a flight path they have 'bought' with full map coordinates and an image of the landscape below.

There have been individuals who have cycled and hiked the length and breadth of our country, or supported events such as the Gibb River bicycle challenge, in which a number of our staff have also taken part, and raised hundreds of thousands of dollars.

There are also many anonymous donors who have pledged their support or provided a carefully considered bequest without any fanfare at all but with a genuine desire to help us in our mission.

Major corporate sponsors have assisted us with vital capital acquisitions. A Flying into the Future campaign at the beginning of the millennium raised a critical mass of funds to enable us to purchase our first Pilatus PC-12 aircraft. It received substantial support from major companies in WA, including Wesfarmers, Woodside, Chevron, Barrick Gold and BHP Billiton. In recent years, Rio Tinto has committed to annual sponsorship of the LifeFlight jet and BHP Billiton made a large contribution to the purchase of four new PC-12 aircraft in 2014.

Expanding horizons
Extending our reach interstate and overseas

The RFDS commenced its work in Western Australia in the most remote parts of the state. Over the years, however, we have grown to meet the needs of the community. We serve all rural areas of the state, including those just outside the metropolitan area and locations such as Rottnest Island. We respond to Australians living and working in Australia's Indian Ocean Territories, assist Kimberley patients to reach a much closer tertiary hospital in Darwin and enable patients with diseases that cannot be managed in WA to receive treatment interstate.

Cocos and Christmas Islands

My first involvement with the Cocos Keeling Islands was in the early 1990s and was quite a challenge. The sole doctor, employed by the Commonwealth Government, lived on the islands and provided a twenty-four hour, seven-day service to Australians working there and to the native Cocos Malay population. He not only provided a general practice service, but also in emergencies could give an extradural (spinal) anaesthetic and then proceed to undertake surgery such as an appendicectomy or even caesarean section.

The Cocos Keeling Islands were originally owned by the Clunies-Ross family but were bought by the Commonwealth Government in 1978. They are situated about 3,000 kilometres northwest of Perth, halfway to Sri Lanka, and offered an important landing point for Qantas aircraft on the Wallaby route to South Africa in the 1950s.

The doctor on the islands became very sick and the island administration needed a means of evacuating him. I received a call at the RFDS in Perth and managed to organise a charter jet and to fit it with our equipment so that we could undertake the flight urgently. After the successful mission, I assisted with finding a temporary doctor for the islands, helping with interviewing candidates and advising on the sort of skill set required for this very remote location. I even considered working there myself.

Following this, we found ourselves being called to assist with evacuations when there was a significant emergency case which could not be held over to the regular charter flights that serviced the islands once or twice a week. The charter aircraft were paid for by the administration of the Island Territories and we provided doctors, initially on a volunteer basis, to assist. They were not short missions – usually consuming an entire day or night – but it was not often that our doctors and nurses had the chance to fly to an idyllic tropical atoll, even if mostly all we saw was the airport.

Christmas Island is a long distance away but much closer to Australia and Indonesia than Cocos. It has a larger population, a more substantial hospital and became much busier during the period when large numbers of asylum seekers were arriving by boat. Our service to the Island Territories has continued to this day, greatly facilitated by having our own medically configured Rio Tinto LifeFlight jet.

Royal Darwin Hospital

When you look at a map of Western Australia, it is obvious that for residents of the Kimberley, Perth is a long way away and Darwin is a much closer capital city. In the 1990s, a number of patients were taken to Darwin by the RFDS. However, with pressure on beds in the Northern Territory health system, their willingness to accept cases from another state declined in the early 2000s. We had situations where patients with critical illness or injury were being flown to Perth, often on multiple flights and sometimes taking up to twelve hours from our call-out to arrival in an intensive care unit. With a small population, around one-tenth of that in Perth, it was not possible for Darwin to provide certain specialties such as neurosurgery or cardiothoracic surgery, but in many cases, patients from the eastern Kimberley could still be in a competent tertiary ICU, able to manage their sepsis or respiratory failure, within a couple of hours.

Despite many requests, WA Health and NT Health kept telling us that we could not take patients to Darwin. I thought this was an unacceptable situation. Australians should be entitled to the best health care, no matter what side of a dotted line on a map they live; so I started lobbying. I wrote to numerous people with data on the number of transfers and gave examples of cases where patients had suffered or died. In the end, I wrote directly to the Minister for Health for Western Australia and started to get some action. A year or two later, a contractual arrangement was established between WA Health and NT Health for the 'purchase' of five beds in Royal Darwin Hospital. WA Health would pay an agreed cost for the care of this many patients and it was up to us all to ensure the beds were fully utilised.

It was a great win. Aboriginal patients would be cared for in a hospital that was much closer to home, rather than down in Perth. It was culturally and environmentally similar, and it was much easier to repatriate people to their towns and communities.

Urgent patients reached treatment more quickly and the substantial costs and resource implications of long RFDS evacuation flights to Perth were reduced. The system has been operating for almost a decade now and works well.

I believe that we need to encourage further development of a northern Australian tertiary hospital centre of excellence, which can serve the Northern Territory, northern Western Australia and northwest Queensland, as well as responding to occasional major incidents in the region north of our nation, such as the Bali bombings or natural disasters. With a larger volume of cases, a critical mass is reached which can lead to more specialised services and infrastructure being provided. At present we are just grateful that many urgent, life-threatening cases have been accepted and managed in Darwin when the patients may not have survived transport to Perth.

Interstate transfers

The hospital system across Australia is universally of a high standard. Other than in a few highly specialised clinical disciplines, patients can be capably managed in any of our tertiary centres. As outlined in the chapter, 'Long distance, small packages', some newborn babies have heart malformations which need specialised care that is only available in one or two hospitals in the country. Likewise, certain complex transplant procedures are best done in dedicated locations nationally.

If a visitor from interstate is ill or injured in Western Australia, they receive treatment here until they are well enough to travel home. State hospital systems do not want to pay the high costs of transferring patients to other states just because they would prefer to be closer to family.

With the commencement of the Rio Tinto *LifeFlight* jet service, the RFDS in Western Australia was able to expand its horizons, offering neonatal transfers to and from the eastern states.

In a few cases where a third party was willing to pay, we were also able to bring critically ill patients back to WA to be closer to family support and rehabilitation. It was gratifying to be able to bring Western Australians home.

There have been opportunities to retrieve patients internationally. While we have done so on a few occasions, mostly we have resisted entering these commercial arrangements as they can impact on our staff and aircraft availability. Our priority is ensuring our resources are always available for Australians on their home turf, though there have been occasional exceptions.

Southern Ocean rescue

On 19 December 2008, around 11.00 pm, my family and I arrived in Melbourne to spend time with relatives leading up to Christmas. After settling in to our apartment and having just gone to sleep, the telephone rang at about 2.00 am. It was Alan Lockwood, a very experienced coordinator at our Coordination Centre in Perth. He had the fleet medical officer (FMO) from the Royal Australian Navy in Sydney on the line asking if we could spare a doctor for a rescue mission in the Southern Ocean – and thought it might be best to put it through to me.

I spoke to the FMO and learned that there was a solo French yachtsman, Yann Eliès, skipper of Generali, *who was competing in the Vendée Globe round-the-world yacht race, a major international race for solo yachtsmen. He had fractured his femur in fierce weather conditions in the Southern Ocean, approximately 800 nautical miles south of Western Australia. They were planning to send a frigate from HMAS Stirling at Garden Island in Perth but didn't have a medical officer available. Could we help? They intended to leave at first light, in less than six hours. I agreed to do my best to find someone.*

As a Naval Reserve doctor, I already had a sense of what was going to be involved in travelling into the Southern Ocean and trying to rescue someone from a yacht in high seas. We would also lose a doctor from our tight roster for up to a week. I needed someone with days off who was willing to volunteer and who would fit in with a naval crew and the physical demands of the mission. Alan read me a list of names of doctors, their shifts over the next week and their phone numbers. While the family slept, I started making phone calls to selected home and mobile numbers.

David McIlroy was a keen Irish-trained doctor working with us as an emergency medicine registrar. I figured he might fit in well on a Navy ship and be up for a bit of adventure. I phoned his home about 1.00 am Perth time and after a long time he answered the phone.

'Good morning, David', I said cheerily. 'Have I got a great opportunity for you! A chance to go on a Navy ship down towards the Antarctic to rescue an injured sailor. It will be exciting and the chance of a lifetime — but we need you to get some medical gear from Jandakot and be down at the naval base by about 5.00 am so the ship can leave at first light.'

The response was a little less lively but, after further discussion, David agreed. We discussed that while the RAN vessel sick bay would be reasonably equipped, there was a range of RFDS equipment and anaesthetic drugs that he should collect from our airport facility. These would be necessary to deal with all eventualities and many days caring for the patient if they rescued him. Within about four hours, he was on board the HMAS Arunta with a collection of RFDS gear, departing Perth at full speed to conduct this rescue.

It was a rough journey. David had no Navy training and the ship's company continued to exercise on the way, planning how to launch and recover the rigid inflatable boat (RIB) and how to board the yacht, and developing strategies for transferring a large injured man on a stretcher across from the damaged yacht to the RIB in rough seas.

The rescue mission turned into a high-profile, week-long media saga. As David had my mobile phone number, he continued to call me regularly from the ship's satellite phone to report their progress. I was able to pass this information on to Lesleigh Green, our Director of Public Affairs, who kept the media informed of the events on the high seas, feeding the global desire for news.

The Royal Australian Navy, with medical assistance from our RFDS doctor, achieved a remarkable rescue in a 3,000-kilometre round trip, with the sailor eventually returned to Perth for surgery. This was not a normal week's work for a flying doctor but undoubtedly a memorable one!

Innovation but not in isolation
Specialisation in medical services

Innovation does not usually occur in isolation. You need to be connected with the rest of the health system and keep up with trends in technology and clinical practice. The same goes for aviation and communication. It is important that the RFDS, working primarily in remote areas, does not isolate itself from the large city medical infrastructure. This is why I have always tried to maintain connections with key players throughout the health system and set up processes to bring on people with experience and expertise, which will benefit our service.

I recognised the need to be more engaged with the specialty of emergency medicine and proceeded on a path to obtain accreditation with the Australasian College for Emergency Medicine. We were proud to receive accreditation for three advanced trainees in 1999, even though we did not have the funds to employ any at the time. The accreditation recognised the quality of clinical experience we could offer and the level of infrastructure and supervision we could provide to doctors who were soon to become specialists in this discipline.

The arrangement is a two-way street. We employ enthusiastic doctors at the top of their game, with high levels of knowledge and skills, preparing to sit their specialty exams. This keeps us current and on our toes. In return, we offer them challenging experiences outside of their comfort zone: operating with limited resources and having to make decisions themselves, as they will need to do when they achieve consultant status. A valuable lesson is the recognition that there is a different world outside the ivory towers of the tertiary hospitals. The trainees observe firsthand that the resources in many country locations are far from ideal but that, overall, health professionals in these settings deal with many challenging situations and in most cases do a very good job.

We also develop lifelong contacts with specialists who will ultimately populate the major hospitals in Perth and elsewhere. This broadens awareness of what the RFDS does and the challenges we face. It provides us with opportunities to organise upskilling in hospital departments for our staff and ensures that, at senior levels, there is a friendly ear when very difficult cases arise.

One of the outstanding achievements of the RFDS is to provide a high standard of hospital-level care to people in the most remote settings. We pride ourselves that the equipment and treatment a patient halfway across the Nullarbor will receive when having a heart attack is little different to that in a major Perth emergency department. Sure, there won't be as many people running around, and only a single doctor and flight nurse involved, but the clinical judgement, the decision-making and the standard of treatment are just as good.

We now have three accredited emergency medicine training positions and one anaesthetic specialty training position, approved by the relevant medical colleges. While we don't have funds to employ doctors in all these training posts, we do continue to maintain a minimum number of retrieval registrar appointments each year. They are highly sought-after positions and we select some excellent applicants. An example was a recent trainee who was the top candidate in the final emergency medicine examinations Australia-wide.

A number of these doctors enjoy the work and make such a valuable contribution that we invite them to rejoin us part time once they have completed their specialty training. As a result, we are very fortunate to have consultants working for us from each of the major emergency departments in Perth. This ensures we maintain our clinical standards and reputation and provides a conduit for feedback regarding the difficult cases we bring in.

People in the most remote parts of the state may benefit from having a specialist from one of the top city hospitals fly in and care for them on our aircraft. Likewise, our rural base doctors have the opportunity to work with people of such calibre and to keep their skills and knowledge honed in a high-performance environment.

We also need to network with other agencies, for example, those involved in rural workforce recruitment and education. Rural Health West, formerly the WA Centre for Remote and Rural Medicine, has recently celebrated twenty-five years in Western Australia. As another non-government organisation trying to deal with the shortage of medical services in rural and remote areas, we have much in common. Our staff regularly attend annual upskilling weekends and, in return, we provide trainers and sessions at some of their conferences. It's a valuable opportunity to promote our messages to country doctors on how best to use the RFDS. In turn, we meet many of the rural doctors we may deal with during the year.

We are often involved in projects of benefit to all rural health services. One in which we had significant carriage was the development of a rural emergency bag, to address a common problem we encountered when trying to give emergency advice to hospitals and nursing posts.

Collaboration on the Parry Pack

Country hospitals and nursing posts in the 1990s had no standard-ised list of emergency medical equipment, or a standard emergency bag that could be taken by doctors to an incident. Medical supplies at each facility were purchased by the matron (now the director of nursing) and the range of items depended on the whims of the local doctors and nursing staff. Following one particular incident in a country town, Dr John Parry, a very experienced and respected GP in Narrogin, approached the Minister for Health, Peter Foss. He asked him to do something to standardise equipment and emergency bags across country health services.

As doctors working in the RFDS, we had considerable interest in this. I had experienced numerous occasions when a patient was seriously ill or injured in a remote setting and a doctor just happened to be available, even in places that normally did not have one. Life-saving interventions would have been possible if basic emergency equipment and supplies had been accessible. However, because the facility was equipped as, say, a remote nursing post, they did not stock the basic equipment and supplies for procedures that would only be completed by a medical practitioner.

A small working group under the auspices of the Department of Health was set up and included Dr Parry, Dr Brian Williams from the WA Centre for Remote and Rural Medicine, emer-gency physician Dr Garry Wilkes and myself from the RFDS. We developed a list of essential equipment, such as laryngoscopes, intraosseous needles, chest drains and various consumables, which were not very expensive but significantly improved the capacity to perform advanced emergency procedures. I identified a locally designed emergency bag, the Marall bag, which contained dozens of clear pouches into which various items could be packed. It could be used just as easily in a hospital setting as at an accident site. The department paid for the bag and the equipment and I had a group of RFDS staff, including my long-term secretary Maureen Prime, spend an entire weekend packing over a hundred of these standardised bags from the basic components.

They were nicknamed the 'Parry Pack'. Thereafter, if we were ever advising a country hospital to perform an important procedure and they told us they didn't have the equipment to do so, we just directed them to find their Parry Pack. The system remained in place for ten to fifteen years and worked very effectively. There is now much greater standardisation of emergency equipment within country hospitals.

Local and international networks

To keep up with technology you need to stay informed and evaluate trends when new technologies arise. It is particularly important that medical staff have the opportunity to attend conferences, including international events, to see what is on the horizon. I introduced innovations such as vacuum mattresses, Propaq portable critical care monitors and iStat point-of-care analysers after attending international conferences. The RFDS in Western Australia has often been an early user of new and innovative technology, which subsequently country hospitals have picked up.

It is also important that our clinical staff have the opportunity to network within Australia, with other branches of the RFDS and other organisations performing similar work, so that we can share ideas. It is sometimes difficult working in a financially constrained, cost-conscious, not-for-profit service to recognise the ongoing long-term value of this.

In the late 1980s the RFDS gave me the opportunity to spend nearly a year studying at the internationally acclaimed Institute of Aviation Medicine at RAF Farnborough in the UK. I had to forgo half a year of salary but the organisation supported me with the course fees and leave of absence, with a modest requirement for a return of service once back in Australia. This foresight ultimately resulted in me remaining in the RFDS for another thirty years. I have used much of the knowledge I gained in formulating our aeromedical operations and passing it on to new clinical staff.

Doctors and nurses working in remote areas need an opportunity for regular upskilling and a sabbatical every five or six years. They can be re-energised and refresh their skills and knowledge, and this benefits our service upon their return. Interestingly, the 1933 draft constitution of the Australian Aerial Medical Service provided for further study for those who had completed their term of service (see 'Championing our challenges' for more detail).

Networking keeps us relevant and ensures that we have the right contacts to deal with major incidents when they arise. Over the years we have been involved in numerous situations with mass casualties. Those I remember most vividly include the Ongerup football pavilion explosion, the hot briquetted iron plant explosion in Port Hedland, various cyclones including Cyclone George, the Qantas Airbus incident at Learmonth, the Christmas Island refugee boat tragedy, the Ashmore Reef refugee boat explosion and a bus smash at Manjimup.

Fortunately, Western Australia has a small medical fraternity with many key players well known to each other. When such incidents arise, despite the official plans, there is still an effective network of informal contacts. For example, Mr Sudhakar Rao, a trauma surgeon and director of the State Trauma Service, is always readily available on his mobile phone. When an incident occurs, I can update him directly on what is happening while the formal arrangements are underway. Likewise, Professor Fiona Woods, an expert in serious burn injuries, can receive an update and provide immediate advice with a similar phone call. Within the Health Department, Dr Andy Robertson is always a useful contact in any major public health outbreak or disaster scenario. We can keep him informed of our status in a major incident or he can provide us with a 'heads up' on a looming issue. For instance, our response to SARS in 2003 and the Ebola virus outbreak in 2014 was very much dealt with through personal networking.

There are times when I think the RFDS has regarded itself as merely a cash-strapped charity doing the best it can in rural areas and is not acknowledged as a critical component of the entire state's medical infrastructure.

While aviation is a key element of how we deliver many of our medical services, we should not forget that our founders' objectives were to provide effective communication and medical services to people who live, work and travel in the most remote parts of our nation. Fixed-wing aircraft and pedal radios were innovative at the time but in the modern environment, helicopters, road vehicles and video-conferencing can, and should, be used to achieve similar ends.

The dates 19 August and 30 October 2015 are significant and mark the eightieth anniversary of the first flights of two RFDS bases in our state. I sincerely hope that we maintain our innovation and relevance as a medical service, as we advance towards our centenary in Western Australia.

Appendix 1
Timeline of significant RFDS events in Western Australia

1928	The Reverend John Flynn establishes the Australian Inland Mission (AIM) Aerial Medical Service in Cloncurry, Queensland. Dr Kenyon St Vincent Welch and pilot Arthur Affleck conduct the first flight on 17 May in de Havilland DH.50A *Victory* G-AUER / VH-UER
1929	Alf Traeger develops the pedal radio
1933	The Reverend John Flynn visits Kalgoorlie to discuss establishing a base there
1934	The Australian Aerial Medical Service (AAMS) Victorian Section is established in Melbourne on 23 August
1934	Alf Traeger installs radio base equipment in Port Hedland, then an outpost pedal radio at Warrawagine
1935	First Victorian Section flying base in Wyndham opens in August, with Dr R. J. Coto and DH.83 Fox Moth *Dunbar Hooper* chartered from MacRobertson Miller Aviation Company (MMA). First flight on 19 August by Captain W. L. B. Reeve and Dr Coto to Halls Creek
1935	Port Hedland Base opens in October with Fred Hull as base radio operator. Dr Alan Vickers, pilot Max Campbell and DH.83 Fox Moth *John Flynn* chartered from MMA. First flight to Warrawagine on 30 October
1936	Western Australian Section formally registered in July
1936	Radio facility opened at Wyndham in September
1937	Eastern Goldfields Section formally established in Kalgoorlie though ad hoc flights occurred before this with Goldfields Airways
1938	Fox Moth at Wyndham replaced by twin-engine DH.84 Dragon in August

1941	WA Section purchases its first aircraft, de Havilland DH.83 VH-USJ for Port Hedland
1942	Australian Aerial Medical Service becomes 'The Flying Doctor Service'
1942	Port Hedland Base transferred to Marble Bar to avoid Japanese bombing attacks. Reopened in Port Hedland in May 1945
1945	Meekatharra Aerial Medical Service operating a base under a local committee, incorporated into WA Section in 1949
1951	The Very Reverend John Flynn dies of cancer on 5 May
1955	Carnarvon Base opens
1955	Prefix 'Royal' added to Flying Doctor Service
1955	Derby Base opened in Clarendon Street by Lady Slim
1956	First RFDS fatal plane crash in WA at the King Leopold Ranges in the Kimberley. All five onboard are killed
1959	First WA School of the Air at Meekatharra opens
1960	Last Fox Moth replaced with a Cessna 180
1963	First Beechcraft Barons purchased by WA and Eastern Goldfields sections
1964	Jandakot Base opens
1964	Port Hedland School of the Air opens
1967	Health Department funds Robin Miller (Sugar Bird Lady) to administer Sabin polio vaccine throughout northern WA
1968	Carnarvon School of the Air opens
1972	First pressurised aircraft adopted by WA Section, the Beechcraft Duke
1973	Eastern Goldfields establishes offices in Piccadilly Street, Kalgoorlie, opposite the hospital
1977	Geraldton Base opens
1978	Introduction of LIFEPAK® 5 portable cardiac monitor defibrillator. Commencement of neonatal transport with the Vickers 77 cot
1980	Derby hangar built. One Navajo and one B80 Queen Air at Derby
1981	New (fourth) Port Hedland Base in Richardson Street opens February
1981	Fatal aircraft crash at Boulder involving Eastern Goldfields Section Piper Navajo VH-KMS. Four killed
1983	Introduction of Oxylog portable ventilators and Aloka ultrasound

1985	RFDS takes on medical staffing of Meekatharra Hospital. Standardised aeromedical records and database established across WA Section
1986	First Cessna C425 Conquest I turboprops acquired by Eastern Goldfields Section
1987	First Cessna C441 Conquest II turboprops purchased by WA Section
1989	Geraldton Base is closed
1990	Wyndham Base is closed
1990	Aircraft replacement appeal is launched and over six years raises $9.5 million to upgrade the aircraft fleet
1990	Upgrade to RFDS Jandakot: two-storey building with auditorium and operations centre built between Hangar 105 and Engineering Hangar
1991	First Propaq monitor acquired with non-invasive BP, pulse oximetry and printer
1992	Statewide 1800 number established for medical advice and evacuation requests
1994	Introduction of Propaq critical care monitors with capnography and invasive pressure, enabling state-of-the-art monitoring of anaesthetised patients
1995	First single-engine Pilatus PC-12 VH-FMC enters RFDS service in South Australia
1995	Formation of a single operating entity, RFDS Western Operations, from amalgamation of three sections in WA
1996	Carnarvon Base is closed
1998	Introduction of i-STAT® point of care analysers enables blood gas and electrolyte testing in flight
1999	New combined base at Port Hedland Airport, in conjunction with School of the Air. Last Piper Navajo VH-LDW leaves fleet
1999	RFDS employs its own doctors in Derby. Base offices established in a house in Loch Street
1999	RFDS is accredited for advanced training of emergency physicians with the Australasian College for Emergency Medicine
2000	Oxylog 1000 transport ventilators replace original Oxylogs
2001	First Pilatus PC-12 aircraft acquired by Western Operations, supported by the 'Flying into the future' campaign
2004	RFDS doctors commence flying on the Perth rescue helicopter

2005	Senior RFDS doctors commence as clinical coordinators at Jandakot to improve the statewide coordination of emergency aeromedical services
2007	Last Cessna Conquest II VH–LFD leaves service, having transferred 6,750 patients
2008	VH–SIM medical simulator constructed for medical training
2008	$5 million upgrade to RFDS Jandakot Base, improving patient transfer area, sleeping accommodation, office and training facilities
2008	Sonosite portable ultrasound enables inflight use for diagnosis and procedures
2009	New Meekatharra Base at Meekatharra Airport established in September
2009	Rio Tinto LifeFlight, the first RFDS jet, commences operations in October. Facility established at Perth Airport with Maroomba Airlines
2010	Last Beechcraft King Air VH–IWO ceases service in November. Western Operations now has a pure PC-12 fleet, except for the jet
2012	Intention to establish a base in Broome announced
2013	Partnership with Edith Cowan University confirmed. Planning and enrolments for first Aeromedical Retrieval courses
2014	RFDS withdraws doctors from Meekatharra Hospital
2014	Purchase of the Pilatus PC-24 jet announced, with Western Operations as lead customer. Aeromedical fit-out planned
2015	Refurbishment of Derby Base at Derby Airport. Construction of Broome Base commences

Appendix 2

Aircraft types used by flying doctors in Western Australia

Type	Comments	Years of operation
de Havilland DH.60M Moth	Flown by George Lewis of Goldfields Airways for ad hoc medical flights before the AAMS was established in Kalgoorlie. Registration: VH-UPD	1934–35
de Havilland DH.83 Fox Moth Single-engine biplane, open cockpit	First aircraft used by Victorian Section at Wyndham, 1935, *Dunbar Hooper*, VH-UTF. Operated by MacRobertson Miller Airways (MMA). Later used in Kalgoorlie from 1938 to 1946. First aircraft used by WA Section at Port Hedland, 1935, *John Flynn*, VH-UVL. Operated by MMA. Damaged by cyclone in January 1939. First aircraft used by Eastern Goldfields (EGF) Section at Kalgoorlie, 1935, VH-UTY. Cockpit had sliding canopy. Operated by Goldfields Airways. The first aircraft owned by the WA Section was VH-USJ, purchased July 1941. Restored and still flying. Registrations: VH-UTF, VH-UVL, VH-UTY, VH-USJ	1935–1960
BA Swallow	Replacement aircraft when VH-USJ was damaged in a crash. Operated by Airlines of Western Australia.	1942
de Havilland DH.84 Dragon Twin engine, closed cockpit	*Dunbar Hooper II* VH-URF replaced Fox Moth at Wyndham. *The Ashburton* VH-UVN was used in Port Hedland and Wyndham. Replaced the Fox Moths in Wyndham and Port Hedland but were pressed into war service. VH-URF was destroyed in a Japanese bombing raid on Wyndham in 1942. Operated by MMA. VH-AGJ *Allan R. Vickers* purchased by WA Section in 1945. Severely damaged in a storm at Marble Bar. Operated until 1950. Registrations: VH-URF, VH-UVN, VH-AGJ	1938–1950

Type	Comments	Years of operation
Various contracted aircraft	Used when the Fox Moth was in Perth for service during the war years. Included a Cessna C37 (operated by MMA) and a Fox Moth (Goldfields Airways).	1942–45
Avro 652A Anson Twin-engine	Acquired from RAAF in 1946 and operated by MMA for flying doctor services. Used in the Kimberley from about 1946 to late 1950s. Also flown in the Pilbara from 1950 to 1956, replacing the DH.83 and DH.84. VH-MMG crashed at Hawkestone Peak, King Leopold Ranges, 4 February 1956. Registrations: VH-MMB, VH-MMC, VH-MMG, VH-MMH, VH-MMJ	1946–1960
Various contracted aircraft	Various types including a DH.82 Tiger Moth, Short Scion, Percival Proctor and Auster, were contracted to provide services from Meekatharra during the latter war years.	1940–1958
Cessna 180 Single-engine	Purchased by WA Section for Port Hedland (1956), Carnarvon (1957), Meekatharra (1958) and spare (1960). FDH fully restored and still flying. Registrations: VH-FDP (changed to FDN), VH-FDG (changed to VH-FDO), VH-FDM, VH-FDH	1956–1963
Cessna 182	Single-engine Cessna, the first aircraft owned by the EGF Section. Registration: VH-FDK	1959–1963
de Havilland DH.104 Dove Twin-engine	Chartered then purchased by Victorian Section. First aircraft owned by the Victorian Section. *H.V. McKay* operated by MMA. Traded in on Queen Air 65. Registration: VH-FDV	1959–1966
Beechcraft Baron 95-A55 and 58 Twin-engine, unpressurised	Eight Barons purchased from 1963 onwards by WA Section. Five Beech 95-A55 (from 1963) then three longer 58 models (in 1981). One Baron 95-A55 by EGF Section. Registrations: VH-FDP, VH-FDG, VH-FDD, VH-FDJ, VH-FDT then VH-FDN, VH-ADB, VH-AYV. EGF Section: VH-FDK	1963–1985

388

Type	Comments	Years of operation
Beechcraft Queen Air 65, 70 and B80	Owned by Victorian Section. Operated by TransWest (SkyWest) on contract. Registrations: VH-FDV, VH-MWJ, VH-FDL	1966–1993
Beechcraft Baron 58	Owned by Victorian Section.	
Beechcraft 60 Duke Twin-engine	First pressurised aircraft in WA Section. Registrations: VH-IFD, VH-UFD	1972–1985
Cessna C421B Golden Eagle Twin-engine, pressurised	Additional aircraft in WA Section. Registrations: VH-ADG, VH-ADK	1975–1988
Piper PA-31 Navajo Twin-engine, unpressurised	Nine purchased by WA Section between 1977 and 1982 and three from 1989 to 1990. Able to carry two stretchers. Latter models included air-conditioning. EGF purchased six between 1968 and 1981. Victorian Section operated two Navajos from about 1981. VH-DEE crashed at Mt Augustus 4 July 1981. VH-KMS crashed at Boulder 30 April 1981. Registrations: VH-ADE, ADI, DEG, DEE, DEH, DEP, DER, AYT, AYS then VH-LDX, LDW, LDZ. EGF Section: VH-KFD, KAD, KMS, EGF, EGK, EGP	1968–1999
Piper PA-31-P 350 Mojave Twin-engine, pressurised	A pressurised version of the Navajo purchased by WA Section. Registration: VH-HFD	1985–1993
Cessna C425 Conquest I Pressurised twin turboprop	First pressurised turboprop aircraft purchased by Eastern Goldfields Section. A total of four acquired between 1986 and 1994. Carried over to Western Operations. VH-EGS *Laverton* flew 3.28 million kilometres over 22 years. Registrations: VH-EGS, EGR, EGQ, EGT	1986–1999

389

Type	Comments	Years of operation
Cessna C441 Conquest II Pressurised twin turboprop	First pressurised turboprop aircraft for WA Section. Longer than the C425 and with Garrett engines. A total of four acquired between 1987 and 1993. Registrations: VH-JFD, LFD, NFD, CFD	1987–2005
Beechcraft C90 King Air Pressurised twin turboprop	Victorian Section replaced Navajos and Queen Airs with a C90 then B200C. Registration: VH-FDT	1986–2004
Beechcraft B200C King Air Pressurised twin turboprop	The first B200 Super King Airs operated from Derby Base by the Victorian Section. Fitted with an AFTS loading system (KFN 1989, FDG 1992). Western Operations bought VH-CWO in 1996. All King Airs replaced in 2010 with PC-12. Registrations: VH-FDG, VH-KFN, VH-CWO	1989–2009
Beechcraft B200SE King Air Pressurised twin turboprop	A special edition King Air with an economical utility interior and a 'flipper' door. Three purchased by Western Operations. Registrations: VH-HWO, IWO, LWO	1999–2010
Pilatus PC-12 Pressurised single turboprop	Initial purchase of four PC-12/45 in 2001, with additional PC-12/45 then PC-12/47 'Next Generation' thereafter. Currently eighteen PC-12s registered for RFDS service in Western Australia. Registrations: PC-12/45: VH-KWO, MWO, NWO, VWO, ZWO; PC-12/47: VH-YWO, OWP, OWQ, OWR, OWB, OWA, OWD, OWG, OWI, OWJ, OWS, OWU, OWX	2001–

Type	Comments	Years of operation
Beech Hawker 800XP Jet	First RFDS jet in Australia – the Rio Tinto *LifeFlight* jet. Purchased and outfitted in the USA in 2009. Registration: VH-RIO	2009–
Piaggio Avanti II Pressurised twin turboprop	Chartered from Susi Air (Indonesia) August 2010 to cover maintenance on Hawker 800XP jet and evaluate for aeromedical use. Registration: PK-BVX	2010
Various charter aircraft	Ad hoc charter aircraft for Indian Ocean retrievals and evacuations in the Kimberley. From Perth includes: IAI Westwind, Citation II, Challenger 600, Beechjet 400. In the Kimberley: Britten–Norman Islander, Cessna Caravan with floats, GippsAero GA8 Airvan and occasional helicopters, including Robinson R22 and R44 through to Super Puma.	
Bell 412EP	RFDS medical staff use Perth rescue helicopter. Registration: VH-EWA	2004–

This table has been derived from multiple sources in an effort to summarise the aircraft types used by flying doctors over the past eighty years for reference. Every effort has been made to ensure accuracy but errors and oversights are possible.

391

Appendix 3

Timeline of RFDS bases across Australia

Year	Location		Notes
1928	Cloncurry	QLD	Closed 1965
1935	Wyndham	WA	Closed 1990
1935	Port Hedland	WA	
1937	Kalgoorlie	WA	
1938	Broken Hill	NSW	
1939	Alice Springs	NT	
1943	Charleville	QLD	
1945	Meekatharra	WA	
1952	Charters Towers	QLD	Closed 1972, consolidated at Cairns
1955	Port Augusta	SA	
1955	Derby	WA	
1955	Carnarvon	WA	Closed 1996
1960	Launceston	TAS	
1964	Jandakot	WA	
1965	Mt Isa	QLD	
1965	Cairns	QLD	
1977	Geraldton	WA	Closed 1989
1987	Adelaide	SA	
1992	Yulara	NT	GP clinic only. Closed 2008
1995	Brisbane	QLD	
1995	Rockhampton	QLD	
1996	Townsville	QLD	

Year	Location		Notes
1996	Bankstown	NSW	
1997	Essendon	VIC	
1999	Dubbo	NSW	
2009	Perth Airport	WA	Jet facility
2016	Broome	WA	

Glossary

Arrhythmia   An irregularity in the electrical rhythm of the heart. Usually results in a worsening in the performance of the heart in pumping blood around the body.

Arterial line   A cannula (tube) and fluid line inserted into an artery rather than a vein. Enables reliable continuous measurement of blood pressure directly inside the artery, which is much more accurate than a cuff on the arm.

Bariatric   Pertaining to patients with morbid obesity, of increased size or weight.

Capnometry   Also called capnography (if there is a graphical representation), or endtidal CO_2. Measurement of carbon dioxide in exhaled air.

Defibrillation   Using an electric shock to convert a patient's heart from a life-threatening abnormal rhythm, such as ventricular fibrillation, to a normal rhythm and contractions.

Endotracheal tube   A tube placed through the mouth into the trachea to enable ventilation of a patient. Usually has an inflatable cuff to ensure a seal.

Endtidal CO_2   Measurement of exhaled carbon dioxide. See *capnometry*.

Hypertension   High blood pressure.

Hypoglycaemia   Low levels of glucose in the blood.

Hypotension   Low blood pressure.

Hypothermia   Low body temperature.

Hypoxia   Low levels of oxygen in the blood.

Intraosseous line   An infusion given through a needle into the marrow space of a bone.

Intravenous line   A soft plastic cannula inserted into a vein and connected to plastic tubing and a fluid bag, for administering fluids, drugs or blood products to patients.

Nasogastric tube   A narrow plastic tube passed through the nose down into the stomach to allow draining of air and fluid.

Oximetry   Measuring the oxygen content of the blood. Pulse oximetry uses a probe, usually attached to the fingertip, and provides a percentage of haemoglobin oxygen saturation.

Point-of-care testing   The ability to perform laboratory tests at the patient's bedside or 'point of care'.

Transcutaneous pacing   Using pads applied to the skin of the chest to provide a small electric shock to the heart, to keep it contracting at a suitable rate. A temporary measure until a pacing wire and pacemaker unit can be inserted by a cardiologist.

Ventilation   Using an external device to breathe for a patient, such as in anaesthesia or intensive care.

Ventricular fibrillation   An abnormal heart rhythm in which the heart is not pumping blood effectively, which quickly leads to death.

Abbreviations and acronyms

Medical

AAMS	Australian Aerial Medical Service
AIM	Australian Inland Mission
ACEM	Australasian College for Emergency Medicine
AEA	Aeronautical Engineers Australia
AED	Automatic External Defibrillator
AFTS	Australian Flight Test Services
AMA	Australian Medical Association
ANZCA	Australian and New Zealand College of Anaesthetists
BCA	Bush Church Aid Society
ECU	Edith Cowan University
EMA	Emergency Management Australia
FSH	Fiona Stanley Hospital
HEPA	High-Efficiency Particulate Arrestance filters
Hib	*Haemophilus influenzae type b*
HIV	Human Immunodeficiency Virus
ICU	Intensive Care Unit
KEMH	King Edward Memorial Hospital for Women
MIMMS	Major Incident Medical Management Support
NETSWA	Neonatal Emergency Transport WA
NICU	Neonatal Intensive Care Unit
PCH	Perth Children's Hospital (opening 2016)
PMH	Princess Margaret Hospital for Children

RFDS	Royal Flying Doctor Service
RPH	Royal Perth Hospital
SARS	Severe Acute Respiratory Syndrome
START	Simple Triage And Rapid Treatment
WACHS	WA Country Health Service
WANTS	WA Neonatal Transport Service

Aviation

ADF	Automatic Direction Finder (a navigation aid)
ADS-B	Automatic Dependent Surveillance – Broadcast
DME	Distance Measuring Equipment (a navigation aid)
EGPWS	Enhanced Ground Proximity Warning System
GPS	Global Positioning System (a navigation aid)
GPWS	Ground Proximity Warning System
IFR	Instrument Flight Rules
NDB	Non-Directional Beacon (a radio navigation beacon)
Omega	A global navigation system which used VLF signals
RNAV	Area Navigation (random navigation in an area using GPS, rather than to or from fixed radio beacons)
TCAS	Traffic Collision Avoidance System
VOR	Visual Omni-directional Radio (a navigation aid)

Communications

DRCS	Digital Radio Concentrator System
HF	High-Frequency radio
SOTA	School of the Air
UHF	Ultra High-Frequency radio
VHF	Very High-Frequency radio
VLF	Very Low-Frequency radio (used for navigation)

Bibliography

Royal Flying Doctor Service

The Best for the Bush. Report of the National Health Strategy Working Group to the Australian Council of the Royal Flying Doctor Service of Australia, Sydney November 1993.

Bilton, John, *The Royal Flying Doctor Service of Australia: Its Origin, Growth and Development*, Halstead Press, Sydney, 1961.

Dicks, Harold G., *The Royal Flying Doctor Service of Australia*, illustrated by Boyd Turner, Oxford University Press, Melbourne, 1971.

Hill, Ernestine, *Flying Doctor Calling*, Angus & Roberston, Sydney, 1948.

Hudson, Harry, *Flynn's Flying Doctors*, William Heinemann, Melbourne, 1956.

Idriess, Ion L., *Flynn of the Inland*, Angus & Robertson, Sydney, 1932.

King, Norma, *Wings Over the Goldfields: The 50-year History of the Eastern Goldfields Section of the Royal Flying Doctor Service of Australia*, Hesperian Press, Perth, 1992.

Langford, S. A., *Preparation of Patients for Transport*, Monograph Series No. 2, Royal Flying Doctor Service of Australia, Sydney, 1991.

Langford, S. A., *Transporting Your Patient: Guidelines for Organising and Preparing Patients for Transport by Air*, 2nd edn, Royal Flying Doctor Service Western Operations, Perth, 2015.

O'Leary, T. J., *North and Aloft: A Personal Memoir of Service and Adventure with the Royal Flying Doctor Service in Far Northern Australia*, Amphion Press, Brisbane, 1988.

Page, Michael, *The Flying Doctor Story 1928–78*, Rigby, Adelaide, 1977.

Royal Flying Doctor Service (Eastern Goldfields Section), *Special 50th Anniversary Publication*, WA Media Promotions, Perth, 1987.

Royal Flying Doctor Service (Federal Council), *Royal Flying Doctor Service of Australia: Australia's Unique Outback Medical Organisation*, RFDS , Sydney, 1990.

Royal Flying Doctor Service (Western Australian Section), *Network '81*, Hampton, Victoria, 1981.

Royal Flying Doctor Service (Western Australian Section), *Special 50th Anniversary Publication*, Australia Wide Promotions and Publications, Perth, 1985.

Woldendorp, R. & McDonald, R., *Australia's Flying Doctors*, Fremantle Arts Centre Press, Fremantle, 2002.

Bush Church Aid Flying Padre and Flying Medical Service

Daniels, L., *Far West*, Church of England Information Trust, Sydney, 1959.

Jones, T. E., *These Twenty Years: A Record of the Work of the Bush Church Aid Society for Australia and Tasmania, 1919–1939*, BCA, Sydney, 1939.

Kirkby, S. J., *These Ten Years: A Record of the Work of the Bush Church Aid Society 1920–1930*, BCA, Sydney, 1931.

Northern Territory Aerial Medical Service

Fenton, Clyde, *Flying Doctor*, Georgian House, Melbourne, 1947.

Moss, Harry, *Ten Thousand Hours*, Hesperian Press, Perth, 1988.

Index

About the author

Dr Stephen Langford joined the Royal Flying Doctor Service for one year in 1983. As a private pilot with an interest in aviation and emergency medicine, the North West of Western Australia seemed a better fit than the sojourn in the Antarctic he was contemplating.

As one of only two doctors employed by the Western Australian Section of the service, he commenced work in the Pilbara. There were no mobile phones, personal computers or internet. Remote communications used HF radio and flights were in piston-engine aircraft. Three decades later the RFDS has changed significantly but is still 'one of the few jobs in medicine where you can really make a difference to people's lives every day'.

In this book, Dr Langford records the modern history of the RFDS in Western Australia, highlighting how the work of a flying doctor has changed substantially in that time. He provides insight into the many innovations and technological developments, particularly in medical care, that have occurred within the service since the late 1970s.